Conjoined Twins
in Black and White

Wisconsin Studies in Autobiography

William L. Andrews
General Editor

Conjoined Twins
in Black and White

The Lives of
Millie-Christine McKoy and
Daisy and Violet Hilton

Edited by

Linda Frost

THE UNIVERSITY OF WISCONSIN PRESS

The University of Wisconsin Press
1930 Monroe Street, 3rd Floor
Madison, Wisconsin 53711-2059

www.wisc.edu/wisconsinpress/

3 Henrietta Street
London WC2E 8LU, England

1   3   5   4   2

Printed in the United States of America

Library of Congress Cataloging-in-Publication Data
Conjoined twins in black and white :
the lives of Millie-Christine McKoy and Daisy and Violet Hilton /
edited by Linda Frost.
p.   cm.—(Wisconsin studies in autobiography)
ISBN 978-0-299-23074-6 (pbk.: alk. paper)
ISBN 978-0-299-23073-9 (e-book)
1. Millie-Christine, 1851–1912.
2. Hilton, Daisy, 1908–1969.
3. Hilton, Violet, 1908–1969.
4. Conjoined twins—United States—Biography.
I. Frost, Linda.   II. Series.
QM691.C66   2009
616′.043—dc22
[B]
2008041889

For

Lucy and **Cora**

Contents

Illustrations

Preface

I witnessed my one and only freak exhibit in a parking lot carnival in Pennsylvania in the early 1990s; the facade of the display sported paintings of hypodermic needles and cannabis leaves and touted the "freak" as "Billy Reed," a man driven savage by illegal drugs. I paid my ticket and walked, a little nervously, into the dark enclosure to see the cage where Billy Reed, long-haired and dirty, rocked snarling on the floor.

The carnival's context obviously represented Billy Reed in a particular way to transmit a social and cultural warning: *don't do drugs.* Before ever plunging into the world of the freak show as a scholar, I had already experienced the role social mores played in the construction of these performances. I certainly didn't believe that the man who was Billy Reed that day was a "real" example of severe drug addiction; showered and shaved, Billy Reed would have looked just like any other nonaddicted twenty-something man I knew. Within the context of freak performance, though, he became a cultural caveat.

Nevertheless, some freak performers, particularly in the nineteenth and early twentieth centuries, indeed had extreme and "real" congenital anomalies, physical configurations that lent these performers a greater sense of authenticity within the world of the "show." Although their managers and biographers also packaged them for particular cultural ends, these performers stood out from their peers, compelling those who fancied themselves normal to look and to wonder. These performers were essentially—because physically—radically different. Such was (and is, still) perhaps most profoundly the case with the "Siamese" or "conjoined" twin.

This book is an attempt to bring together some of those culturally determining voices, like those of nineteenth-century physician William

Pancoast and twentieth-century showman Myer Myers, with the voices we most need and want to hear—those of the conjoined twins them-selves, Millie-Christine McKoy and Daisy and Violet Hilton. I have annotated the texts where necessary to facilitate a smoother reading ex-perience for the reader; I have not tried to provide an exhaustive back-ground to what are mostly self-explanatory texts or tried to determine the accuracies or inaccuracies of the different versions of these women's life stories. Rather I want to encourage the reader to see how these auto-biographies work to create new identities for these women, even as the biographical works included here—whether show history, medical ar-ticle, or novelization—stumble over or directly threaten them.

Minor typographical errors have been, for the most part, silently corrected; where a correction is a guess given the poor print quality of the original, I have indicated this in brackets (in the case of the McKoys' autobiography and biography, I have used other versions of the texts to make decisions about some of these questionable instances). Photo-graphs have been taken from a variety of sources and do not, except in a few clear instances, stem directly from the texts reprinted here. My introduction attempts to provide both a historical and a critical context for the documents, providing a way of reading and thinking about them that highlights their significance to the study of autobiography in partic-ular, although their interest to scholars and readers will certainly extend beyond that category. While one possible analytical framework, my ap-proach is hardly exhaustive and the collection will be most successful if it is reread and rewritten by other interested readers. Of course, the sto-ries contained here are just plain interesting, so one can always happily ignore those sections of the introduction that don't capture one's atten-tion and get right to the good stuff.

As always, there are many people to thank: for this book, I am happily indebted to a wide range of crucial supporters. Thanks to Jason Blaine Baker, Michael Flannery, Fred Griffin, Eddie Luster, Joanne Martell, Dawn Pekarek, Kathryn Pitt, Lia Rushton, Debra Scarbor-ough, Lindsay Swain, Pratik Talati, and L. Lewis Wall, some of whom helped me find texts and others, my way through them. All the fine folks with the Cornell University Asian American Studies Program, particu-larly Derek Chang, Viranjini Munasinghe, and Shelley Wong, were crucial in letting me try out my ideas early on in the process and encour-aging me to do so. I could never have imagined this collection, both intellectually and practically, without the foundational scholarship and overall generosity of Robert Bogdan who, with infinite trust and good-will, lent me his personal copy of the Hilton autobiography, a text that is still not, to my knowledge, catalogued in any conventional collection. Amy Fulkerson and John Spencer from the Witte Museum in San Antonio were just great—incredibly helpful, completely accommodating, and very kind, indeed—and Nicholas Graham, Mike Millner, and Jason Tomberlin at the libraries of the University of North Carolina at Chapel Hill also cheerfully provided essential assistance. Funding for the project was provided largely by the University of Alabama at Birmingham Office of Graduate Study; thank you, Bryan Noe, for your very significant support! The support of everyone in the UAB University Honors Program, where I was housed for four years, and of my new colleagues at Eastern Kentucky University has also been crucial to the book's coming-to-be. Margaret Harrill gave me the support I needed to stay on the computer; Sue Kim, as usual, read everything with her big loving heart; and David Basilico listened, as he always does, with an extremely patient ear. My readers at the University of Wisconsin Press were exacting and gave me the criticism I needed to make the work better as well as the support I needed to keep going; I hope all are content with what they helped birth (while it is understood that all mistakes are only mine). Raphael Kadushin, Todd Dresser, and the staff at the University of Wisconsin Press have been wonderful from my very first querying email. William Andrews in particular was the best kind of mentor possible for this project—not only did he remind me of the existence of the McKoy twins' autobiography, he remained genuinely interested, enthusiastic, and particular. I've been very fortunate indeed to be able to work with him.

Finally, as always, I thank my husband, Russell Helms, with whom I share a necessarily intense, sometimes stressful, but still deeply satisfying interest in book making. We also share the privilege of raising two amazing daughters, and it's to them, Lucy and Cora, the sisters in *my* house, that I dedicate this book; despite where your lives may take you, may you never be separated!

Conjoined Twins
in Black and White

Introduction

Peculiar Intimacies

The phrase "Siamese twins," the colloquial term for conjoined twins, first appeared in the nineteenth century as the public nomenclature for Chang and Eng, twins of Chinese heritage born in Siam in 1811 and connected by a band of flesh at their chests.[1] They were, according to cultural critic Robert Bogdan, "the vanguard of joined twins," being as they were "the first put on display in this country"; in a very real way, our current conception of the public and exceptional nature of the Siamese twin was born with them.[2] They had a long, prosperous career, played to large audiences, and fully assimilated to life in the United States, acquiring citizenship, assuming the surname "Bunker," marrying, in this case, sisters Adelaide and Sarah Ann Yates, and moving onto adjoining plantations in Mount Airy, North Carolina, where they both owned slaves. They each fathered over ten children and spent alternating three-day periods at one another's farms in order to appease what have been described as their understandably disgruntled wives. They both died on January 17, 1874, Chang first, from pneumonia, and Eng several hours later from systemic complications.[3]

The story of Chang and Eng is just one of the many of extraordinary and extraordinarily represented people who made their livings as "freak" performers, playing to audiences at country carnivals, traveling circuses, and museums like Barnum's American Museum.[4] As Bogdan

3

observes, "although freak shows are now on the contemptible fringe, from approximately 1840 through 1940 the formally organized exhibition for amusement and profit of people with physical, mental, or behavioral anomalies, both alleged and real, was an accepted part of American life."[5] Conjoined twins were of course among the rarest and most fascinating of these performers. It was because of the voracious interest in what the lives of people like these were really like that "freak" histories, pamphlets that recounted the biographies of these exhibited people, were produced and sold at exhibitions and performances of figures like Chang and Eng.

These publications, or "show histories," attempted to satisfy the public appetite at the same time that they worked to create and whet it; a show history was as much an advertisement and an inducement to future viewings and show goings as it was then a souvenir. As well as these show histories, most major freak performers of the nineteenth and early twentieth centuries sold copies of their photographs as postcards, commonly known as *carte de visites*. Mary Hilton, the midwife who delivered Daisy and Violet Hilton and then adopted them from their distraught mother, sold two-penny postcards of the twins in their baby carriage from the backroom of the Brighton bar, The Queen's Arms, where the girls were first shown to the public. Millie-Christine McKoy sold "her" photos, signing them alternately "Chrissie-Millie" or, as in the case of at least one postcard from 1873, "with Millie Chrissie's love."

Certainly both the McKoys, born in 1851, and the Hiltons, born in 1908, had such histories written and photos taken of them; today these bits of "freak memorabilia" continue to attract a pretty penny on eBay. But while the memorabilia of the McKoys and Hiltons share common ground with other such freak, circus, and show performers, there is still one striking difference between them. Each set of twins wrote an autobiography of their own during their lifetimes, memoirs that begin to answer the kinds of questions those of us who are not conjoined have about what it must be like to live every single moment in physical connection to someone else. Here in the United States, where privacy and individuality are nominally prized and exalted, life as a member of a set of conjoined twins flies in the face of almost every understanding we have of what it means to enjoy a "normal" and "desirable" existence. Nevertheless, one of the first things we learn from these self-told tales is how "normal" the life of conjoined twins feels to those born into it. As medical historian Alice Domurat Dreger puts it, "most such twins, like most of us singletons, grow up accepting the basic bodies they were born with as necessary to their selves. Most people who are conjoined, given the opportunity to do so, accept and embrace a life of two minds in one packaging of skin."[6] However normal their lives and bodies seemed to themselves, though, the stories of Millie-Christine McKoy and Daisy and Violet Hilton remain tantalizing to the general public.

Of course, conjoined twins are of such great interest in part because they are rare. According to M. H. Kaufman, "the spontaneous incidence is about 10.25 per million births."[7] Dreger notes that we "can be fairly confident about a few general facts: the phenomenon is unusual but occurs with some regularity; roughly two-thirds of conjoined twins are female; 40 percent or more of conjoined twins are stillborn; another 35 percent die within one day as a result of profound medical problems stemming from their anomalous development."[8] Films like the 2005 mockumentary *Brothers of the Head* about two punk-rock conjoined brothers, the 1997 musical *Sideshow* based on the lives of the Hiltons, and documentaries that constitute in part a kind of autobiographical account of the lives of contemporary conjoined twins Reba and Lori Schappell and Abigail and Brittany Hensel have continued to pique the public's interest in this phenomenon. The same can be said regarding recent attempts to surgically separate conjoined twins. The 2005 case of Clarence and Carl Aguierre is one example. Filipino brothers joined at the top of the head, Clarence and Carl were separated in a yearlong series of experimental surgeries performed by and under the direction of Dr. James Goodrich at Montefiore Medical Center in the Bronx. The surgery, Dr. Goodrich, and the Montefiore Medical Center all received significant media attention at the time it was undertaken.[9] Certainly readers and viewers remain fascinated by these stories and their implications. The freak show may be gone, but public intrigue in the lives of conjoined twins remains.

Within the realm of academic scholarship, certainly Robert Bogdan's landmark *Freak Show: Presenting Human Oddities for Amusement and Profit* (1988) is largely responsible for moving the study of exhibited people like conjoined twins into the realm of serious scholarship and the field of cultural studies in particular. A host of other critics, led or joined in part by the work and example of Rosemarie Garland Thomson, who edited the anthology *Freakery: Cultural Spectacles of the Extraordinary Body* (1996) and published her own *Extraordinary Bodies: Figuring Physical Disability in American Culture and Literature* (1996), began in earnest to investigate the ideas of freak performance within the realm of cultural criticism and to consider disability as a larger theoretical category. But for the most part, the words written by these exhibited people themselves have not been moved into the realm of scholarship.

In fact, almost every claim that theorists of autobiography have made or are now making is either subtly complicated, or completely turned on its head by the autobiographical writings of Millie-Christine McKoy and Daisy and Violet Hilton. According to Georges Gusdorf, one of the foundational theorists of the field, the necessary cultural prerequisite for autobiography is a foundational understanding of individual existence: "a conscious awareness of the singularity of each individual life."[10] James Olney has claimed that for the autobiographer, "separate selfhood is the very motive of creation"; autobiography is propelled by "a single, radical and radial energy originating in the subject center, an aggressive, creative expression of the self, a defense of individual integrity in the face of an otherwise multiple, confusing, swarming, and inimical universe."[11]

Feminist critics of autobiography, scholars like Margo Culley, Susan Stanford Friedman, Mary G. Mason, Nellie McKay, Nancy Miller, and Sidonie Smith, have worked hard to dismantle this idea that a singular, individuated consciousness is necessary to the work of the autobiographer; their work has opened up the field as a result. Friedman, for instance, has argued that a female consciousness is to some degree necessarily collective, whether forged from the psychodynamics described by psychoanalytic scholars like Nancy Chodorow or from the cultural condition of being continuously projected upon as a feminine subject in a patriarchal world.[12] Certainly these theorists have made way for readings that allow for a much wider range of conscious acts of self-telling. As have critics of African American autobiography like William Andrews, these feminist scholars have also helped clear the path for a better understanding of work by nineteenth-century American slave narrators for whom, as McKay notes, the autobiographical self and personal black female identity is "a process of ongoing reinvention of self under the pressures of race, class, and gender oppression."[13] Theorists of Native American autobiography like Hertha D. Sweet Wong assert the need for a better understanding of collective identity that allows for both the idea of the individual self as collectively constituted as well as a reconsideration of the different kinds of collective selves that result from varying tribal communities.[14] The work of Judith Butler and others has brought the idea of the body to the forefront of the discussion of how we tell our stories, and particularly the way in which the bodies that "fail to materialize provide the necessary 'outside,' if not the necessary support, for the bodies which, in materializing the norm, qualify as bodies that matter."[15] Feminists have done and are continuing to do crucial work in understanding how women writers understand themselves, as well as how writers who are not privileged to be able to assert an uncontested and autonomous "individual integrity" in the face of "an otherwise multiple, confusing, swarming, and inimical universe" have nevertheless written their own selves and therefore reframed the conversation. In fact, all these voices and their critical contributions have been crucial in bringing us to a point where we may now be able to posit some kind of critical understanding of the self-told stories of two sets of conjoined twins.

Many of the issues with which theorists of autobiography, and particularly feminist theorists, grapple are literalized in the work and writings of the McKoys and the Hiltons. Rather than a self that is theoretically devised as collective, these women both were in some sense, and describe themselves as being, at once both two and one; in fact, our very definition of the body is confounded when dealing with women like Millie and Christine McKoy, who often hyphenated their *first* names and performed under the stage name "the Two-Headed Nightingale." Daisy and Violet Hilton famously claimed that they would never allow themselves to be guinea pigs for a medical separation, despite the fact that the film in which they starred, and that they claimed in many ways did represent their own lives, depicts the sisters as miserably unhappy in their connectedness. As readers, we have to think about how these writings change the way we understand our basic sense of human self, of the subjectivity we imagine our very skins—or skin—to provide. When two people are physically, anatomically joined together, what constitutes their "body" exactly? For that matter, what constitutes "a" body for a conjoined twin? Just how many bodies does a set of conjoined twins have? And when the bodies that come to configure the "necessary 'outside'" for the normal bodies that matter are not in fact immaterial at all, but bodies with more materiality than we might be able, or even want, to grasp, what is the matter about which we're talking? What does "individuality" in such a case mean? Indeed, this collection pulls together both autobiographical and biographical writings that show us the most basic and troubling ways in which our definitions of subjectivity, theoretically inclusive though they might be, still have to struggle to explain this particular incidence of "self," that of the conjoined twin.

The Biographies

Complete biographies of both the McKoys and the Hiltons have appeared only recently. Pieced together from texts like the ones contained in this collection, contemporary newspaper coverage, and interviews with surviving family members and friends, these texts offer one important context in which to consider the autobiographies written by the twins themselves and the biographical pieces written about them by their contemporaries.

Joanne Martell uses a line from one of the McKoys' show tunes for the title of her biography; she calls it *Millie-Christine: Fearfully and Wonderfully Made* (2000), referencing the twins' description of their own unique physiology. As Martell suggests, although their physiology was indeed extraordinary, the life journey the McKoys undertook from their birth in slavery to their status as world-class entertainers may well have been the most "wonderfully made" thing about them.

Born slaves in 1851 to mother Monemia and father Jacob, Christine weighed an estimated twelve pounds at birth and the diminutive Millie, five; they were born as property into the slaveholding family of Jabez McKay, a blacksmith living in Columbus County, North Carolina.[16] Ten months after they were born, McKay sold the twins and entrusted the rights to "show" them to others, namely John C. Pervis, who sold the twins back to McKay after fourteen months, and a man described by Martell simply as "Brower," who was to manage them with the backing of Joseph Pearson Smith from Wadesboro. (The cost of the twins at this point is reported in different publications as alternately ten, thirty, and forty thousand dollars). Despite initial success exhibiting the girls, Brower hit a dry spell in New Orleans and opted to sell the girls to someone known to Martell simply as a "Texan." This "Texan," perhaps not surprisingly, took the girls without paying, leaving Brower to deliver the bad news to Joseph Smith, who went ahead and paid off his promissory note to McKay, hiring a private investigator to find the twins. What follows this is the most sensationalized portion of the sisters' lives—a series of cross-Atlantic, cross-country kidnappings, with Smith and his investigator in hot pursuit. In a climactic moment of triumph, Smith and

Monemia are described as reclaiming the twins at one of their performances in Liverpool; according to the *Biographical Sketch*: "no sooner . . .
had the keen eye of the mother caught a glimpse of her long-lost child
than she uttered a scream of such heart-rendering pathos that the audience simultaneously rose to their feet, wondering and astonished. The
mother, overpowered, fell fainting to the floor. When resuscitated she
wildly threw her arms about, crying in most piteous tones. 'My own
child! O! give her to me! Do not take her away again; she needs my care!
Where is she? Where is she?'"[17] The British court system recognized
Monemia's claim to her children, ignoring the master who brought her
there and, after the trial, took them all back to the United States. Despite
his initial discomfort with it, Smith eventually assumed the role of the
twins' manager himself and, with the assistance of his able and instruc-
tive wife, transformed the two little girls into an internationally recognized entertainment duo.

Smith himself toured with the girls for the next five or so years, assisted by T. A. Vestal, the patient and now trusted private investigator
from Selma who had helped him find the two in England.[18] They managed a wide Southern circuit until the Civil War, when Smith removed
the McKoys from public life. In 1862, in an attempt to solicit money
from extended family to improve his own failing finances, Smith went to
North Carolina but died before he could return. Emancipation at this
point being no kind of reality for Southern slaves despite Lincoln's proc-
lamation in January of that year, Mary Smith auctioned off thirteen of
hers at a family estate sale in March 1863; she used the proceeds from
the transaction of her "people" and most of her farm's goods to pay off
their debts. Millie and Christine remained with the family they often described as their own.

After the war, the twins toured with Jacob, Monemia, Mary Smith,
and Mary's son, Joseph Junior. It was at this point, according to Martell, that the twins not only claimed a portion of their own wages, but
also "insisted on one big change [for their performances]. . . . [T]here'd
be no more intimate examinations by curious doctors in every town."[19]
Physicians continuously were disappointed by this decision; during one
stop in Washington, a doctor noted that the girls' "keeper, Mr. Smith,
would not allow me to see them naked nor place my hand under their
clothes to examine the pelvis."[20]

The twins' parents eventually returned to their home in Welches
Creek, North Carolina.[21] Meanwhile, the "Two-Headed Nightingale"

was claiming a position for "herself" as a well-established theatrical act.[22] Chang and Eng Bunker were forty years old when Millie and Christine were born and had already retired from their life in show business. But even though they were no longer actively touring, the original Siamese twins had set a kind of precedent for their American and European audiences. Showmen and publicity agents time and again noted the grace of, and overall pleasure induced by, the McKoys' appearances in comparison to the Bunkers'. The *Liverpool Daily Courier* claimed that the McKoys were "certainly a rival to the famous Siamese Twins and very much more attractive in appearance than Messrs Chang and Eng. Those who saw the Siamese Twins during their presence in England will have a vivid recollection of the pained look that their features bore, and the constrained movements of their bodies while walking in any direction."[23] According to the *Courier*, the McKoys boasted "four bright black eyes and dazzling rows of pearly-white teeth" that helped to light up their "fair Creole complexion with an animation that is really attractive."[24]

The twins toured all over the Northeast, including an engagement at P. T. Barnum's American Museum in 1866. The following fall, their New York manager, Judge H. P. Ingalls, put together a new troupe that included the McKoys and the Bunkers; Ingalls continued to manage the McKoys even after Chang and Eng retired permanently when Chang suffered a stroke. It was during this period of the twins' career that they again encountered Dr. William Pancoast, a prominent physician in Philadelphia who had examined them earlier in their career and who they now called upon to treat them for a fistulous opening.[25] Pancoast notes that "this case of pygopagus symmetros came under my professional care January 18, 1871 in consequence of an abscess forming near the genitals."[26] He took the opportunity to convince Mary Smith and the twins to allow him to shoot a semi-nude photo of Millie-Christine for an article he published in the *Photographic Review of Medicine and Surgery* later that same year (see fig. 6 in the image gallery).

After their enormous success in the Northeast—according to Ingalls, 150,000 people had come to see Millie-Christine's troupe of performers during their eight-week stay in Philadelphia and 10,000 one day alone in New York—the twins and their touring group headed for Britain and Europe, where they stayed for seven years. They traveled and performed widely, attended weddings of fellow show performers, giants Anna Swan and Martin Van Buren Bates, and visited the queen of England, who presented them with "a matched pair of diamond-studded hair clips."[27] In France, they disappointed Pierre Paul Broca, founder of the Anthropological Society of Paris and the surgical pathologist who would discover the speech production center of the brain, who wanted to examine the twins more thoroughly than they wanted him to (Broca nevertheless remained intrigued by what he described as the McKoys' racial makeup). The twins continued to perform in the United States and Cuba on their return, in part with Batcheller and Doris's Great Inter-Ocean Railroad Show, a competitor of Barnum and Bailey's Greatest Show on Earth, with whom they cleared a cool $25,000. They divided the end of their lives between the road and the land that road had brought to them in North Carolina: the farm that their father insisted in his will must stay in the McKoy family. During these years, the twins gave significant contributions to various educational institutions, including a school for African American children established in 1880. According to family lore, all of these contributions were made anonymously; for us today, this detail clearly suggests the McKoys' desire to do all they could to increase the political and economic freedoms of African Americans in general.

Millie was diagnosed with tuberculosis sometime in 1911 and died peacefully on October 8, 1912. Dr. Crowell, the family's physician, called the governor's office to receive the state's permission to provide euthanizing opiates to Chrissie once Millie died. The governor's permission was granted, and Chrissie died hours later—seventeen according to one account.

The title of Dean Jensen's recent biography of Daisy and Violet Hilton, *The Lives and Loves of Daisy and Violet Hilton* (2006), plays on the title of their autobiography— *The Intimate Loves and Lives of the Hilton Sisters*— contained in this collection. In his biography, Jensen tells the story of a show career gone very wrong and the ways in which a normalized public consumed performers like the Hiltons, who were seen as anything but "normal." For the McKoys, who were born into slavery, a career in show business ironically but eventually brought security and familial comfort. For the Hiltons though, an initially successful life in show business ended in financial ruin and never brought the Hiltons the one thing for which they longed the most—the love and comfort of family.

Daisy and Violet were born to the unwed twenty-one-year-old Kate Skinner in the resort town of Brighton, England, on February 5, 1908.[28]

Mary Hilton, Brighton's best-known midwife, assisted at the birth;
she and her husband, Henry, with their daughter Edith, ran a pub there
called The Queen's Arms, where, according to Jensen, Mary "paid" her
pregnant barmaids with her midwifery skills. Kate was horrified at the
"monstrosity" of her twin daughters and was easily convinced to give the
girls up in legal adoption to Mary and Henry. At the time of a carefully
publicized christening when the girls were seven weeks old, Mary Hilton
already had her first penny postcards available to present to the attending clergyman as a memento of the extraordinary infants and the service
he performed for them. As Jensen depicts, Mary Hilton was clearly invested in the girls' well-being as a business proposition. She kept them in
a room at the back of her bar, where they were always available for exhibit; when the twins were two, she and her daughter Edith took them
on the circus and fair circuit in Britain for the first time.[29]

What follows then is a sizeable period of touring under the guardianship of Mary Hilton; Henry died in 1912 when the family was touring
the twins in Germany, but Mary went on to take the girls throughout
Europe—at this point, they were being tutored closely in dancing, singing, and playing musical instruments—on to Australia, and eventually
to the United States. During their time in the Australian Outback, Mary
hired as troupe companion Myer Myers, a balloon and candy vendor
who traveled the same circus circuit as the Hiltons. In 1915, after two
years of touring and working together, Mary's daughter Edith married
Myers, who would eventually replace Mary as the twins' manager.

Life with Myers and Mary was secure in some ways, as Jensen notes,
but certainly not pleasant. Like the McKoy twins, the Hiltons were carefully educated and tutored in order to make them an acceptable and successful act—and successful they were. But the social restrictions placed
upon them would ultimately produce a kind of endless and unfulfilled
need for human affection: according to Jensen, when touring with
Wortham's World's Greatest Shows on the West Coast of the United
States in 1916, the girls had no freedom to develop relationships with
anyone other than the Myers family:

> Money was gushing into the show daily, thanks to Daisy and Violet, so
> that in the course of just a month or two, Myer Myers was transformed
> into a parvenu. The sisters did not benefit in any direct way from their
> growing wealth, however, nor did their lives change much. The rules
> had been laid down earlier by Myer and Mary: They were not to asso-
> ciate with other children, especially those from outside the carnival.

Actually, they were forbidden by Myer and Mary from being seen by
the public anywhere outside their tent. The twins weren't allowed to do
anything or go anywhere that might risk tarnishing their aura as the
rarest of sideshow attractions and possibly discourage some townies
from paying to see them.[30]

This is the kind of life the twins describe in their memoir that eventually led them to a lawsuit against Myers. After the twins attempted an
escape after Mary's funeral in 1919, Myers allegedly told them, "'You
girls belong to me now. . . . You'll do just as we say. See here? Auntie left
you to us. You and her jewelry and her furniture are now ours. Do you
understand?'"[31] As Jensen notes, to Myers and Mary Hilton, "Daisy
and Violet were a business, a cottage industry on which they depended
for their livelihood."[32]

The Hilton twins did eventually win their freedom in 1931 in San Antonio's Bexar County Courthouse when they sued Edith and Myer
Myers for an equitable portion of the assets listed in the names of the
Myers family but acquired through the twins' earnings.[33] They won their
lawsuit but lost a significant portion of the assets when presiding Judge
W. W. McCrory claimed that Myers had earned that money. "Jack
Dempsey was nothing but a ham-and-egger until Jack Kearns took hold
of him and developed him into a national champion," the judge announced, adding that "the Hilton twins would not be where they are
today had [Myers] not managed their affairs and proved himself a good
promoter."[34] Indeed, the cost of the Hiltons' freedom was in part the loss
of a stage manager with tremendous foresight and ability. Myer Myers
may have acted in many ways like a slaveholder—keeping the girls with
him against their own will, deciding their every move and action, refusing them the right to their own earnings, even beating them, according
to the twins, on a regular basis—but he was also a shrewd manager. And
while they did gain their freedom, in doing so, the twins also lost the only
familial environment they'd ever known, dysfunctional and scarring
though it might have been. Despite a trip the twins later made back to
their hometown of Brighton, Jensen notes that there is no evidence to
suggest that any members of Kate Skinner's family attempted to contact
them during their time there. As Joseph Haestier, son of the twins' aunt,
says, "the poor girls must have been heartbroken upon realizing that,
after all those years, they were still regarded as untouchables by all of
their blood relatives."[35] Daisy and Violet's almost desperate search for
love seems in part only a logical consequence of this lack of family.

Indeed, Jensen relates a long and sad search for relationships by the Hilton twins. While affairs of the heart never seem of any centrality in the story of the McKoys, it is in fact—as the title of their memoir shows—the defining framework for the Hiltons' life stories. Violet first carried a torch for the married Blue Steele, then in Britain became engaged to boxer Harry Mason, later falling in love with bandleader Maurice Lambert. Daisy fell in love with Don Galvan, then later Chicago bandleader Jack Lewis, then later Harry Mason after Violet ended her relationship with him. According to Jensen, both Daisy and Violet had lovers in the Dale Stevens Orchestra in 1936 when Daisy discovered she was pregnant. Jim Moore, one of Jensen's informants, himself played the groom in a publicity-driven marriage to Violet at the 1936 Dallas Cotton Bowl.[36] Also according to Jensen, Daisy gave her baby up for adoption and later, in 1941, married Buddy Sawyer, only to be abandoned in the days that followed.

In addition to being unlucky in love, the twins were too trusting and unwise with their finances. Giddy and extravagant in their newfound freedom, the twins lost their remaining fortune in the period following their lawsuit with Myers. In 1937, they returned to the carnival circuit to regain their financial footing. Although they did work their way back into the public eye, history intervened and World War II took the audiences that had kept the Hiltons on the entertainment circuit. As Jensen explains, the 1940s witnessed a decided shift in public attitudes about the exhibition of extraordinarily different people like the Hiltons. Certainly this was one of the reasons Tod Browning's film *Freaks* horrified rather than captivated audiences, another bad financial venture in which the Hiltons were involved. It's perhaps not surprising then that the Hiltons turned to the burlesque stage in 1943, performing at times as "The World's Only Strip-Teasing Twins."[37] Despite these troubling circumstances, the Hiltons did eventually regain their financial footing in the mid-1940s, only to become prey again—this time to booking agent Ross Frisco, who introduced the twins to the idea of a film starring them, a screenplay on which he claimed he already had a lead called *Chained for Life*.

While the story of *Chained for Life* follows the fictional Hamilton twins, who become the target of a publicity-stunt marriage by managerial agents, the Hiltons themselves became a similar kind of target for Frisco. The film ushered in the end of the girls' life in show business, draining their newly reconstituted savings in the film's production and digging a new pit of debt out of which they were forced to try and fight their way. As Jensen describes it, the twins' sense of financial propriety—they underwrote the entire production, relieving producer George Moskov of all fund-raising responsibility—was a defining problem with the film's making, given that they were continuously providing advice and direction where and when they shouldn't have been. About the director hired for the film, Harry L. Fraser, Jensen claims that the twins were drawn to the fact that "unlike the other directors who had been brought in on the project earlier, [Fraser] was a director who could be directed."[38] Jensen describes the cast as "comprised of actors and actresses who could be placed in the categories of has-beens, never-beens, and never-would-bes."[39] Although the Hiltons relished their time in Hollywood, once the film was finished, Eagle-Lion Studios, with whom they had contracted for the movie's production, refused to release it until the thousands of dollars still owed on it was paid. Once it was finally released, *Chained for Life* only showed at drive-ins and obscure movie houses, often, as Jensen notes, "as part of a double and triple feature with *Reefer Madness, Test Tube Babies,* or the twenty-year-old *Freaks*."[40]

The twins never recovered financially from the catastrophe of *Chained for Life*. Having lost most, if not all, of their drawing power as entertainers, they opened the Hilton Sisters Snack Bar in Miami in 1956. That business failed within a year, and after struggling for employment in entertainment for another five years, they wound up essentially homeless in Charlotte, North Carolina. Made the subject of charity by several interested parties, the Hiltons' final jobs were as cashiers in a grocery store where once, desperate for employment, they had appeared to promote packs of twin potato chips. On January 4, 1969, both twins were found dead in the cottage into which they'd recently moved; Daisy had been sick with the Hong Kong flu since Christmas, and although their physician recommended hospitalization, the two had refused. A neighbor donated the cemetery plot in which they were buried in Forest Lawn Cemetery in Charlotte.

The Autobiographies and Related Texts

According to Martell, the McKoys' autobiography, *The History of the Carolina Twins,* was probably written at the suggestion of a new agent hired by the Smiths in 1869, in part to help revive interest in what was then a slow period in the twins' performance history (see fig. 1 in the image gallery). Thirty-two pages long and 4½ by 7 inches in size, the booklet sold for twenty-five cents at the twins' shows. Dicksie Cribb, the Smiths' great-granddaughter, notes that "Christine did all the writing; she was the correspondent. The other, Millie, crocheted and dictated to Christine what to write."[41] The *History* was published in Buffalo by publishers Warren, Johnson and Company.

Also according to Martell's and others' research, at least five versions of the McKoys' show history were produced during their lifetimes. *Biographical Sketch of Millie Christine, the Two-Headed Nightingale* appeared in 1871 in London and was an updated and locally engineered account ordered by then show manager Judge H. P. Ingalls. During the twins' time touring with the Batcheller & Doris Great Inter-Ocean Show, another version was published in 1882 in New York by Torrey & Clark, and other versions appeared in or around 1889 and early in the twentieth century. The version reprinted here was one of these last, appearing sometime between 1902 and 1912 and published by Hennegan & Co. in Cincinnati. While much of the text in these different versions remains largely consistent, the title and other smaller details are altered in later versions. For instance, the line "each mouth is adorned with such a set of brilliant ivory, as an American dentist observed, that many of his patients would be glad to purchase for twenty-five thousand dollars" that appeared in the 1871 British edition was changed in later U.S. editions to read, simply, "each mouth is adorned with a set of brilliant teeth." The extra matter included with the histories—for example, newspaper stories, physicians' testimonies, songs, and advertisements—is also somewhat different from version to version.

William Pancoast's article "The Carolina Twins" appeared in 1871 in *The Photographic Review of Medicine and Surgery*. The text is at once a medical account of the twins' physiology as well as a record of the numerous and invasive explorations Pancoast made of the bodies of the McKoys, forays in which he was often accompanied by a host of his friends and medical associates. Indeed, the original publication includes not simply the only photograph known to exist that illustrates the twins' actual physical point of connection but also an explicit woodcut of the twins' lower torso with a detail insert of their vulvae.[42]

While the twins successfully assert their unique subjectivity in their autobiography, stressing their connectedness and unity of feeling at the same time they matter-of-factly affirm their duality, the *Biographical*

Sketch and Pancoast's "Carolina Twins" display the various ways in which the public, in the forms of the twins' managers and the larger medical community, chose to limit and redefine that subjectivity for their own purposes. In fact, the greatest achievement of the twins in their autobiography is their ability to highlight and make familiar the quandary that was their personhood without diminishing its exceptionality, claiming for themselves an identity of two women who simultaneously constitute one being, one united emotional and spiritual force. In doing so, the McKoys become a powerful and literal example of two sisters, born in slavery, who refuse under any circumstances to be separated. To fully appreciate the significance of this refusal one need only remember the history of family separation that was the criminal hallmark of slavery in the United States. In other words, in a world in which black families had been intentionally torn apart for centuries, in part to weaken the African American community, the image of two sisters who repeatedly avow that they will not be separated—and whom even the press describe as being "an indissoluble union"—is a powerful statement of solidarity indeed.[43]

The first sentence of the twins' memoir plants us firmly in this unfamiliar territory of conjoined subjectivity and leaves us there: "We are, indeed, a strange people," the twins say, emphasizing at once not just their complete difference—their identity as "a strange people," unlike any seen before—but also their simultaneous state of singularity *and* multiplicity: *a people* they are, neither pluralized people nor individualized persons.[44] The second sentence unsettles the reader's assumption coming to the text that there might be something wrong with their physical state: "Physicians who have examined us," they note, "say our formation— or rather malformation—is much more remarkable than the physical condition of the Siamese twins" (40). There is nothing "mal" for the McKoys about their physical state; the term "malformation" enters their sentence as an afterthought, an ironic self-correction. In fact it is this very "malformation" that will induce the twins' master, Smith, to purchase not just the girls but their entire family as well.[45] And it is their family that Millie-Christine credit with the decision to see the twins as people at the moment of their birth:

> We made our *entrée* into this breathing world in 1852. Our coming in such "questionable shape" created as great a *furore* in the cabin, as our appearance has since, wherever we have been. "Old Aunt Hannah," a faithful nurse, whose specialty was to be around and to discharge the

first hospitalities to new comers of our complexion, couldn't for "de life or soul of her" tell whether we was a "young nigger" or "something else." But the "something else" soon gave unmistakable evidences that it could *viva voce* intimate a desire for maternal comforts, just as well as the best developed young African on the premises. So our mother and the rest of the family came to the conclusion that "a child was born." (40–41)

By alluding to another amazing child who was born into humble circumstances, the twins once again refute any possibility that their exceptionality can be regarded as anything other than wonderful, even divine.

The drama contained in the autobiography centers on the ways in which the twins are taken from "friends, kindred, or any one who had a *right* to feel an interest in us," including the Smith family who owns them (42). In fact, readers today may be surprised at the way slavery is represented in all the McKoy texts. In an odd distortion of the by-then familiar scene of slaves and enslaved children being sold away from their families, both the autobiographical *History* and the *Biographical Sketch* capitalize on the dramatic appeal of Millie and Christine's early "kidnapping" away from their Southern master. When the twins are about to be recovered from their time in what is in actuality their secondary captivity, Smith, the girls' owner, uses Monemia to force the hand of the British courts to reinstate the children to her. There seems to be little awareness in the texts of the profound hypocrisy in using the twins' enslaved mother to foil the courts in emancipated Britain, which would not—could not, legally—send the McKoys back to their slaveholding master but were forced to return them to their biological mother. One can't help but wonder what strictures were put on Monemia—a woman traveling alone across the ocean with her master to reclaim part of her children while leaving the rest of her family, including her husband, behind in North Carolina—to make this happen.[46]

Rather than the abusive or sexually predatory master we might today expect to encounter in an abolitionist-driven slave narrative of a slightly earlier date, Smith is depicted instead as a hero, working selflessly to reunite the "stolen" twins with the tragically distraught Monemia. Early on in their account, the twins describe Smith as the one responsible for keeping their family together when he purchases their parents and siblings after buying Millie-Christine (41). And when Smith dies during the war that the twins refer to simply as "the domestic political troubles," they note that they were old enough "to mourn the loss of our good master, who seemed to us as a father, and we here would render a grateful tribute to his memory, by saying that he was urbane, generous, kind, patient-bearing, and beloved by all" (45–46). (In the *Biographical Sketch*, we are told that "Christine Millie desires particularly that it be inserted in this sketch of her life, that she experienced at his death rather the affliction of one who had lost a beloved father rather than a master" [69].)[47] The twins also describe their relationship to their mistress in nothing short of glowing terms: "None can mistake our determination in remaining under the guardianship of Mrs. Smith. Our object is two-fold: *We can trust her*, and what is more, we feel grateful to her and regard her with true filial affection. We will not go with any one else; where she goes there will we go; where she tarries there will we halt" (46).[48] One wonders here if in fact the definitive nature of their decision—to stay with Mrs. Smith because *"we can trust her"*—may speak to an implicit fear of being sold or taken away from this apparently generally happy home. Likewise, they reference their increased independence when they talk about returning to England to see the "many things of interest" they missed when they were there before; "now, that we are 'grown up girls,' and like the rest of our sex, with tongues, and a knowledge of their use, we may go across the water once more" (44). Indeed, the twins' signature song reprinted toward the end of the text following a list of physicians who vouch for their physical authenticity begins with the stanza, "It's not modest of one's self to speak, / But daily scanned from head to feet / I freely talk of everything—/ Sometimes to persons wondering" (48). Despite the claim the McKoys make to "freely talk of everything," the reader can't help but wonder what all they might have left out. A kind of Reconstruction-era slave narrative, the *History* necessarily contains an encrypted version of the McKoys' life story, something that is especially evident when we look at the medical statements of "authenticity" included at the end of it.

Many if not most slave narratives begin with a prologue written by a prominent white man or woman, usually an abolitionist, that acts as a verification for the white reader, skeptical that a slave could tell their own story and tell it truthfully. In a variant of this gesture, the McKoys include "some medical testimony of a most positive and unmistakable character" to verify that they should be "viewed as something entirely void of humbug—a living curiosity—not a sham gotten up to impose upon and deceive the people" (47). This testimony appears in the form of a letter addressed to "Mrs. James P. Smith" and signed by a list of five physicians, including Dr. Ellershe Wallace, Professor of Obstetrics at Jefferson Medical College, and Dr. William H. Pancoast. It states that "a number of medical gentlemen" have examined the twins and found "a thorough fusion of the lower portion of the trunk, osseous and fleshy; the two spinal columns uniting together at the base, forming but one large bone common to both" (47). They note that the upper bodies and heads of the McKoys are "perfectly separate, as though belonging to a distinct individuality, forming the most interesting monstrosity, morally and physically considered, on record" (47). The twins do not allow this intrusive statement to be the final word on their lives; rather, they sum up by again asserting their exceptionality, claiming that, "although we speak of ourselves in the plural we feel as but *one person*. . . . We have but *one heart*, one feeling in common, one desire, one purpose" (48). They conclude with a song they say "conveys a good idea of our feelings" (48). Unlike the rest of the autobiography, the song only relies upon the first person singular pronoun to express the twins' feelings; nevertheless, it ends with the following stanza that again leaves the question of the McKoys' subjectivity wide open:

> I'm happy, quite, because I'm good;
> I love my Savior and my God.
> I love all things that God has done,
> Whether I'm created *two* or *one*.
>
> (49)

Once again, as they did when telling the story of their birth, the McKoys here link themselves to divinity, to the love of God, and to the power of God to create them as "happy" and "good," regardless of whether they are seen as "*two* or *one*." For the McKoys, it is this distinction that is "immaterial."

This powerful assertion by the twins of their unique subjectivity, particularly given the pervasiveness of the forces that worked to contain or dismantle it, may well be one of the first things a reader sees when she or he looks at the show history, *Biographical Sketch of Millie-Christine, the Carolina Twin.*[49] Here already in the title, the twins have been boiled down to one person, merely a "twin" rather than the marvelous duality they claim for themselves in their own life story. From the notices that open and close the text announcing that it is "customary for Millie-Christine, the dual woman, to require but one ticket" when riding the train to the epithets the writers use to describe her at the beginning of the narrative proper—"The Two-Headed Lady, the Double-Tongued Nightingale, the Eighth Wonder of the World, the Puzzle of Science, the Despair of Doctors"—to the text itself, which singularizes the twins as simply "her" throughout, the McKoys are literarily reduced to one person in the biography (52–59, 60). In fact, singularity is where the text rests: "There are marvels of nature, science and art, of all which the world knows; but there can only be one NONPAREIL, one UNEQUALLED, and that is the subject of our brief sketch, for only one living creature is like Millie Christine and her name is Christine Millie" (60). Despite the effort to reduce the twins to one person, however, the *Biographical Sketch* contradicts itself: the last epithet to be included on this list is in fact "the Dual Unity" (60). Whether it's "Millie Christine" or "Christine Millie," the question remains unanswered as to whether the reader should or can understand the McKoys to be either one or two people. In one of the numerous newspaper notices reprinted in the *Biographical Sketch*, writers from the *Liverpool Mercury* comment that "the question which naturally arises, and which it seems difficult to solve, is, whether this is one being, or whether, in some extraordinary manner, two persons have thus marvelously joined together" (74). The answer for this observer comes perhaps in the next sentence when an account of the many medical examinations the McKoys underwent is summarized: "The lungs, heart, and functions of digestion are those of two persons, apparently perfect and healthy in each, but that the whole of the lower organization of the body is that of one female, with the exception of the four legs" (74).

The question of whether the McKoys are one person or two people captivates and distracts another writer from the *Liverpool Leader*:

> We can testify that no person of ordinary intelligence can be in her company for half an hour without yielding to the charm of her manner and the fascination of her double smiles. She has you on both sides. If you remove your head from one position you are immediately the victim of another pair of eyes, which fix you and, in fact, transfix you. We candidly admit that we were fascinated, and that we immediately lost sight of the phenomenon and became overpowered by the influence of this dual brain. (78)

Clearly the fascination of the twins has to do with the impossibility of not being watched by them—of the doubling of a mentality and physicality that somehow pleasurably, erotically "victimizes" the observer here. It's not the twinning that enthralls this reader but rather the doubling of the

McKoys, one woman made two. For him, it is both "fascinating" and "transfixing."

Indeed, the decision to see the McKoys as one woman seems to be settled largely in the public's eye due to the twins' gynecological physiology—and not surprisingly, really, given both the cultural history of women depicted as inherently more bodily than men and the specific U.S. cultural history of black women as inherently sexually rapacious. This is certainly how the writer from the *Liverpool Leader* seems to see the twins—a sexually doubled single woman.[50] As the authenticating "Certificates of Eminent Medical Men" that appear in the *Biographical Sketch* explain, in the twins "there are separate bladders, but one common vagina, one uterus to be recognized, and one perfect anus" (82). The *Biographical Sketch* includes a number of these notices and it takes a moment before the reader realizes the significance of all these "certificates," signed by long lists of physicians from all over the United States and Britain and each of which includes some permutation of Pancoast's statement above, that the twins have "one common vagina, one uterus to be recognized, and one perfect anus." The magnitude of this exploitation—that each of these signers apparently conducted or were privy to a gynecological exam of the twins—is nothing short of staggering; it is of course to what the twins refer when they note that they are "daily scanned from head to feet." More, it is blatant evidence of the sexual economy of slavery and the pornographic and sexual appropriation of black women's bodies that were foundational not just to slavery or the racist terrorism that followed its demise but also to institutions of popular entertainment like the freak show.[51]

It is therefore ironic that the only text that treats the twins as predominantly individualized is Pancoast's disturbing "The Carolina Twins."[52] While initially referring to the McKoys as "this case of pygopagus symmetros" that he is able to examine when "*it* was on exhibition" in Philadelphia, Pancoast mostly focuses on the differences between the two and where those differences eclipse into something else (99, emphasis mine).[53] But in a way neither of the other texts do, Pancoast focuses first on one twin ("Chrissie can now, as she has always been able to do, bend over and lift up Millie by the bond of their union" [101]) then the next ("Millie, though the weaker physically, has the stronger will, and is the dominating spirit"), keeping them distinct and separate (101). Even though he openly acknowledges the McKoys' individual personalities and physicalities, Pancoast's essay does not confer a greater sense of humanity on the twins as a result but instead enacts an appropriation and, more, a violation of them. In fact, there is something about the kind of separation that Pancoast performs in his writing that feels akin to the surgical parting the twins refused to consider in their own lives. No doubt Pancoast harbored his own fantasies about executing just such an experimental division himself.

The imagery in the article is as demeaning and dehumanizing as anything else about it. Pancoast presents the engraving of the two women lying naked on a bed preparing for a gynecological exam; underneath that image is an enlarged detail of the women's vulvae. In the accompanying text, Pancoast goes on to describe what he finds as he probes them:

> On examining the vagina, which gave them more annoyance than pain, I found no hymen present, but the orifice naturally small and contracted, as that of an ordinary young unmarried woman. I readily passed my index finger up its whole length. I found only one vagina, and no bifurcation of it, only one womb. (103)

After completing his description of his examination, Pancoast adds that "to establish the accuracy of my examination, I invited upon one occasion Prof. Pancoast [his father, also an eminent physician in Philadelphia], Prof. Gross, Dr. Seavy, of Bangor, Maine, and Dr. T. H. Andrews; and upon another, Dr. R. J. Levis and Dr. S. H. Dickson, Jr. These gentlemen agreed with me that there was but one vagina, but one womb to be recognized, but one perfect anus" (104). The sense of violation is multiplied here by every name listed.

Not surprisingly, it is also Pancoast who publishes the only image of the twins that shows their physical bond, one that is also necessarily partially nude (see fig. 6 in the image gallery). He is careful to describe their distinct displeasure at having this picture taken: "They clung to their raiment closely, as may be seen, and it was only by earnest entreaty that they were willing to compromise by retaining the drapery as photographed. The expression of their countenances shows their displeasure, as their features ordinarily express great amiability of character" (99). Why Pancoast includes this information is unclear; while he seems to want to protect the twins' reputations by assuring his readers of their sexual purity and physical modesty (he notes that while he does not find a hymen in his investigations of their bodies, the twins have the physiology of "an ordinary young unmarried woman" [103]), his inclusion of images that undoubtedly excited an already existing pornographic interest in these women works to contradict that impulse. But of course, as he indicates early on in the article, these are in the end black women, figures for whom sexual autonomy and even possession of one's own body are not guaranteed.

While occupying a relatively minor place in the McKoy biographies, marriage is another issue that Pancoast raises. He notes that he believes in regard to the possibility of the twins' future nuptials, "physically there are no serious objections," but "morally there are insuperable ones" (108). Despite this inquiry and the extended investigation into the twins' gynecological makeup, the issue of the twins' future as wives is practically ignored. As African American women after Emancipation, the McKoys certainly would have had a legal right to marry. And in fact, one of the most intriguing things for audiences about Chang and Eng was the reality of their married lives. Nevertheless, the history of slavery hangs over these women and their life stories; in the *Biographical Sketch* and Pancoast's "Carolina Twins," the McKoys' sexualized bodies remain in the possession of the general public, the numerous physicians who examined them, and the audiences and readers who were informed by these examinations. Surely the uncompromising subjectivity Millie and Christine McKoy carve out for themselves in their *Biographical Sketch* is all the more remarkable for this.

The three documents included here that pertain to Daisy and Violet Hilton stretch the generic limits of conventional autobiography and biography; nevertheless, all three are treated by a range of interested parties as viable representations of the lives of Daisy and Violet Hilton. In 1925, tour director and manager Myer Myers produced *Souvenir and Life Story of San Antonio's Siamese Twins, Daisy and Violet Hilton*, a 9-by-12-inch show history of the girls over whose lives Myers had assumed control (see fig. 8 in the image gallery). Myers's text is practically the inverse of the autobiography the Hiltons composed themselves, published first in six Sunday issues of the *American Weekly* in 1943. Again according to Jensen, this serialized memoir, "The Private Life of the Twins," was "represented by Daisy and Violet Hilton to be a 'true and full double autobiography,' as told to Ethelda Bedford, apparently a staff writer for the *American Weekly*."[54] Published by the Hearst Corporation from 1896 to 1966, the *American Weekly* was a Sunday newspaper supplement that published largely sensationalized writing. Nevertheless, the autobiography permitted the Hiltons the opportunity to refashion themselves during a time in their lives when, having slipped from public view and acclaim, they were starting to experience an upswing in their career, a new start that the story in the *American Weekly* helped relaunch.[55]

When *Chained for Life* was finally released in 1953, the twins republished their *American Weekly* memoir in a small booklet—*Intimate Loves and Lives of the Hilton Sisters*—that they sold for two dollars from card tables set up at concession stands at drive-ins and movie theaters (see fig. 7 in the image gallery). In Jensen's words, "to help justify the $2 cover price for the forty-eight page potboiler, they threw in a second publication, a recreation in novella form of *Chained for Life*."[56] While certainly not a biographical account of the twins' lives in any direct or factual way, the novella is nevertheless represented by the Hiltons to be illustrative of their lives. The caption to a sketch of the twins that opens the pamphlet explains that the photo stills that pepper the text "although borrowed from scenes of the motion picture entitled 'Chained for Life,' in which the Hilton Sisters play the leading role, nevertheless depict actual events in their lives."[57] The memoir actually instructs the reader to read *Intimate Loves and Lives of the Hilton Sisters* and the novelization of *Chained for Life* as two versions of the same story. Given the crushing legacy the twins inherited from the film's awful failure, the novelization becomes a disturbing endnote to the ways in which the Hilton twins had their so-called "biography" turned against them.

Rather than linger on the question of whether the Hiltons constitute one or two people, Myers instead steeps his biography of the Hiltons within the context of demonstrable virtue, repeatedly affirming how moral the girls are, how morally they're being raised, and how "their ambition to achieve is the natural result of their living clean lives, thinking wholesome thoughts and cultivating noble purposes" (162). Myers describes how the twins climbed "from the pit of the street carnival where they began their careers to the pinnacle in the amusement world" and casts that ascent as a tribute to "the children's willingness to sacrifice, to work, to study and to aspire" (160). Myers alters the story of the girls' familial background to make it more respectable: he tells the reader that the Hiltons are "the daughters of an English Army officer" who "was killed in Belgium in 1914" and that "their mother died a year after their birth" (160). From a patriotic origin to the "pinnacle of the amusement world," Myers emphasizes at every turn the virtue the girls

exemplify. At times, those turns are decidedly abrupt. In an example of
how they have been raised by the Myers family to ensure this purity of
heart and mind, Myers claims that "their minds are supplied with those
things that stimulate the mind and body with high ideals and healthful
thoughts. If a young unfortunate jazz-crazed girl kills her mother there
is every effort made to keep this sordid story from lodging in the minds
of these little innocent girls" (161). The specificity of this example is intriguing to say the least. Perhaps more a preemptive strike on the part of
Myers than anything, if indeed the girls ever turned on him, such an action could only result from the corruption of the world of the popular
press, not from the girls themselves or anything from their lives with the
Myers family. The story of the "jazz-crazed girl" obviously indicates one
of the seamier elements of society that, if the twins were to leave the "protection" of the Myers circle, may well infect them as well.

    In fact, "Mr. and Mrs. Myers," who are described as having adopted
their orphan "nieces" in order to "devote their entire time to the girls
and their activities," have actually realized a better marital life because
of this assiduous care:

> Mrs. Myers will tell you that she and her husband have tried to
> show the Hilton Twins every care and devotion, and that they have
> been paid back with every ounce of love that these little bodies hold.
> Those who will tell you that not only has this devotion been rewarded
> by a deep, abiding love that these little girls have for their adopted par-
> ents, but that while training and caring for these little girls who came
> into the world so handicapped for life's race, they have brought them-
> selves to the same standard that they sought for the girls, and as a result
> Mr. and Mrs. Myers have found married life to be one of pleasure and
> understanding. They have found a unity in purpose in doing for the little
> twins that has smoothed the path of life over which they themselves are
> traveling. (162)

As Myers and his wife emphasize their parenting skills, they infantilize
the Hiltons in the process. Doing so benefits them in a couple of different ways. The emotion invoked by *Souvenir and Life Story* is primarily pity;
as long as the readers see the Hiltons as disabled and somewhat pathetic
children rather than women with complex sexualities, the reader will be
moved to wonder at their beauty and talent rather than linger on these
more complicated questions. In fact, in the images that appear in the
center of the booklet, every photograph is labeled as to the age of the
girls when it was taken—"Six Months," "Three Years," "Six Years,"

and so forth (see fig. 9a in the image gallery).[58] The final such labeled image is of the girls at fifteen with the accompanying caption: "A proper home atmosphere—care and devotion, developed the sisters and the girls radiate happiness—Sweet sixteen around the corner."[59] The facing page includes several more photographs, but their age is now omitted from the captions; they are simply "young ladies" who "enjoy all the good things in life that other girls enjoy" (see fig. 9b).[60] In fact, as we learn at the very end of the text, the girls are "past 20 years of age," although again, Myers is careful not to specify exactly how far past (170). By denying the girls full womanhood, Myers maintains not only a kind of paternal posture for the reader in relation to them but also an implicit authorization on his part to continue to control their lives; as the Hiltons themselves noted in *Intimate Loves and Lives*, Myers forced the girls to continue to sleep in his and his wife's bedroom until they were in their early twenties, clearly to ensure constant surveillance and control of their movements, movements that might well have included some kind of exploration of their own sexuality.

Despite the apparent desire to contain this sexuality, though, Myers's final comment here is about marriage and the twins. As Myers explains, "there is always the possibility that one of these twins, who are separate individualities despite their legal status of a single being, will suddenly fall in love some day" (170). Myers records a conversation the girls reportedly have about two newlywed friends. Daisy declares that "Tom is a great, big dear, so direct and sincere and faithful. He reminds me of a loyal affectionate Newfoundland" (170). Violet, however, imagines that puppy Tom's concern about his new wife's spending and her tendency to ignore him may be the result of Tom's own behavior: "Tom loves to regard her as a child" (171). In fact, Myers seems to be carefully allowing the girls to mature on the page; rather than an impossibly wholesome family environment, we have entered into a different place with a more powerful undercurrent. What Myers finally describes as the "keen observation facilities" of the Hiltons inadvertently becomes something a bit more charged, more alluring:

> The outstanding fact about Violet and Daisy is that they are normal girls, who, by the very nature of their physical tie, have had more time for study, reading and serious conversation with older people than have most other girls of their ages. So obvious is this rather mature mental state that people who come to see them, prepared to treat them as abnormal children, almost instantly drop that attitude in quick confusion,

> for the gaze of the twins' thoughtful, observing eyes is not that of artless
> children,—not that at all. (171)

Like the Liverpool reporter who was "victimized" by the McKoy twins'
double stare, so, too, will the casual observer of the Hiltons quickly realize the deep water into which any possible intimate of Daisy and Violet
must find himself. But Myers firmly brings us back to the land of moral
compass; about marriage for conjoined twins, Violet notes that, yes, she
has heard of the conjoined Blazek sisters, one of whom mothered a child,
but as she explains, "our way can't be their way. We can't be separated,
no matter how the future may force such a desire upon us, so there is no
way for either of us to find happiness that others find in marriage" (172).
    Myers's control of the girls' sexuality is both evident and carefully fi-
nessed. But in fact, we can see where he has learned such lessons about
sales because he tells us:

> In the methods used to elevate the Hilton Sisters to the pinnacle of fame
> and fortune there is an absolute similarity with the way Henry Ford
> raised the fliver from a freak to where last year it earned him, his wife
> and son, Edsel, $115,000,000.00 profit and won him the greatest popu-
> larity ever enjoyed by a rich man in the history of the world. (161–62)

It's a little startling to see the wanton desire for profit so openly espoused
here by Myers. Not only does he loudly and unabashedly celebrate himself as a savvy seller of the disabled, he goes on to note that "psychologists will tell you that not over one-fifth of what anything costs is represented in actual value; four-fifths are in the mind; four-fifths have been
created by mental processes. In the case of the Hilton Sisters it is more
than nine-tenths created value. It takes imagination and enthusiasm to
create those intangible values and convert them into realities. That is
showmanship in its highest sphere. It is salesmanship in its highest
phase" (162). While the girls are the main subject of the pamphlet, a
prominent subplot is the Myers family's own remarkable ability to sell
them. A "freak" with "nine-tenths created value," Daisy and Violet Hilton constitute little more than a sexualized product Myers successfully
markets, a virgin that pops open to reveal the whore hiding inside. The
fact that Myers can announce this and do so with pride tells us pretty
clearly what the Hiltons' audiences expected and allowed.
    Although the Hiltons themselves play on this sexualized possibility,
doubling and redoubling their romantic status, their autobiography is

an attempt to establish themselves as individual yet linked beings who desire love and the moral possibility that a text like Myers'—despite its proclaimed moral code—ultimately denies them. The title of the twins' memoir reprint—*The Intimate Loves and Lives of the Hilton Sisters*—plays on the idea of a tantalizing sexual exposé, and indeed, both of the stories contained in that booklet make the sisters' intimate lives their focal point. But the intimacy that is highlighted in the twins' autobiography is less sexual than emotional—how they must maneuver to maintain privacy within the context of their relationship with one another, the peace they have achieved in their shared intimacy, and their desire for an extension of that relationship into romance and family. Although it is not nearly as intentional and clear-cut as it is in the McKoys' autobiography, the Hiltons also provide their readers with a newly conceived subjectivity, one perhaps not so much asserted as assembled over the pages.

The first three paragraphs of the autobiography outline its major themes: first, as the twins note, "the eyes of a curious world have been focused on us almost from the moment of our birth;" next, due to their physical connection with one another, whether "there could be no such thing for either of us as a private life;" and finally, "how two human beings can endure constant, continuous living together harmoniously" (131). For the Hiltons, the issue is privacy, whether that means having an autonomous social life beyond the control of Myers, preserving the harmonious emotional relationship they share with one another, maintaining a sense of separateness from one another particularly in moments of sexual intimacy, or questioning whether in fact their lovers can negotiate—or more accurately bear—the lack of privacy that romantic involvement with a conjoined twin requires. And although it seems less conscious an attempt here than in *The History of the Carolina Twins*, the Hiltons, too, weave a complex interchange between singularity and duality, between harmony and discord, between separateness and togetherness.

In fact, each of these positions seems to create and call up its own narrator. The autobiography begins with a joined speaker ("the eyes of a curious world have been focused on *us* almost from the moment of *our* birth"). While immediately establishing a relationship with the reader ("you are undoubtedly wondering"), the text moves from we-ness to oneness by the end of the fourth paragraph: "The truth is that we are as different in our reactions as day and night. I, Violet, often weep over something which makes my sister chuckle" (131). This is the dialogic

nature of the autobiography: from "we are as different" to the more
stilted, "I, Violet." It continues like this throughout the autobiography:

> We never consult or advise. We simply tell each other our wishes.
> For instance, I, Daisy, may want to go shopping when my sister, Violet,
> has a headache.
>   I, Violet, tell Daisy that at a certain time the following day I'll go
> shopping with her. Having once given her my word, nothing will stop
> me—at least, nothing ever has. (131–32)

Rather than one or even two voices, the Hiltons' autobiography uses
three: one for Violet, another for Daisy, and a third that indicates when
the two speak as one. In essence then, rather than a new subjectivity de-
fined in terms of their exceptionality, such as occurs in the McKoys' account of their lives, the Hiltons multiply theirs, granting themselves the
license to move back and forth between these positions at will. In fact, it
is the loss of any of these subjectivities that troubles them most, whether
it be due to the Myers family's attempts to squash their social movements and collect their own earnings or the moves of the men who love
them yet want to contain and control them. (Daisy is at once thrilled
and dismayed when her lover Don Galvan asks her to marry him:
"Even as he asked me," she says, "he took the cigarette from my hand,
pushed my wine glass aside. Even he would suppress me!" [152].) The
essence of the subjectivity the Hiltons claim is a lack of containment, a
tripling even, rather than a doubling, and the ways in which this expan-
sion functions without discord or strife. This last is a key idea reiterated
throughout the text: "It is as though some Power, greater and stronger
than ourselves, has given us this inner harmony to compensate for our
being forced to live constantly as an entity. And that harmony has been
with us through the years—a harmony that has amazed many who have
known us" (132).

In fact, the emotional interconnectedness of the Hiltons dominates
the descriptions they provide of themselves. They note that their early
thinking was unusually, but necessarily, mature: "As strongly as we have
fought against being separated, we have determined to live harmoniously in our bond. . . . In order to do this, there are many rules we are
forced to follow. Among them [are] not to seek advice from each other,
not to advise, ever, and not to speak aloud our thoughts" (136). When
after the death of "Auntie" they discover that she has in essence willed
them to her daughter and son-in-law, they in fact credit this sense of

togetherness with their very survival: "Our minds grew strong and our Siamese bond of flesh and bone became one of real understanding between us. Our desire to harmonize with each other was, indeed, our real salvation" (141). During their trial, Violet describes the power she absorbs from her sister in order to speak there: "As I, Violet, did most of the talking, I was stimulated and strengthened by my twin's concentration. My answers came clearly and quickly. When I hesitated only slightly Daisy would prompt me by the movement of her arm against mine, or shrug her shoulder. There are, you see, many times when being a Siamese twin has its peculiar advantages" (150). Throughout the text, the twins' emotional connection is depicted as their saving grace, their life force.

This harmony and sense of interconnectedness, of course, stems from their physical bond, and they talk about that as well—how they preferred the sound of the violin to the piano because they "liked the vibration of the violin as it traveled over our connecting bridge. The piano was too detached" (137). And when Daisy finally shares a fleeting moment of physical intimacy with Don Galvan as their hands clasp "for a throbbing second" offstage, she hears "my sister gasp for me. The surge of emotion swept through both of us as Edith elbowed Don away from me" (142). In fact, it is this shared sense of sexual intimacy that Allison Pingree argues shows us how the doubling of the twins' sexuality and female force were part of a larger conversation about the figure of the newly independent and resourceful "New Woman" and all that she promised—and threatened. Pingree highlights a moment from the Hilton's first film appearance in Tod Browning's *Freaks* when, during a passionate kiss between Violet's character and her fiancé, Daisy's character "looks up in surprise, closes her eyes, and relishes the erotic pleasure right along with her sister."[61] According to Pingree, "such a sequence serves, once again, to reveal the frightening prospects that the twins pose—prospects such as women sharing simultaneous sensual enjoyment, or husbands unable to control altogether when, where, and how their wives experience sexuality."[62] Indeed, the Hiltons include a still from *Chained for Life* in *Intimate Loves and Lives* that depicts Violet/Vivian smiling as Daisy/Dorothy kisses her publicity paramour, Andre Pariseau.

Despite the emphasis they place on the intimacy between them, and unlike the McKoys' text where the twins' sexual desire is practically erased, Daisy and Violet do long for love. "We still long to find real romance and love equal to our own tolerance and forgiveness," the Hiltons

reiterate at the end of their memoir (158). Indeed, they say it quite
clearly: "We dream of having homes and families" (158). But the last
sentence of the text is in some ways the most intriguing plea of all:

> Perhaps you have seen through this story that life has given us
> plenty of problems, and that we have adjusted ourselves to most of
> them. And somewhere still, *we believe and hope we will find the right mates, to
> whose understanding and love we can entrust our private lives.* (158, emphasis
> mine)

Not only do the Hiltons seek to redefine the permeability and flux of the
boundaries of personal identity, an identity that is, like the McKoys, both
one *and* two, they also inadvertently reposition the private: no longer an
individualistic space, the private lives of the Hiltons constitute the environment where this identity can be explored, embraced, accepted.

   While the Hiltons' autobiography uses a sentimentalized discourse
appropriate for popular magazine publication, the *Chained for Life* novelization reads slightly more like erotica. The text tells the story of a set of
Siamese twins and their money-hungry (but not entirely heartless) manager Ted Hinkley, who arranges a publicity marriage for Dorothy Hamilton, Vivian's twin, with another showman—a sharpshooter, Andre
Pariseau, who is unquestionably heartless. Despite the facade of the arrangement, Dorothy falls in love, and when, after the hugely successful
and hugely promoted wedding, Andre abandons her, Vivian eventually
revenges her sister's broken heart with one of Andre's own pistols. Much
of the story in fact parallels the twins' failed attempts at marriage, including Violet's own staged wedding at the Cotton Bowl. But the details
that stand out for the modern reader from this poorly typed piece are
those that linger on the question of the twins' sexuality. As Dorothy lets
her "mind dwell on how Andre had looked at her," the prose turns blue:

> Relaxed and languid from the warm bath, she could feel the warm
> inner sides of her thighs pressing together under the warm silk. Her
> eyes were brilliant, and unconsciously, she was smiling, her small white
> teeth biting her lower lip. She wondered if Andre was as powerful as he
> looked. (186)

The text allows the reader to remain in the world of fiction with
these overt sexual references in a way the memoir prohibits; in this fictional space, morality is less a shaping force than it was in the memoir
or Myers's show history. Indeed, even the character of Mabel, the

Hamilton twins' rough but caring assistant, serves as a kind of echo of the sexuality the twins ended up performing in their real life. A reporter who barges into the twins' dressing room rebukes Mabel with her own past when she tries to throw him out: "'You were a strip-tease queen, weren't you?'" (194). In effect, the sexuality that is implicit in the Hiltons' memoir and even eventually in the earlier show history by Myers becomes explicit in this fictionalized piece. Here, at least part of the truth resides more resolutely within the fiction.

Despite the hasty and generally poor quality of the prose, the deeply flawed typesetting of the text, and the sensationalism for which the whole thing reaches, many of the issues the Hiltons themselves address in *Intimate Loves and Lives* recur: the question of the twins' completion as individuals versus their interconnectedness, what constitutes privacy for them and how they achieve it, and the overriding concern of their singularity or duplicity. (The judge at the end of the trial actually acquits them because, as he notes, "'I cannot pass sentence and deprive an innocent person of her liberty and her life! Therefore, a higher court than mine will have to impose the final judgment!'" [231].) Even the issue of the control men have over women—a decisive one in the twins' own autobiography—crops up. At a critical point in the text when it appears that stage-groom Pariseau may in fact attempt to assume control over the Hamiltons and usurp the power their manager has had over them, attorney Price makes clear to the twins' manager what precisely he has done by putting such a rogue in the position of Dorothy's husband:

> "Well," Price said with finality, "don't be surprised if after the marriage—provided Birnham gets her a license—Andre Pariseau takes over. You've handled the girls for years without a contract, haven't you? See where that leaves you?"
> "They wouldn't stand for anything like that," Hinkley said heatedly. "They love me . . . they're like my own children! They wouldn't know what to do without me!"
> "No . . . But Pariseau would! And remember, he'll have certain rights as Dorothy's husband!"
> And in his heart, for the first time in his life Ted Hinkley felt the clutch of an icy dread. (216)

Despite the sometimes familiar topics, the reader does not see through the eyes of the twins here; this gaze remains stymied at the question of whether these women constitute one or two people and inserts, in distinct contradiction to the women's own memoir, their burning desire to separate. After a dream in which she sees herself as a singular person with Andre, Dorothy tells Vivian, "'I know the only way I can be happy is to be alone with the man I love! I want to be free!'" (210). In *Chained for Life,* only the probability of death keeps the twins from attempting such a surgical separation. In their own memoir, the Hiltons proclaim that, even if they could be separated, they wouldn't want to be: "'Siamese Twins' . . . 'cut apart' . . . 'doctor' are the first words we seemed to re-member. They stood for fear and created our longing [to] remain joined by our birth-bond of flesh and bone" (135). While the noveliza-tion ends again essentially where all of these third-person accounts begin—with the question of how many bodies and how many women a set of conjoined twins contains—the Hiltons, like the McKoys, claim their identity as both—without apology, without hesitation, and with-out fail.

Conclusion

What finally do these lives and stories of lives tell us? Do they underscore that, despite constructionist ideologies and understandings of social en-genderings, bodies do, as Judith Butler put it, matter? That for these conjoined twins, the vagina did indeed "make the woman," answering the question, perhaps, of why Millie-Christine was seen as one double-headed female while the Hiltons counted for two "stuck" together? That when it comes to the conjoined twin, the idea of the body demands a dif-ferent kind of identity and a very different autobiography; that the writ-ings of these women show the mapping of a newly and uniquely forged subjectivity that confounds our current categorizations? And don't these texts also suggest that the power of autobiography here is the textual embodiment of this very act of self-empowering self-definition—a power that autobiography has and continues to grant countless disen-franchised, formerly invisible, socially stigmatized people?

I think all these things are true, as is the claim that according to Alice Domurat Dreger and all available evidence,

> the desire to remain together is so widespread among communicating conjoined twins as to be practically universal. In other words, people who are conjoined and able to communicate seem to be almost as dis-inclined to be surgically separated as singletons are to be surgically joined.[63]

The question for Dreger is not how the medical community can help conjoined twins lead normal lives as singletons (a terrifically challenging and, in the right circumstances, often noble enterprise) but, rather, what kind of reorientation do those of us in the "normate" realm have to undertake in order to grant conjoined twins their own full humanity—the "validated sense of normality" and "reasonably wide degree of self-determination" we claim to celebrate as part of the American promise?[64]

Dreger makes one other crucial point, one that the readers of this collection may well come to on their own. She notes that "after reading many biographies and autobiographies of people who are conjoined, one has to wonder whether we might not *all* benefit from more twin-type behavior in this world—that is, whether we might not all benefit from a little *less* 'individuation.'"[65] Indeed, Daisy and Violet Hilton stress the absolute necessity for harmonious cooperation between them, a skill they develop as children before they can even put words to it. And the McKoys close their *History of the Carolina Twins* with the clarity they feel in their dual existence: "We have but *one heart*, one feeling in common, one desire, one purpose" (48). It is this sensibility in the end that perhaps feels as peculiar to us as the intimacy that brings these women to it, a way of being in the world that is nevertheless anything but monstrous.

Notes

1. "Conjoined" has replaced "Siamese" as the more acceptable term, although it is no more technically accurate. For recent theorizing regarding the appearance of such births, see M. H. Kaufman, "The Embryology of Conjoined Twins" *Child's Nervous System* 20, nos. 8–9 (August 2004): 508–25.

2. Robert Bogdan, *Freak Show: Presenting Human Oddities for Amusement and Profit* (Chicago: University of Chicago Press, 1988), 201.

3. When they died, a plaster cast was made of Chang and Eng's bodies that is still on display—along with their preserved joined livers—at the Mütter Museum at the College of Physicians of Philadelphia.

4. Bogdan is careful to note that the exhibition of these people termed freaks depended for its success as much if not more on their performance as it did on whatever actual physical anomaly they may (or may not) have had. In fact, many "freaks" had no physical anomaly at all but were simply discursively and performatively cast within this realm; it was common, for instance, to see Pacific South Islanders displayed as Fiji cannibals and shown within an exotic setting performing what would have seemed to viewers to be exotic activities. See Bogdan, *Freak Show*, 1–21.

5. Bogdan, *Freak Show*, 2.

6. Alice Domurat Dreger, *One of Us: Conjoined Twins and the Future of the Normal* (Cambridge, MA: Harvard University Press, 2004), 43.

7. Kaufman, "The Embryology of Conjoined Twins," 508. According to Kaufman, about 20 percent of that figure result in pygopagus twins such as the Hiltons and the McKoys—conjoined twins joined at the rump. See ibid., 514.

8. Ibid., 31.

9. Scholars and activists like Dreger have questioned the desirability of such separations, particularly in light of other analogous body-altering surgeries involving the intersexed. Dreger and others point to the case of twenty-nine-year-old Laleh and Ladan Bijani, the only pair of conjoined twins on record to actually request and consent to a separation surgery. The Bijani twins died fifty hours into their surgery when, after the final cut to separate them, they hemorrhaged uncontrollably. In fact, although the plotline in the novelization of *Chained for Life* (the film the Hilton twins made at the end of their show career) depends upon the desire of the lovesick Dorothy Hamilton to be physically separate from her conjoined sister, such a desire is practically nonexistent in the Hiltons' actual autobiographical text. For more on this issue, see Dreger, *One of Us*, particularly 51-112.

10. Georges Gusdorf, "Conditions and Limits of Autobiography" (1956), translated by James Olney, in *Autobiography: Essays Theoretical and Critical*, ed. James Olney (Princeton, NJ: Princeton University Press, 1980), 29.

11. James Olney, ed., *Metaphors of Self: The Meaning of Autobiography* (Princeton, NJ: Princeton University Press, 1972), 23 and 15.

12. Susan Stanford Friedman, "Women's Autobiographical Selves: Theory and Practice," in *Women, Autobiography, Theory: A Reader*, ed. Sidonie Smith and Julia Watson (Madison: University of Wisconsin Press, 1998), 72-82.

13. Nellie McKay, "The Narrative Self: Race, Politics, and Culture in Black American Women's Autobiography," in Smith and Watson, *Women, Autobiography, Theory*, 100.

14. Hertha D. Sweet Wong, "First-Person Plural: Subjectivity and Community in Native American Women's Autobiography," in Smith and Watson, *Women, Autobiography, Theory*, 168-78.

15. Judith Butler, *Bodies That Matter: On the Discursive Limits of "Sex"* (New York: Routledge, 1993), 16.

16. For the following section, see Joanne Martell, *Millie-Christine: Fearfully and Wonderfully Made* (Winston-Salem, NC: John F. Blair, 2000). The very slight difference in name between the slave family and that of the slaveholder suggests that one stemmed from the other; according to a family descendent of the McKay family, it was Joseph Pearson Smith who actually changed their name from "McKay" to "McKoy." Also, while the McKoys spell their mother's name "Menemia" in their autobiography, in most other texts, including Martell's biography, it is spelled "Monemia," which is how I have decided to spell it here.

17. *Biographical Sketch of Millie Christine, the Carolina Twin, Surnamed the Two-Headed Nightingale, and the Eighth Wonder of the World*, this volume, 66. For works reprinted in this volume, page numbers refer to the current volume rather than the original publication unless otherwise noted.

18. See Martell, *Millie-Christine*, 77–123.

19. Ibid., 109.

20. Ibid., 113.

21. Relying on land records and information recounted in *Biographical Sketch of Millie Christine, The Carolina Twin*, Martell writes that Jacob and Monemia indeed bought the McKay plantation for themselves; in private correspondence, descendents of the McKay family contest this claim, arguing that the McKay family has retained legal ownership of the farm to this day. See Martell, *Millie-Christine*, 208, and *Biographical Sketch*, 70n8.

22. See Martell, *Millie-Christine*, 121–39.

23. *Biographical Sketch*, 76.

24. Ibid.

25. Pancoast later went on to become Professor of the Philadelphia Medico-Chirurgical College in 1886. He was also the physician who performed Chang and Eng's autopsy.

26. William H. Pancoast, "The Carolina Twins," 99.

27. Martell, *Millie-Christine*, 166.

28. For the following section, see Dean Jensen, *The Lives and Loves of Daisy and Violet Hilton* (Berkeley, CA: Ten Speed Press, 2006).

29. See ibid., 1–28.

30. Ibid., 78–79.

31. Daisy and Violet Hilton, *Intimate Loves and Lives of the Hilton Sisters*, 140.

32. Jensen, *Lives and Loves*, 81.

33. The twins likewise sued to terminate a "contract" that they claimed was invalid, committing them to work for Myers until at least March 31, 1937. For more on the trial and case, see Jensen, *Lives and Loves*, 166–89.

34. Daisy and Violet Hilton, *Intimate Loves and Lives*, 151–52.

35. Jensen, *Lives and Loves*, 228.

36. Ibid., 261.

37. Ibid., 306.

38. Ibid., 331.

39. Ibid.

40. Ibid., 350.

41. Ibid.

42. I have chosen not to include the woodcut in this collection in part because it so forcibly undermines the very subjectivity the McKoys claim for themselves in their own writing; its authenticity is also questionable: according to Pancoast, the image was "drawn by the artist, Mr. Faber, from my description" (102 in this volume). The Pancoast photograph is included in part because, although they were unhappy about it, the McKoys did consent to have it taken.

43. Thanks to Shelley Wong for this observation.

44. *The History of the Carolina Twins, Told in "Their Own Peculiar Way" by "One of Them,"* 40. Further references to texts reprinted in the current volume will be included parenthetically.

45. The twins refer to Joseph as James throughout their account.

46. In fact, when one of these "kidnappers" ventures back to the United States and to Charlotte to try again to claim the McKoy twins, we are told in *The Biographical Sketch*

that the locals conclude "to give them an admirably fitting suit, composed of good *tar* and excellent *feathers*" (68). Catching wind of this plan, the kidnappers "decamped by night" (68).

47. Smith is actually treated by the twins in their memoir as a kind of victim himself, "being a 'Southern gentleman from the country,'" rather than a "practical 'showman,'" and therefore "very liable to be imposed upon" (41–42).

48. This is a direct reference to the book of Ruth in the Bible; the allusion underscores at once the twins' sense of familial dedication to Mrs. Smith and the thoroughness of the religious training she undertook for them.

49. Mostly for expediency's sake, I have forgone discussion of the songs and poetry included in the *Biographical Sketch*; I hope these pieces provide fodder for other and future discussions.

50. In this case, the most obvious predecessor to the McKoys has to be Saartje Baartman, known as the freak exhibit the "Venus Hottentot." A Khoikhoi woman with steatopygia, or enlarged buttocks, Baartman was put on display in London from 1810 to 1811. For more on Baartman, see Bernth Lindfors, "Ethnological Show Business: Footlighting the Dark Continent," in *Freakery: Cultural Spectacles of the Extraordinary Body*, ed. Rosemarie Garland Thomson (New York: New York University Press, 1996), particularly 207–11, and Rachel Holmes, *African Queen: The Real Life of the Hottentot Venus* (New York: Random House, 2007).

51. For more on slavery and freakery, see my discussion of the Circassian Beauty phenomenon in *Never One Nation: Freaks, Savages, and Whiteness in U.S. Popular Culture, 1850–1877* (Minneapolis: University of Minnesota Press, 2005), particularly 56–85.

52. Pancoast was a surgeon and professor of medicine but he is also noted in the annals of medical history for his involvement with reproductive technology. According to his former medical student, Addison Davis Hard, Pancoast was the first physician to perform a successful artificial insemination by donor. In their article "The Impregnators" (*Fertility and Sterility* 16, no. 1 [1965]: 130–34), A. T. Gregoire and Robert C. Mayer summarize that a couple "complaining of primary infertility," including "a successful Philadelphia merchant 10 years the senior of his wealthy Quaker wife," came to Pancoast, who, after thoroughly examining the woman, collected semen from the "best looking member" of his class of medical students and, "while the woman was anesthetized with chloroform," inseminated her (131). Neither husband nor wife were told about the procedure at the time, although Pancoast later did tell the husband; apparently Hard, "to assure himself that the artificially sired offspring was of sound character and good health," traveled to New York twenty-five years later to meet the experiment's result (131). Gregoire and Mayer provocatively suggest that indeed it was Hard who was "the best looking member of the class" and, therefore, the father of the child.

53. Pancoast's racism is evident in the article when he notes that despite the fact that the twins' "complexion was of the dusky brown of the American negro, . . . the expression of their faces was so amiable and intelligent, and their manner so well bred, that they produced a most pleasing impression upon me" (100).

54. Jensen, *Lives and Loves*, 311.

55. Ibid., 311–12.

56. Ibid., 348.

57. Daisy and Violet Hilton, *Intimate Loves and Lives of the Hilton Sisters* (Hollywood Books, 1953?), i (original publication).

58. Myer Myers, *Souvenir and Life Story of San Antonio's Siamese Twins* (San Antonio: Naylor Printing Co., ca. 1925), 8–9.

59. Ibid., 8.

60. Ibid., 9.

61. Allison Pingree, "The 'Exceptions That Prove the Rule': Daisy and Violet Hilton, the 'New Woman,' and the Bonds of Marriage," in *Freakery: Cultural Spectacles of the Extraordinary Body*, ed. Rosemarie Garland Thomson (New York: New York University Press, 1996), 182.

62. Ibid.

63. Dreger, *One of Us*, 46.

64. Ibid., 16. While I obviously have a great deal of sympathy for Dreger's point of view, the physicians who undertake these separation surgeries—many of which seem imperative to the parents and medical staff who facilitate and propose them—do so with tremendous concern, apprehension, and preparation. See James L. Stone and James T. Goodrich ("The Craniopagus Malformation: Classification and Implications for Surgical Separation," *Brain* 129 [2006]: 1084), who highlight that, given that 40 percent of conjoined twins are in fact stillborn, only approximately 25 percent who survive the first twenty-four hours of life can even be considered for separation surgery. See Stone and Goodrich, "The Craniopagus Malformation," 1084–95, for more on the issues and complexities of separating craniopagus twins (those joined at the head).

65. Dreger, *One of Us*, 44.

The History of
the Carolina Twins

Told in "Their Own Peculiar Way"
by "One of Them"

Warren Johnson and Company published this booklet in Buffalo probably in 1869. The cover
says the booklet was "Sold by their Agents for Their [the Twins'] Special Benefit, at 25 cents."

History of the Carolina Twins

WE are, indeed, a strange people, justly regarded both by scientific
and ordinary eyes as the greatest natural curiosities the world has ever
had sent upon its surface. Physicians who have examined us say our
formation—or rather malformation—is much more remarkable than
the physical condition of the Siamese Twins.[1]

We made our *entree* into this breathing world in 1852. Our coming in
such "questionable shape" created as great a *furore*[2] in the cabin, as our

1. Chang and Eng Bunker.
2. British usage; furor.

40

appearance has since, wherever we have been. "Old Aunt Hannah," a faithful nurse, whose specialty was to be around and to discharge the first hospitalities to new comers of our complexion, couldn't for "de life or soul of her" tell whether we was a "young nigger" or "something else." But the "something else" soon gave unmistakable evidences that it could *viva voce*[3] intimate a desire for maternal comforts, just as well as the best developed young African on the premises. So our mother and the rest of the family came to the conclusion that "a child was born."

Our parents were named Jacob and Menemia, and at the time of our birth were part of the family of a Mr. McCoy.[4] Shortly afterwards we and our parents changed owners, and were taken to Anson County, North Carolina. There we became separated from our parents, and after a few more transfers in the way of ownership, became the property of Mr. James P. Smith, who gave for us, two strange lumps of humanity, the sum of $6,000. He, with a goodness of heart, which in after life developed itself in more ways than one towards us, ascertained where our parents were, went to their owners, purchased them, and all our little brothers and sisters, thus bringing a long separated family together, and the making of more than one heart rejoice in gladness.

When we were infants, not much more than fifteen months old, Mr. Smith, yielding to the advice of a number of his friends and well wishers, made arrangements for starting upon an exhibition tour through the Gulf States, intending to show us at all the principal cities and towns. Our local fame was communicated to the press generally throughout the South, and soon the "South Carolina Twins," or "double headed girl," became a magnet of attraction to the lovers of the curious in nature.

Perhaps it would not be improper to remark here, *en passant*,[5] that Mr. Smith was not in those days a practical "showman," but being a "Southern gentleman from the country," was very liable to be imposed

3. By word of mouth; orally.

4. Names and their spellings are problematically fluid in the case of Millie and Christine, or Millie-Christine. The McKoys spell their mother's name "Menemia" in their autobiography; in the biographical show histories and in Martell's biography, it is spelled "Monemia." Likewise, according to the McKoys' biographer, the name of their master at the time was Jabez McKay. Here, though, the twins refer to him as "McCoy." In my discussion I have chosen to use the spellings most current scholars and writers use—Monemia, McKoy, and McKay.

5. In passing.

upon. A speculator, one of those "smart" men, ever ready to take all undue advantage of his fellow man, came to Mr. Smith at New Orleans, and made a proposition to become our exhibitor. This man had a persuasive address, spoke as one having authority, and great influence with the "press and the public," so the consequences were [that] Mr. Smith hired the fellow to exhibit us, rather to "put us properly before the public." The man was to get a percentage of the receipts, Mr. S. to bear all the expenses. For a while things worked agreeably, until one day Mr. S. was called to his home in North Carolina to attend to some pressing business. Taking advantage of the absence of our kind master and guardian, the man absolutely kidnapped us, stole us from our mother, and bore us far away from friends, kindred, or any one who had *a right* to feel an interest in us. The man who took us away could not, or rather *did not dare* to publicly exhibit us, but gave private exhibitions to scientific bodies, thus reaping quite a handsome income off of "two little black girls" whom he had stolen away.

Finally, when we had been thus dragged over the country for nearly two years, the one who had surreptitiously became our custodian, disposed of us to another speculator, who was unacquainted with the fact that we were *originally* and then the legal property of Mr. Smith. He took us to Philadelphia and placed us in a small Museum in Chestnut Street, near Sixth, then under the management of Col. Wood, who is, we believe, somewhat known as a showman.

While there, a party saw us, and hearing that we were born South, came to the conclusion to get possession of us. He went to the authorities and said we were slaves, brought into a free State, where we were unjustly deprived of our liberty. He prayed the Court to exercise jurisdiction in the premises, take us away from the party who held us, and to appoint a guardian for us. This dodge did not work well, for the man who had us spirited us away before the necessary papers could be served, and in a few hours we were upon the basins of the broad Atlantic *en route* for Europe.

By this time Mr. Smith had gained tidings of us, and in company with his Attorney, Luke Blackmar, Esq., of Salisbury, and a friend, J. Vestal, Esq., came North to reclaim us. He and his friends arrived in the city of New York the day after the Baltic sailed with us. Friends who took an interest in Mr. Smith's misfortunes, told him that all attempts to claim us as his property would prove futile in England; but that no one could restrain us, provided our parents claimed us as then infant children.[6] Quick as thought he acted upon the suggestion, started for our home in the "Old North State," got our mother Menemia, and was soon *en route* for "Merrie England," where he and our mother shortly arrived in safety.

Mr. Smith was not long in discovering our whereabouts. The fact of our being in England was soon known, as the parties who had carried us there thought that they could, any where out of the United States, show us with impunity. They influenced a colored woman, under the promise of a rich reward, to testify upon oath that she was our mother; but the woman, anticipating the enormity of the crime, ran away; not until, however, she had received in advance a portion of the wages of sin. Another woman yielded to the temptation of gold, and did in open court perjure her soul, and swear that she had given us birth. But her carefully told and well rehearsed *lie* would not stand the close scrutiny of the Ministers of Law, who listened to the plain and well-told narrative of our mother, who evinced a mother's tenderness for *us*, her little deformities, and imparted a pathos to those utterances when she, in a natural unassuming way, begged for the custody of her children, from whom she had so long been separated, but from whom she could never feel estranged. The law vindicated itself, and gave us to our mother.

As soon as the decision was made manifest, then those who had stolen us the last time endeavored to prevail upon our mother to *hire* us to them, offering her a large sum to allow us to travel over the country, and to go upon the continent. This she refused to accede to, until some outside parties succeeded in inducing Mr. Smith to consent to some copartnership arrangement, by which both he and us would be the recipients of fine receipts. Mr. S. then consented to mother's signing a three years' agreement, the effects of which we need not here give. But, suffice it to say, that soon the cloven foot of the man who wanted us, showed itself; he tried to vitiate the contract, so as to get things his own way, and thus deprive us of our rights. He abused our mother, and applied the most revolting epithets. He threatened the life of Mr. Smith, and refused

6. Slavery had been outlawed on British soil in 1772, and the Atlantic slave trade outlawed in 1807. At the time of the twins' reclaiming in Britain in 1857, therefore, no British court would have honored the "ownership" of a slave by a Southern slaveholder from the United States.

to allow us to receive the attention and luxuries which children of tender age require. Our mother got afraid, and begged our good master to assist her and us children to reach the shores of our own beloved America. He yielded to her prayers and entreaties, and determined to set us free from a bondage so repulsive. Becoming familiar with the running time of all the railway trains, and becoming cognizant of the exact time when the steamer would leave her dock at Liverpool, he made all arrangements for a speedy departure. Getting a trusty cabman to come to our lodgings, where all our things were in readiness, we were at the depot in London before any one surmised our intentions. The steam cars moved, and after a rapid journey (for steam cars do travel in England) we arrived at the Americanized city of Liverpool just half an hour before the steamer Atlantic was ready to leave her docks.

With grateful hearts we turned our backs upon Albion's shore, not but that the people treated us well enough, and would have paid liberally to have seen us; still, we had enemies there who we thought would injure our master and protector, and act in bad faith toward us.

There are many things of interest we missed seeing in England, on account of the brief time we had to stay there. Perhaps, now, that we are "grown up girls," and like the rest of the sex, with tongues, and a knowledge of their use, we may go across the water once more. A gentleman who called to see us when we were on exhibition in Baltimore, told us that the "double headed girl" was often inquired after, and that he thought we would prove a "good card" there. At present our business relations are such that we feel in duty bound to stay at home.

We might, could we feel disposed, tell many anecdotes of our travels, but we think a simple narrative of ourselves is all that at present those of our patrons who buy our little book will require.

But our visit to the Queen and the Royal Family at "Osbourne House," we shall never forget. Her Majesty had, "signified her pleasure" to have us brought before her. Our good mother wrapped us up in real southern style to shield us from the heavy fogs of London. We nor she did not comprehend the glory of the errand we were bent upon, only she knew that a grand and good lady wanted to see us. When we arrived, the pomp and circumstances of the surroundings dazzled our young eyes, and we wondered what was to be done with us. But we can say that "Victoria was a woman" for she talked tenderly to us, and to our mother, and when we left we bore away abundant tokens of her good feeling and queenly liberality. A great many artists boast of having been before the

Queen. Perhaps they have, and employed great diplomacy to get there. But with us the case was different. Poor little monstrosities, and black babies at that; we were sent for, and that without any influence at court to gain for us a Royal summons.

When we arrived home again at New York, Mr. Smith took us under his cloak and carried us on the Ferry Boat to Jersey City, where he got us on the cars and never stopped until we reached the Monumental City,[7] where we felt safe from pursuit.

There we rested for a few days under the hospitable roof of Barnum's Hotel and then left for our own dear home. It was a joyous night when we arrived there and found our "white ma," Mrs. Smith, waiting to secure us. Of course we then did not appreciate her worth for we were babies when we left her; but we soon learned to regard her with the most tender feelings. She taught us our first precepts of religion, and assumed the duties of preceptress, our ideas of a Deity were very imperfect. We had heard the Supreme Being alluded to, but not in tones of love and reverence, but to give force to some angry expression. She gradually imparted to us such ideas as our crude minds could comprehend, until such times as we could begin to understand the fundamental principles of the doctrine of the established church of England. Now, although we do not wish to speak Pharisaical,[8] we think we can safely call ourselves really Christian children. Mrs. S. instructed us to read and write, to sing and dance, and thus while being able to enjoy ourselves, and to employ our time usefully, to contribute in no small degree to the amusement of those who called to see us.

In 1860 we were in New Orleans when the domestic political troubles commenced. Mr. Smith, who had heavy responsibilities resting upon him, was obliged to withdraw us from public life and take us home. Shortly after that, he was taken ill, and after a few weeks' suffering died, leaving his widow to look after his people and the estate. We were old enough then to mourn the loss of our good master, who seemed to us as a father, and we here would render a grateful tribute to his memory, by

---

7. Baltimore. In 1827, in a toast at a dinner given in his honor after touring the sights of the city, President John Quincy Adams said, "Baltimore, the Monumental City—may the days of her safety be as prosperous and happy as the days of her danger have been trying and triumphant!"

8. To go by the letter of religious law rather than spiritual content; to be hypocritical and/or self righteous.

saying that he was urbane, generous, kind, patient-bearing, and beloved by all. We trust, in fact believe, that he has gone to that heaven we have heard him so often describe to us, when he would impress upon our minds the necessity of leading a good life in the hope of gaining a blessed immortality hereafter.

Master had always been liberal to others, and had, upon frequent occasions, lost heavily in business transactions. These circumstances and the results of the war, left us and his widow and children to a certain extent in straightened circumstances. The only alternative was for us to again go upon exhibition, and by our humble efforts contribute to the happiness and comforts of the surviving members of our late master's family. We are *interested* pecuniarily in the "show," and are daily receiving and putting away our share of the proceeds. None can mistake our determination in remaining under the guardianship of Mrs. Smith. Our object is two-fold: *We can trust her,* and what is more, we feel grateful to her and regard her with true filial affection. We will not go with any one else; where she goes there will we go; where she tarries there will we halt. We shall endeavor to imitate that deep devotion which Ruth evinced toward Naomi.[9]

Having thus spoken of ourselves and given you a very plain, and perhaps, a very uninteresting autobiography, we will give you a few extracts from letters and opinions which have been uttered and expressed relative to us:

The editor of the Louisville *Journal* said, "The exhibition of these remarkable twins is characterized by the peculiar delicacy, modesty and ingeniousness of these *young girls* themselves. Nothing occurs nor can occur offensive to the most fastidious sense of propriety, or refined taste." Mr. Prentice, we have always heard, could say pleasant as well as very witty and cunning things. We thank him for the handsome manner in which he has thought proper to speak of us.

"Brick Pomeroy," of the LaCrosse *Democrat,* came to one of our *levees*[10] last winter, and shortly after our secretary received a paper from Wisconsin which contained the subjoined: "We have seen the Carolina Twins, or the 'Double-headed Girl' as they are styled on the bills. We

9. See the Book of Ruth, 1:17–18.

10. A reception held in honor of a particular person; the term stems from the reign of King Louis XIV when the king's rising from bed was itself raised to a ceremonial venture called a "levée."

can in truth say we were pleased with them, particularly with the manner in which they conversed. They are not impudent, but they are not foolishly retiring. They sing well, in fact excellent; and dance divinely, considering the manner in which their limbs and body are constructed. They know they are a curiosity, and feel anxious that the public should appreciate their attractiveness. We have no hesitation in declaring them to be the most extraordinary exhibition of a peculiar and 'indissoluble union' we have ever witnessed. The Siamese twins in the way of strange formation cannot bear any comparison to them."

That editor fully knows how we feel in regard to the public. We wished to be viewed as something entirely void of humbug—a living curiosity—not a sham gotten up to impose upon and deceive the people. We are indeed a strange freak of Nature, and upon the success of our exhibition does our happiness and the well doing of others depend. We have been examined most scrutinizingly by too many medical men to be *regarded* as humbugs by any one. Still there are many persons who will not believe anything, no matter how strong the facts may be presented to them. If there be any such who have been to see us, and into whose hands this little book of ours may chance to fall, we beg most respectfully to offer them some medical testimony of a most positive and unmistakable character.

PHILADELPHIA, May 30th, 1866.

MRS. JAMES P. SMITH:

Madam:—A number of medical gentlemen having been invited to examine the North Carolina Twins now upon exhibition at the Assembly Buildings, say they found a thorough fusion of the lower portion of the trunk, osseous and fleshy; the two spinal columns uniting together at the base, forming but one large bone common to both.

The limbs and upper part of each trunk and the heads are perfectly separate, as though belonging to a distinct individuality, forming the most interesting monstrosity, morally and physically considered, on record. Among the gentlemen who are willing to allow their names to appear and give tone to the above statements are:

DR. S. H. DICKSON,
Professor Practice of Medicine, Jefferson Medical College.

DR. ELLERSHE WALLACE,
Professor of Obstetrics, Jefferson Medical College.

DR. JOHN B. BIDDE,
Professor Materia Medica, Jefferson Medical College.

DR. J. AITKIN MEIGS,
Lecturer Summer School.

DR. WILLIAM H. PANCOAST,
Demonstrator of Anatomy and Lecturer Summer School.

All these gentlemen are well known, not only in Philadelphia, but throughout a great portion of the country, and it is not at all probable that they could be deceived, and it is still more unlikely that they would lend their countenance to an imposition.

Although we speak of ourselves in the plural we feel as but *one person*; in fact as such we have ever been regarded, although we bear the names Millie and Christina. One thing is certain, we would not wish to be severed, even if science could effect a separation. We are contented with our lot, and are happy as the day is long. We have but *one heart*, one feeling in common, one desire, one purpose.

The song we sing, we have so often been requested to give copies of, that we have concluded to insert it in our book. We must admit that, as a literary production, it has not much merit, but it conveys a good idea of our feelings.

It's not modest of one's self to speak,
But daily scanned from head to feet
I freely talk of everything—
Sometimes to persons wondering.

Some persons say I must be two,
The doctors say this is not true;
Some cry out humbug, till they see,
When they say, great mystery!

Two heads, four arms, four feet,
All in one perfect body meet;
I am most wonderfully made,
All scientific men have said.

None like me, since days of Eve,
None such perhaps will ever live,
A marvel to myself am I,
As well to all who passes by.

I'm happy, quite, because I'm good;
I love my Savior and my God.
I love all things that God has done,
Whether I'm created *two* or *one*.

Those who are in attendance upon us can, perhaps, give the public some information that we have overlooked. Hoping our little book will be found well worth the money, we conclude our plain unvarnished tale.

Biographical Sketch of Millie Christine, the Carolina Twin

Originally appearing in 1871, the version of the *Biographical Sketch* reprinted here was published between 1902 and 1912 by Hennegan & Co. in Cincinnati. The full text of the original title page appears on the facing page.

BIOGRAPHICAL SKETCH

OF

MILLIE CHRISTINE,

THE CAROLINA TWIN,

SURNAMED

THE TWO-HEADED NIGHTINGALE,[1]

AND THE

EIGHTH WONDER OF THE WORLD.

––––––

"None like me since the days of Eve—
None such perhaps will ever live."—Except Christine Millie.

––––––

At each Levee[2] MILLIE CHRISTINE will sing some of the Songs
and Duets which will be found at the end of this book.

HENNEGAN & CO. PRINT, CINCINNATI, OHIO

1. An allusion to Jenny Lind, the "Swedish Nightingale," who enjoyed tremendous
success and fame as a vocalist in the United States and Europe.
2. A reception; see current volume, 46n10.

Southern California Railway Company. Passenger Department.[3]
H. G. Thompson, Gen'l Pass. Agt.
H. K. Gregory, Ass't Gen'l Pass. Agt. Los Angeles, Cal., Jan. 30, 1895.

To Conductors, Los Angeles to Santa Ana, San Bernardino via Orange, San Bernardino to Redlands, and Redlands to Los Angeles:

It is customary for Millie Christine, the dual woman, to require but one ticket. Please be governed accordingly when Millie Christine is making a trip over any of our lines as above indicated.

Yours truly,

H. G. Thompson, G. P. A.

The Pennsylvania Railroad Co.
Phila., Wilmington & Balt. R. R. Co.
Alexandria & Fredericksburg Railway. Co.
Camden & Atlantic Railroad Co.
Northern Central Railway Co.
Baltimore & Potomac R. R. Co.
West Jersey Railroad Co.
Office, 233 South Fourth Street.
Passenger Department.
J. R. Wood, Gen'l Pass. Agent.
Geo. W. Boyd, Asst. Gen'l Pass. Agent Philadelphia, June 10, 1894.
Subject: Refunding extra fare.
J. P. Smith, Esq., Grand Central Hotel, New York City.

Dear Sir:

Referring to your call at this office a few days since I enclose herewith order No. 25286 on our Treasurer for $4.71, covering refund of extra fare paid

3. It is unclear exactly why these notices appear in the McKoys' biography; while they function as further authentication of the sisters' anomalous physiology, they also may well have had the practical intent they declare—to assure conductors that the sisters only require one ticket to travel, the text therefore in particular circumstances acting as both show history and traveling pass. These railway notices in fact pepper the text, appearing at the beginning, again at the middle, and at the end. For ease of reading, all of them have been moved to the beginning of the text, starting here.

from Washington, D. C. to Philadelphia, June 4th, by Millie Christine, the dual woman, in connection with one first-class ticket between same points, which the conductor lifted on the ground that two fares were necessary to cover passage.

Please sign and return enclosed form of receipt, and oblige,

Very truly,

Geo. W. Boyd, A. G. P. A., Wash.

❧

Baltimore & Ohio Southwestern Railroad.
Passenger Department.
City Office, Southeast Corner Fourth and Vine Streets.
O. P. McCarthy, General Passenger Agent.
Chas. H. Koenig, District Passenger Agent. Cincinnati, O.,
April 13, 1892.

Conductors B. & O. S. W. and connecting lines:

This is to certify that Manager Smith has purchased three (3) tickets, Cincinnati to New York, in connection with Millie Christine, the dual woman, this person being included. It is customary to require but one ticket for her passage. Kindly be governed accordingly.

Chas. H. Koenig, D. P. A., B. & O. S. W.

❧

Treasurer's Office, T. H. Gibbs, Treasurer.
Columbia, Newburg & Laurens Railroad Company.
Columbia, S. C., Sept. 8, 1893.

Conductors S. A. Line and connecting lines:

This is to certify that J. P. Smith, Esq., has purchased three (3) tickets from Columbia, S. C. to Lincoln, Nebraska, in connection with Millie Christine, the dual woman, this person being included. It is customary to require one ticket for her passage.

B. F. F. Leaphart, Ticket Agent. C. N. & L. R. R.

❧

BURLINGTON, CEDAR RAPIDS AND NORTHERN RAILWAY.
LOCAL FREIGHT AND TICKET OFFICE.
A. F. PILCHER, Agent. Sioux Falls, So. Dak., Oct. 5, 1895.

TO CONDUCTORS:

It is customary to carry Millie Christine on one ticket.

Respectfully,

A. F. PILCHER, Agt.

❧

SOUTHERN RAILWAY CO., Office of Division Passenger Agt.
R. W. Hunt, D. P. A.
S. H. Hardwick, G.P.A., Washington, D.C.
W. H. Taylor, A.G.P.A., Atlanta, Ga. CHARLESTON, S. C.,
December 13, 1902

To Conductors—It is customary for Millie Christine, the dual woman, to travel on one ticket. Please be governed accordingly when she is traveling over the Southern Railway.

Yours very truly,

R. W. HUNT, D. P. A.

❧

ATLANTIC COAST LINE, Traffic Department.
T. H. Emerson, Traffic Mgr.
H. M. Emerson, G. F. & P. A. WILMINGTON, N. C., December 10, 1897.

To Conductors—Millie Christine, the dual woman, is transported over these lines for one ticket, notwithstanding the fact that she has two heads.

Yours truly,

H. M. EMERSON, G. P. A.

❧

BALTIMORE & OHIO RAILROAD, Passenger Department, J. H. Cowen & O. C. Murray, Receivers.

S. D. Hege, D. P. A

H. R. Hoser, Ticket Agent, 619 Pennsylvania Ave. WASHINGTON, D.C.,
June 9, 1898.

Conductors B. & O. R. R.—This is to certify that Manager Smith has purchased four tickets, Washington, D. C., to Zanesville, Ohio, in connection with Millie Christine, the dual woman, this person being included. You will accept one ticket for the passage of Millie Christine.

Yours truly,

J. N. SCHRYVER, G. P. A.

Per S. B. H., D. P. A.

&

PLANT SYSTEM OF RAILWAYS.

B. W. Wrenn, P. T. M. SAVANNAH, GA.,
November 22, 1900.

To Conductors—It is customary for Millie Christine, the two-headed woman, to travel on one ticket. You will please govern yourself accordingly.

Yours truly,

B. W. WRENN, P. T. M.

&

SEABOARD AIR LINE RAILWAY.

To Conductors—It is customary for Millie Christine, the two-headed woman, to travel on one ticket. You will please govern yourself accordingly.

Yours truly,

A. O. MACDONALD, A. G. P. A.

&

ATLANTIC, VALDOSTA & WESTERN RY. Traffic Department.

Smith D. Pickett, G. F. & P. A. JACKSONVILLE, FLA.
November 30, 1900.

To the Conductors, A. V. & W. Ry.—It will only be necessary for Millie

Christine, known as the dual woman, to present one ticket for her passage over our line.

S. D. Pickett, G. P. A.

✍

Southern Ry. Co. Office of Trav. Pass. Agent.
W. A. Turk, G. P. A., Washington, D.C.
C. A. Benscotter, A. G. P. A., Chattanooga, Tenn.
J. C. Lusk, T. P. A. Selma, Ala., January 11, 1901.

To Southern Railway Conductors—It is the custom for Millie Christine, the dual woman, to travel on one ticket. Please be governed accordingly.

Yours very truly,

J. C. Lusk, T. P. A.

✍

The Missouri Pacific Ry. Co., St. Louis, Iron Mountain and
Southern Ry. Co. and Leased, Operated and Independent Lines.
August Sundholm, P. & T. A.
G. E. Richie,
Guy E. Thompson, Ass'ts, S. W. Cor. Markham & Louisiana Sts. and
Union Depot. Little Rock, Ark., February 19, 1899.

Conductors S. L., I. M. & S. Ry. and Connecting Lines—It is customary to carry Millie Christine on one ticket.

Respectfully,

August Sundholm, P. & T. A.

✍

Norfolk & Western Ry. Co. Norfolk & Richmond Vestibuled Limited,
Fastest Train in the South, Virginia and Ohio Line, West and Northwest.
C. H. Bosley, D. P. A.
John E. Wagner, C. P. & T. A. 838 Main St., Richmond, Va.
W. E. Hazelwood, P. A., 95 Granby St., under Monticello Hotel,
Norfolk, Va.

To Conductors Norfolk & Western Railway Company:

Gentlemen—For your information, I beg to advise that the manager of

Millie Christine, a dual woman, is in the habit of only purchasing one ticket for her. This custom has been adhered to and recognized by all lines.

Yours truly,

W. E. HAZELWOOD, P. A.

NASHVILLE, CHATTANOOGA & ST. LOUIS RAILWAY.
W. L. DANLEY, Gen'l Pass. and Ticket Agent. Nashville, Tenn.,
Oct. 20, 1892.

CONDUCTORS N., C. & ST. L. RY.:

This is to certify that Manager Smith is authorized to purchase *one* ticket good for ten seats Nashville to Atlanta, in connection Millie Christine, the dual woman, this person being included. It is customary to require but one ticket for her passage. Kindly be governed accordingly.

W. L. DANLEY, G. P. & T. A.

CHICAGO, MILWAUKEE & ST. PAUL RAILWAY CO.
OFFICE OF DIVISION FREIGHT AND PASSENGER AGENT.
425 PIERCE ST., IOWA SAVINGS BANK BUILDING.
Sioux City, Iowa, Sept. 30, 1895.

TO CONDUCTORS:

It is customary for Millie Christine, the two headed woman, to travel on one ticket. You will please govern yourself accordingly.

Yours truly,

E. W. JORDON, D. P. A.

THE PHILADA. & READING RAILROAD CO. WILKESBARRE,
B. STATION, Jan. 22, 1893.

TO CONDUCTORS:
It is customary for Millie Christine, the dual woman, to require but one ticket. Please be governed accordingly.

S. S. CHASE, C. T. A.

dp

OLD DOMINION STEAMSHIP CO. S. S. "JAMESTOWN,"
Oct. 4, 1897.

The dual woman, Millie Christine, travels on this steamer on one ticket as one person.

FORD KUISKENE, Purser.

dp

LOUISVILLE & NASHVILLE RAILROAD CO.
PASSENGER DEPARTMENT, 114 NORTH FOURTH STREET, St. Louis,
Mo., Feb. 4, 1889.

CONDUCTORS of L. & N. R. R. and connecting lines:

This is to certify that J. P. Smith, Esq., has purchased three (3) tickets St. Louis to Columbia, S. C., in connection with Millie Christine, the dual woman, this person being included. It is customary to require but one ticket for her passage. Kindly be governed accordingly.

Very truly yours,

JOHN W. MASS, D. P. A.

dp

CENTRAL RAILROAD AND BANKING COMPANY OF GEORGIA.
H. M. COMER, Receiver. Macon, Ga., Nov. 3, 1892.

CONDUCTOR NO. 1:

It is customary for Millie Christine, the dual woman, to require but one ticket. Please be governed accordingly.

J. C. HAILL, G. P. A.

dp

NORTHERN PACIFIC RAILROAD COMPANY.
THOMAS F. OAKES, HENRY C. PAYNE. HENRY C. ROUSE, Receivers.
TRAFFIC DEPARTMENT.
I. A. NADEAU, General Agent. Seattle, Wash., July 28, 1895.

CONDUCTORS:

It is customary for Millie Christine, the dual woman, to require but one ticket. Please govern yourself accordingly.

I. A. NADEAU. Gen'l Agent.

SKETCH OF THE LIFE

— of —

Millie Christine; or, Christine Millie, The Carolina Twin.

The Two-Headed Lady, the Double-Tongued Nightingale, the Eighth Wonder of the World, the Puzzle of Science, the Despair of Doctors, the Dual Unity.

All of these names has she earned at various times, with the final title which we claim for her in defiance of any other or others:

THE MOST WONDERFUL BEING ALIVE.

There are giants and giants, dwarfs and dwarfs, fat men and women, living skeletons of both sexes, hirsute monsters and baldheads by the century; there are marvels of nature, science and art, of all which the world knows; but there can only be one NONPAREIL, one UN-EQUALLED, and that is the subject of our brief sketch, for only one living creature is like Millie Christine, and her name is Christine Millie.

But, says the curious reader, was there ever such another heard of before?

Only one is on record, attested as a fact, and leaving out of the question fabulous monsters. The first year of the eighteenth century witnessed the birth of a similar phenomenon in Hungary, the sisters Helen and Judith, born in the year 1701.[4] These girls were united at the lower

---

4. Called typically just "The Hungarian Sisters," Helen and Judith of Szony, Hungary, were born on October 26, 1701, and were one of the first documented conjoined twins to be exhibited in Europe. Like the McKoys and the Hiltons, these pygopagus twins were a musical duo. They died at 22 in a convent; Judith, seen as the weaker of the sisters, died of some kind of "brain trauma," while Helen died hours later. According to George M. Gould and Walter L. Pyle, authors of *Anomalies and Curiosities of Medicine* (New

part of the body only, and were perfectly distinct beings in every way. Helen was larger, stronger, and better-looking than Judith, besides being much more active and intelligent. These girls lived to their twenty-second year, when Judith fell sick and died, Helen following her within a few minutes of her demise. And all this, you remember, happened more than a century since, so that it takes Nature a hundred years at least to produce such a marvel again. Helen and Judith died at twenty-two years of age, while Millie Christine still lives, healthy and happy, at thirty-eight, and bids fair to attain a ripe old age as easily as less wonderful beings. The following pages, confined to a simple record of the facts in her career, will therefore prove of interest and value.

Miss Millie Christine, or Christine Millie, was born of slave parents, on the plantation of Mr. Alexander McCoy, near the town of White-ville, Columbus County, North Carolina, on July 11, 1851. At her birth her mother was in her thirty-second year. She was a handsome woman, finely formed and in excellent health. Millie Christine's father, of Moorish descent, slender and sinewy, with the powerful activity characteristic of his race. Prior to the birth of Millie Christine, her mother had borne seven other children, five boys and two girls, all of ordinary size, with no peculiarities of conformation, and some of them are still alive.

York: Bell Publishing Co., 1896), although Alexander Pope and other poets spoke of them in verse, "A description of them can be best given by a quaint translation by Fisher of the Latin lines composed by a Hungarian physician and inscribed on a bronze statuette of them:

> Two sisters wonderful to behold, who have thus grown as one,
> That naught their bodies can divide, no power beneath the sun.
> The town of Szoenii gave them birth, hard by far-famed Komorn,
> Which noble fort may all the arts of Turkish sultans scorn.
> Lucina, woman's gentle friend, did Helen first receive;
> And Judith, when three hours had passed, her mother's womb did leave.
> One urine passage serves for both;—one anus, so they tell;
> The other parts their numbers keep, and serve their owners well.
> Their parents poor did send them forth, the world to travel through,
> That this great wonder of the age should not be hid from view.
> The inner parts concealed do lie hid from our eyes, alas!
> But all the body here you view erect in solid brass."

                                                                    (177–78)

Gould's text can be found in its entirety at the Electronic Text Center at the University of Virginia Library; see: http://etext.lib.virginia.edu/toc/modeng/public/GouAnom.html (accessed August 23, 2008).

The wonder of the family, Millie Christine, weighed seventeen pounds when she entered the world, and, although her mother was only attended by a colored midwife, no serious consequences attended such a remarkable birth.

But, when the child was once fairly in the world, how rumor flew about the township of Whiteville,[5] and spread from thence over the whole country! "Have you seen the girl?" was the first question asked of every one by every one, and pilgrimages to visit her became all the rage in the country side.

The old nurse who had superintended her introduction into this world was doubtless awestruck at the anomalous and wonderful addition she had made to her master's property, and not unnaturally prided herself on having assisted Nature to produce a phenomenon; but the master himself, and his amiable lady, without stopping to question the designs of Providence, immediately surrounded the extraordinary infant with such care and attention as enabled it to thrive and grow. The dual-headed child was taken from the cabin to the mansion, and Mr. McCoy's family commenced then a course of care and attention to her health and welfare.

During the first eighteen months of her life nothing of importance occurred to Millie Christine worthy of note. She grew as other girls grow, learned to walk at twelve months old, was of a lively and agreeable disposition, and at fifteen months began to talk with both her mouths. She was cheerful and active as any girl of her age, with every appearance of robust health. Her vivacity and goodness, together, no doubt, with her peculiar formation, rendered her the almost idolized child of the mother and a general favorite of both old and young, and every attention and kindness was bestowed upon her.

At this time Mr. McCoy, being a man in very moderate circumstances, a plain farmer, thinking the girl would become a burden to him, and annoyed with the frequent visits of strangers to see her, determined to dispose of her. He was not long in finding for her a purchaser, a person of the name of Brower, who offered $10,000 for her, seeing the possibilities of the child in the way of an exhibition. But inasmuch as this Brower was not possessed of the requisite cash to back his faith, and only offered to give a note of hand for the purchase money, Mr. McCoy

5. Ten miles from Jabez McKay's farm; also the county seat of Columbus County, North Carolina.

naturally desired some responsible person to whom to look for the money in case of the non-payment of the note when due. This person was ultimately found by Brower in Joseph P. Smith, of Wadesboro, North Carolina, and Mr. McCoy finally parted with Millie Christine, in consideration of Brower's note for $10,000 endorsed by Mr. Smith.

The happy Brower, in full possession of his prize, at once departed for New Orleans, in obedience to a request from the medical faculty of that city asking that she be brought there for a scientific examination.

Rooms were taken and every preparation made for the contemplated examination, after which she was to be placed on public exhibition. It had been arranged, prior to their leaving home, that their presence in the city should be kept as quiet as possible, as the desire to see her would undoubtedly be very great and might interfere with the examination. This precaution was not strictly regarded, and soon the rooms and the passages leading thereto were literally besieged with anxious crowds of people eager to get a sight of her.

The examination, however, at length took place and proved most satisfactory, every physician in attendance concurring in pronouncing her Nature's greatest wonder. Being endorsed by the medical faculty, she was now put on public exhibition, but from want of proper management she succeeded but indifferently.

Mr. Brower, being quite ignorant of the business he had undertaken, despaired of success after a few more efforts. About this time he became acquainted with a certain adventurer who hailed from Texas and boasted of his immense tracts of land in that State. This swindler proposed to purchase the girl by giving for her lands, at a fair market valuation, to the amount of forty-five thousand dollars, and Brower, having full confidence in the would be millionaire, concluded the bargain by giving possession of the girl, and was on the following day to receive the deeds in due form. The day arrived, but neither the Texan nor the deeds were forthcoming, and then for the first time the unpleasant fact broke upon him that he had been completely duped. To gain some knowledge of her whereabouts was now his first effort; but so adroitly was everything pertaining to her abduction managed that no clue to her, or even the direction she had been carried, could be gained, and every effort for a time to learn anything of her proved futile.

Mr. Brower, after weeks of useless search, becoming convinced that, for the present, further efforts to regain her would only prove useless, determined to return to North Carolina and impart to Mr. Smith his loss, and to the mother the sad intelligence of the abduction of her daughter. Words are inadequate to describe the anguish of the parent on learning the fate of her child. For a time she was perfectly frantic, during six days refusing food and for the same number of nights her eyes did not close in sleep. Her excellent character, uniform kindness and amiable disposition had made her a general favorite, so that everything that could be was cheerfully done to comfort and soothe her mind. She was promised that no amount of money should be spared, no effort left untried to procure her much-cherished child. How truly this promise was kept the sequel will prove. Brower and partner were bankrupt, and Mr. Smith expected no assistance from them. But before anything could be done to recover the child it was necessary that her original owner should be compensated for his loss in the transaction. Christine Millie had been spirited away to parts unknown, and all that Mr. McCoy had to show for her was Brower's note for $10,000; and as Brower could not pay this money his endorser, Mr. Smith, became the responsible party and accepted the responsibility. He at once paid the purchase money in full to Mr. McCoy, and took from him a deed which made him the exclusive owner, under then existing laws, of the person of Millie Christine. The proviso, "wherever he could find her," was of course understood, and in order to quiet the mind of her mother and convince her that, whenever found, the child would be restored to her care, Mr. Smith at the same time purchased the father, mother and seven children, a transaction of course involving a large sum of money, all of which was dependent for its recovery on the recovery of Millie Christine herself.

The question then arose, where was she, and if found, how was she to be recovered, if at all?

Mr. Smith found in the person of Mr. T. A. Vestal of Selma, Alabama, one of the shrewdest detectives in the country, and Vestal at once commenced operations, with the assistance of two other detectives, and ultimately gained intelligence of her in the city of Philadelphia, though not before the lapse of some fifteen or eighteen months.

Vestal heard from a negro barber, whose confidence he had obtained, that about a year ago a child answering her description had been in the city, and for a time had been secreted in a cellar on Pine Street. The cellar was found, and, through the influence of bribes, it was ascertained from an old woman still living in a portion of the house to which the cellar belonged that the child had been carried to New York. The next day Mr. Vestal started for that city to prosecute his search, and remained there five weeks. Every effort was made, but no further intelligence of her could be learned. If any one knew of her or had seen her there, their mouths were sealed to the influence of money or persuasion. Mr. Vestal began almost to despair, yet determined not to yield his cherished object. He had every reason to believe she was alive, for when taken from New Orleans she was in excellent health. The papers had been watched closely by him, and no account of the death of any one answering her description had been noticed, which certainly would have been the case had she died. From New York he proceeded to Boston; from thence to Philadelphia, and ultimately to Newark, New Jersey. There, for the first time, he got definite information of her. He learned from a man then keeping a drinking house that at one time, when engaged as a cabman in the city of New York, he had been hired to convey a girl answering her description to a sailing vessel, the name of which he did not remember, bound for and ready to sail for Liverpool; that he had seen the vessel depart, and knew the child was aboard of her when she sailed. Acting on this valuable information, Mr. Vestal immediately returned to North Carolina and urged on Mr. Smith the necessity of following her. Mr. Smith determined to make the attempt, and accordingly prepared for the journey. Accompanied by the mother of Christine Millie, he reached New York, took the steamship Atlantic, and after a pleasant voyage reached Liverpool. There they learned that the child had been on exhibition in that city; also in London, Leeds and other places.

Seated in a promiscuous crowd of traders and traveling clerks one evening, in front of his hotel, her name was introduced, and he learned that a short time before she had been on exhibition in Glasgow, Scotland. Immediately they started for that city, but on arrival found that a short time before she had been taken back to England, and was then in Birmingham. So to that city they posted, and on their arrival, to their joy, found she was then on exhibition. It now became necessary that extreme caution should be used, lest their long-cherished object would be frustrated on the very eve of consummation. The impatience of the mother knew no bounds: scarcely could she be restrained from rushing to the exhibition room and defiantly claiming her child, supposing the party who then had possession of it would recognize her claim. She was, however, at length convinced of the imprudence of such a course, and submitted until the case had been placed in the hands of the proper officers. Accordingly the Chief of Police and a select body of assistants were called and a true statement of the affairs given. The American Consul was also waited upon and consulted. He immediately took a lively interest in the matter, and advised that the arrival of the American party be kept unknown to the exhibitor until they, in company with a protective force of police, should enter the hall that evening; and should the child recognize the mother among the audience, it would be *prima facie*[6] evidence of the facts attempted to be established by them, and used as such in case of litigation. Accordingly, the impatience of the mother was restrained until the hour of the gathering of the visitors, when a portion of the police (selected for the purpose and disguised), Mr. Smith and the mother procured tickets of admission and entered the hall, as casual visitors impelled only by the general curiosity. No sooner, however, had the keen eye of the mother caught a glimpse of her long-lost child than she uttered a scream of such heart-rending pathos that the audience simultaneously rose to their feet, wondering and astonished. The mother, overpowered, fell fainting to the floor. When resuscitated she wildly threw her arms about, crying in most piteous tones. "My own child! O! give her to me! Do not take her away again; she needs my care! Where is she? Where is she?" While this scene of excitement was going on, the exhibitor attempted to secrete the girl in an adjoining room; but an honest Scotchman, divining his intentions, placed his back against the door, and bringing himself into a position that would have delighted a pugilist, cried out: "Ye'll nae tak' the bairn ayant the door, maun ye wallop me first, and I'm nae thinkin' ye'll soon do that."

Such a scene of excitement as this denouement created has seldom been witnessed. The women fainted, and the men, learning the true state of affairs from the Chief of Police, who mounted the stage for the purpose, threatened with immediate and summary punishment the sordid villain who had stolen, for the purpose of gain, a helpless child. He managed, however, to escape by jumping from the second story window, which hazardous feat alone, for the time, saved him from certain and well-merited punishment.

6. Latin for "at first appearance or instance"; *prima facie* evidence is the evidence required to prove that a case indeed exists. The girls' immediate recognition of their mother, from whom they were being kept, would have been regarded as *prima facie* evidence.

The mother, recovering, took the child, and they were conveyed to the hotel, where, for the first time in three years, she slept with it in her arms, forgetting, in the possession of the fondly-loved and long-lost one, the days and nights of anguish she had spent during its absence, and dreamed of naught save happiness and pleasure to come. But her troubles were not to end here. The prize was too rich to be thus easily given up by interested ones. So, on the following morning, a writ of *habeas corpus*[7] was served upon them, requiring the appearance of mother and child before the Court of Admiralty, to show cause why she was taken from the custody of the exhibitor. Here the Consul again proved a friend and true American by demanding the child as an American citizen, and requiring it, as a minor, to be placed in charge of the mother, and that protection be given her to maintain her maternal rights.

Voluminous proofs, giving an accurate description of mother and child, together with all necessary facts bearing upon the case, had been carefully procured and carried there, in case of necessity. Upon these the Consul spoke a short time, when the judge, arising, declared it useless to occupy more time, for from the opening of the court the case had been decided by the Bench. "The child should be given into the custody of its lawful mother. If it was not the child of the defendants, then mother never bore a child. Every lineament, every feature, every look betokened it; every spectator in his inmost heart felt, yes, knew it to be her child, almost as certainly as though they had seen it every hour since its birth." A long and hearty shout of approbation at this decision ascended to the dome of the stately old building.

As soon as order was restored, the plaintiff determined to make one more effort; so, calling the attention of the Court to the fact of his ability to perform all he promised, he said he was ready then and there to settle upon the mother the sum of ten thousand pounds sterling, and deed to her an elegant house, in which she could spend the rest of her days in luxury and comfort if she would remain in England and give him possession of the child until she was eighteen, to all of which flattering offers she only turned a deaf ear, preferring, as she said, "to return and live, as she had done, in the land of her birth, with those she had known from infancy, and among her kindred and her friends."

7. Latin; "you have the body." The legal move by which a detainer of another person is brought before the court to prove that they indeed have the right to keep him or her.

It should have been remarked before that the Texan, although shrewd enough to dupe Brower, was in turn made a dupe himself. Arriving in Philadelphia, on their way from New Orleans, he fell in with two showmen, Thompson and Miller, who soon succeeded in getting possession of the girl, and it was they who had carried her to, and in whose possession she was found, in England. As Thompson and Miller had been most successful in their exhibitions of her (in the course of three years arising from poverty to comparative affluence), it was not to be presumed they would willingly abandon the hope of again possessing her, be the means of possessing what they would.

Mr. Smith, the mother and the subject of our sketch, being now free to depart, made their preparations openly to return. The Atlantic had made a return trip and was then at the Liverpool docks. The now happy party again took passage upon her, and after a prosperous voyage reached New York. There they took the cars and were soon landed safely in the good old State of North Carolina.

Astonishing as it may appear, scarcely had the party reached home when those who had caused so many sleepless nights and days of anguish and trouble made their appearance in Charlotte, distant from the girl's home fifty-five miles, evidently intent upon another attempt to regain the rich prize they so fraudulently had possession of for a time, but now wrested from their avaricious grasp. The citizens of Charlotte, learning of their presence and intentions, concluded to give them an admirably fitting suit, composed of good *tar* and excellent *feathers*, and the freedom of the streets for promenading, with the company of a lusty negro to keep time to *quickstep* on the end of a large tin kettle.

Thompson and Miller, by accident, learning the intentions of the Charlottins, concluded "discretion was the better part of valor" and decamped by night, and since then nothing has been heard of either in North Carolina, and the only thing to remind you of their visit to that section is the chorus of a negro song heard at the corn shuckings:

> Massa Tomsin run a race;
>   Oh! oh! o-o-o yah!
> He beat de fastest hoss in de place;
>   Yah, oh yah! O ha!

Millie Christine grew and flourished, when Mr. Smith, yielding to the earnest solicitation of friends who knew him to be possessed of the world's greatest marvel, allowed her to be taken upon a tour through the States of South Carolina, Florida, Georgia and Louisiana. At the close of that tour, in the City of New Orleans, an incident occurred which, for a short time, made shipwreck of the happiness of Millie Christine, and which, but for the affection of Mr. and Mrs. Smith, and the persistence which that affection inspired, would probably have altered the whole life of the child for the worse. She was again kidnapped and for months was hurried over the country, from place to place, and deprived of the fostering care of her natural guardians. Ultimately, however, Mr. Smith's anxiety and determination were rewarded, and the child was restored to the arms and heart of Mrs. Smith, whom it soon came to regard and denominate its "white mamma." Under her care the girl was reared to regard with reverence and love the Supreme Father of all mankind, and speedily grew up into an intelligent Christian child. She not only became proficient in elementary education, but, showing a high appreciation and taste for music, soon became an object of great interest to all visitors at Mr. Smith's home by the rapid progress she made in that accomplishment.

The year 1860, the dreadful year which brought so much pain and suffering to the United States of America, brought its own individual sorrow to the home of Millie Christine. Mr. Smith, after a few weeks of suffering, passed quietly away to a better world, mourned by all who knew him, and by none more than those who called him master. Indeed, it is only due to Mr. Smith and his wife to state, and Christine Millie desires particularly that it be inserted in this sketch of her life, that she experienced at his death rather the affliction of one who had lost a beloved father rather than a master. Not only this, but other families on [the] estate of the Smiths, while calling the owner and his wife master and mistress, always regarded them in the light of protecting parents.

But the war came on, and with it came those heavy losses which prostrated the fortunes of the Smith family, making of the once prosperous plantation an untilled waste, over which the restless hand of the armed spoiler worked its will. It was then that the kindness of the past found its fruit in the devotion displayed by Millie Christine towards her only living protector, Mrs. Smith, whom she regards with filial affection, and from whom she was fully determined never to separate herself. To retrieve the fallen fortunes of the family she, now free, consented to place herself on exhibition, and afford the world the opportunity of seeing the most marvelous physical development which has ever existed in the human family.

It may be mentioned here as an interesting fact, showing the strange mutability of human fortunes, that Jacob, the father of this wonderful being, once the slave of the planter McCoy, now owns, with his wife Monemia, the very plantation on which he was once a bondman, and on which Millie Christine first saw the light of day, the same having been purchased by her with the proceeds of her exhibitions as a present to her father and mother.[8]

It will be necessary to append to this sketch a few of the medical and surgical reports on Millie Christine's physical organization; but it may not be uninteresting to give a brief description of her as she strikes the mind and eye of a familiar friend. Millie Christine, physically, has but one existence; mentally, she has two, perfectly developed. From the middle of the single spine grow two perfectly developed busts, each of which has a pair of fine arms, and terminates in an interesting head. Both heads are adorned with curling black hair; each has a pair of sparkling black eyes, constantly lit up by intelligence, which, at any out-burst of fun and humor, seem literally to dance with glee; while each mouth is adorned with a set of brilliant teeth. The two faces are bright and interesting, but differ materially in features, one resembling Jacob, the father, the other Monemia, the mother. There is very little distinc-tion to be made in the two developments. The two sets of brains always agree in forming the same conclusions; equally amiable, and equally agreeable in character, they never form different ideas on the same sub-jects, and the thoughts of each are characterized by that independence which is usually exhibited by natives of America. The tastes and habits of the two are alike; both are fond of music and dancing, both take interest in the same amusements; indeed, this marvelous organization shows its wonder in nothing more evidently than its perfect happiness. The two minds can converse each through its own lips. The being is never at a loss for society or for company, for each has, attached to itself, another existence; and yet in no single instance has a particle of disagree-ment ever occurred to conflict with the happiness or comfort of either. If the one mind formed the fancy to be in London, and the other desired its body to proceed to Paris, a conflict might ensue; providentially, this seems impossible, and has never occurred. Christine has a soprano

8. Descendents of the McKay family argue that they have retained legal ownership of the farm. See Joanne Martell, *Millie-Christine: Fearfully and Wonderfully Made* (Winston-Salem, NC: John F. Blair, 2000), 208, and the current volume, 37n21.

voice. Millie a contralto; and they sing duets together with exquisite taste and sweetness. Their natural taste for music has been conscientiously and carefully cultivated by their kind protectress, and the public will not be slow to discover that they have as much power to please and amuse as a very large number of artistes of established reputation. It should now be stated that Millie Christine has four legs, on which she walks with grace and ease; but she can use the outer ones only for purposes of locomotion. She is a very graceful dancer, and executes the schottische, polka or waltz with equal ease. Her manners in the presence of strangers are most engaging. She does not object to speak of herself or her own peculiarities, and her two minds are always as one on these points. The two minds composed some verses descriptive of herself, which the two voices repeated in unison, and, although of no great literary merit, they are simple and expressive. The verses are as follows:

'Tis not modest of one's self to speak;
But, daily scanned from head to feet,
I freely talk of everything,
Sometimes to persons wondering.

Some persons say I must be two,
The doctors say this is not true;
Some cry out humbug till they see,
When they say—great mystery!

Two heads, four arms, four feet,
All in one perfect body meet;
I am most wonderfully made
All scientific men have said.

None like me since the days of Eve—
None such, perhaps, will ever live—
If marvel to myself am I,
Why not to all who pass me by?

I'm happy, quite, because content,
For some wise purpose I was sent;
My maker knows what he has done,
Whether I'm created *two* or one.

The medical reports on the anatomical construction of this extraordinary phenomenon are published separately for the benefit of the scientific and the gratification of the curious, but sufficient may be here stated to satisfy the ordinary interest of the public. A number of gentlemen connected with Jefferson Medical College, in the city of Philadelphia, examined Christine Millie. Among them were Drs. Pancoast, Meigs, Bidde, Wallace and Dickson, all well known in the medico-scientific world. *Forney's Press* contains the following report of the clinic:

At a special clinic recently held at the Jefferson Medical College, "Christine Millie" was submitted to a scientific anatomical examination.

Assembled at the clinic we found Professors Pancoast, Ormsby, Rand and Gross and Drs. Meigs, W. H. Pancoast, Gardette, Ray, Turnbull, Atkinson, Barson, Bache, Dickson, Cohen, Altee, Andrews and others, well known to surgical fame.

The double-headed girl was introduced by Dr. William H. Pancoast, the demonstrator of anatomy at the College, and a general feeling of astonishment was felt when it was discovered that, instead of a monstrosity there was exhibited to the professional talent assembled a well-educated, intelligent, quick witted girl, with nothing about her that was repulsive or calculated to offend the most fastidious, but which at once stamped her as a wonder and a source of scientific information to these learned in anatomy.

Dr. Pancoast stated that the body had been placed under his professional care, and, owing to the important questions involved, a private examination had been made by Professors Pancoast and Gross, and Drs. Sevie and Andrew, which had verified all the opinions expressed as to her duality.

It was then stated that this remarkable freak of nature was united at the lateral posterior portion of the pelvis, while above that point they were separated—had separate chests, two pairs of fully developed arms, but only one trunk.

The double-headed possessed separate intellectual faculties as entirely distinct as was the brain power of two different individuals, while their faces indicate, to a remarkable degree, intelligence of a high order and amiability. The lower portion of the body had inclined outwards from each side, and the lower limbs were inferior, and not so fully developed as the arms.

A series of experiments was then made under the direction of Professors Pancoast, Atlee, Maury, and others, calculated to demonstrate the construction of the nervous system, which showed that while above the junction the sense of feeling was separate and distinct in each, below the union it was in common. A touch upon the foot of one would be instantly detected by the other, while a hand placed upon either shoulder was only noticed by the one touched.

The pulse of Millie was found to be about four beats slower than that of Christine, while the beat of the two hearts was nearly the same.

An impromptu performance was given at the clinic in order to show the agility of the girl, and, to the astonishment of the audience, dances were executed, conversations carried on between the two heads, and conversations with two different persons at one and the same time. They stood upon their outer limbs, walked about with a pleasing undulating motion, and Christine lifted the other by the ligature at the pelvis merely by inclining her body to one side. To cap the climax, a duet was executed by the girl, displaying musical knowledge, culture, perfect time and tune, one head taking the soprano and the other the alto; and then, in order to show the sympathetic nature of their voices, "Sweet Spirit, Hear my Prayer," was given in admirable style.

Some of the leading statesmen in Washington manifested great interest in the case, and two of the most eminent physicians in the city were afforded an opportunity to make an examination. Respecting it, the *Washington Republican* says: "The examination by Dr. Bliss and Dr. Borland was most satisfactory, and revealed the fact that the representations made by the young lady's guardians are entirely correct, the girl being but of one body, with two heads, four arms, four feet, two sets of lungs, two hearts, but only one physical organization. The doctors express themselves as entirely satisfied that the young lady is the most wonderful human being on the face of the earth."

The *Baltimore Sun*, a paper of very high standing in Maryland, says: "There is, at the juncture of the trunk, but one spinal column. The nervous system seems to be identical, but each possesses individual consciousness, and each head does its own thinking. On the other hand, the appetite is the same; when one is hungry the other is the same. The digestive organs are independent. As she moves about she looks like two bright young copper-colored girls tied together in the middle, in the same dress, which is cut short so as to display the movements of four feet. The busts of each are very nearly symmetrical; the heads and necks, shoulders and arms, are perfect. The faces are round, bright and intelligent; eyes large and clear; hair black and glossy."

The press of all the large cities in America bore similar testimony.

During the past few months Millie Christine has received an enormous number of visitors. Christine Millie's receptions have always been attended by great numbers of people. In the city of Washington, during a fortnight's stay, thirty thousand persons attended her receptions; in

Philadelphia, during eight weeks, a hundred and fifty thousand visited her; in Boston, seventy thousand in three weeks; and in New York, in a single day, ten thousand persons flocked to see her. Christine Millie has made an extensive tour of Europe, and remained there several years. The *Liverpool Mercury* has the following regarding her:

Extraordinary Physical Phenomenon.

Since the days when the Siamese twins arrived in this country and occasioned so much excitement in medical circles, no illustration of the freaks of nature has been found at all approaching in its remarkable character to that given in the person of Christine Millie, a native of North Carolina, who arrived at this port on Tuesday, per City of Brussels, from New York. The young person who is about to proceed to London for exhibition, is the child of parents formerly slaves in North Carolina, still living, and having several other children, and was herself born a slave. It is scarcely possible by a written description to convey anything like an adequate idea of the marvelous physical organization of this extraordinary being. In figure, Christine Millie, who is 19 years of age, is rather short, and possesses two heads upon one body, with two well-developed chests and four arms. This portion of the frame is as perfectly distinct in each figure as if the upper part were the heads of two persons; but at the lateral posterior portion of the pelvis there is but one body, with one spine, the lower parts of which gradually incline outwards from each side, and terminate with four legs. The faces are of the African type, with thick lips and large mouth, denoting the race from which the girl has descended; but in conversation the countenances brighten with intelligence, and those who have had the opportunity of seeing the girl could not fail to be pleased with the geniality of her manner and with the store of information which she has at her command. The question which naturally arises, and which it seems difficult to solve, is, whether this is one being, or whether, in some extraordinary manner, two persons have thus marvelously joined together. A very careful anatomical examination, made by the professors at Jefferson Medical College, America, has led to the discovery that the lungs, heart, and functions of digestion are those of two persons, apparently perfect and healthy in each, but that the whole of the lower organization of the body is that of one female, with the exception of the four legs. Each head is said to possess separate intellectual faculties, as entirely distinct as the brain power of two different individuals, and the volitions of the will are independent, but very much in harmony with each other. In proof of this the two mouths will at the same time converse with different persons upon topics of a widely different character, and will join in singing a duet, one taking the soprano and the other the contralto part. Experiments have been tried with a view to demonstrate the nervous system, which showed that whilst above the junction the sense of feeling was separate and distinct in each, below the point of union it was common. Thus, a hand placed upon the shoulder of either was noticed only by the one touched, but a pressure of the foot was instantly felt by each.

Yesterday a private party of ladies and gentlemen had an interview with this extraordinary person at the Washington Hotel, and were both astonished and pleased. She seems remarkably cheerful, suffers no inconvenience or pain from peculiar physical organization, dances with freedom, and, for one of her race, sings with considerable taste and expression.

The editor of the *Liverpool Daily Post* says:

THE NEW PHENOMENA.

A numerous party assembled yesterday at the Washington Hotel to "interview" a most extraordinary natural Phenomena who is about to be exhibited in London as the "Two-Headed Nightingale."

Christine Millie is a phenomenon of the Siamese twin order, but far more wonderful, for instead of two bodies connected with a ligature, there is only one *torso*, the body separating a little above the waist. There are two distinct busts and pairs of shoulders, two heads, four arms, and four legs. Anatomical examination has proved that the young lady—she is nineteen years of age—has two sets of lungs, and two digestions. It is certain there are mentally two perfect individualities, for conversations may be carried on with each of the two persons so mysteriously blended in one; and, each having a very pretty gift of singing, they perform duets in parts. Christine Millie also dances very gracefully, and appears to have no difficulty in moving about, and in no way differs in appearance from two animated and engaging young negresses, who for sport have agreed to pass an hour tied together nearly back to back. The exceedingly amiable and merry disposition of the mysterious pair deprives the exhibition altogether of that painful element which was present even in the case of those practical philosophers, the Siamese Twins. Christine Millie "first saw the light" as a slave in North Carolina, and the lady on whose estate she was born, and by whom she has been most affectionately and successfully educated, accompanied her to England. All who met Christine Millie yesterday must have felt interested in her fortunes, and well disposed to meet her again.

From the *Liverpool Daily Courier*:

ARRIVAL OF CURIOSITIES OF NATURE.

Amongst the visitors who arrived at Liverpool from New York on Tuesday in the Inman steamer City of Brussels, was a party of ladies and gentlemen, whom the indefatigable Mr. Barnum,[9] of showman notoriety, has nothing to do with, though here for the edification of the curious.[10]

The most singular and physiologically interesting member of the party is a young lady, between eighteen and nineteen years of age, or rather, two young ladies rolled into one, who is certainly a rival to the famous Siamese Twins, and very much more attractive in appearance than Messrs. Chang and Eng. Those who saw the Siamese Twins during their presence in England will have a vivid recollection of the painful look that their features bore, and the constrained movements of their bodies while walking in any direction. There is a total absence of this in the young lady who bears the name of Miss Christine Millie, whose four bright black eyes and dazzling rows of pearly-white teeth light up a fair Creole complexion with an animation that is really attractive. This singular *lusus naturae*[11] is the offspring of parents who were slaves in North Carolina previous to the American civil war, and has several brothers and sisters who are like ordinary humanity. During the struggle the family suffered considerable privations; but as a curious illustration of the changes which have taken place in Southern society, through the war and the declaration of freedom from slavery, it may be mentioned that

9. Phineas T. Barnum of the American Museum in New York City; Barnum was not the first, but certainly the most successful and famous showman and entertainment manager of his time. For more on Barnum's role in U.S. entertainment history, see Bluford Adams, *E Pluribus Barnum: The Great Showman and the Making of U.S. Popular Culture* (Minneapolis: University of Minnesota Press, 1997).

10. The following additional text appears here in the 1882 version of the pamphlet published by Torrey & Clark: "It will be remembered that a year or two ago Mr. Barnum was burnt out, his museum being utterly destroyed, and the results of a lifetime of collection of various oddities—with the exception of the human specimens—consumed. To most men this would have been irretrievable ruin, but Mr. Barnum is made of other stuff. He set to work with renewed energy to make a more attractive collection than ever, and he is once again to the fore as the world's unrivalled showman. He has not come over to this country with his batch of 'specimens,' but has entrusted them to the care of gentlemen who have been here before, and who are thoroughly conversant with the customs of the country."

11. Latin; "freak of nature."

the father of Christine Millie is now the owner of the plantation on which he was once a slave. As to the young lady herself—for we have surgical authority for describing her—she has bodily only one person, though possessed of two heads, two pairs of shoulders, four arms, and two pairs of legs, amalgamated curiously with one trunk. We can only say that an hour's audience with her yesterday afternoon proved her to be a cultured, self-possessed and accomplished person, who had a most singular attribute of being able to hold two totally distinct conversations at the same time with different persons, or the same person, can sing a duet very tastefully and tunefully in two voices, soprano and contralto, and can dance a mazourka[12] with singular grace and facility. There was no difficulty made in exhibiting the upper portion of the dorsal connection, and it was done without any infringement of modesty.

From the *Liverpool Leader*:

"MOST EXTRAORDINARY."

In the steamship City of Brussels, from New York, on the 2d of May, 1871, arrived a cargo which, in the words of Mr. Toole, may be termed "most extraordinary." Of all the curiosities ever unearthed by the immortal Barnum, none can compare in the most minute degree with Millie Christine, a daughter or daughters—whichever the fastidious please—of the State of North Carolina. They first saw the light nineteen years ago, and the mother is presumably the founder of that gigantic Woman's Rights Association in America, which has lately made formidable inroads upon English society. Here we have a young lady with one body, but two distinct minds, borne by two separate heads. All the intelligent men who saw her at the Washington Hotel the other day, can bear witness to the marvelous intelligence which predominates in both brains; the conversational powers of the two heads at once in communication with two different persons, upon different topics, would sufficiently testify it. But the marvel did not stop here; some of the sweetest duets in the language of music were sung by a high soprano and a pure contralto. The notes issued from two heads, and yet but one trunk supplied the *verve*.[13] It may now be added that this extraordinary trunk has two pairs of perfect legs, terminating in symmetrical and very pretty feet, and that, moving upon their pedal extremities, the trunk exhibits

12. A Polish dance or the music for such a dance; the second beat is particularly heavy.

13. Animation or actual life.

the very poetry of motion. The polka, the mazourka, the schottische, are delineated by these two pairs of pretty feet, in perfect time and harmony, and the spectator is rewarded not by one smile, as in the case of ordinary young ladies, but by two distinct smiles, winked at you by two pairs of sparkling and roguish eyes, and thrown at you by two different sets of the purest ivory that ever adorned the mouth of an Indian Sultana. There are a lot of people here, or elsewhere, always ready to strain at the smallest gnat and swallow the biggest camel, who will doubtless put this young lady down as outside the pale of ordinary humanity. If this prejudice should carry one so far as to avoid her, they alone will be the losers. We can testify that no person of ordinary intelligence can be in her company for half an hour without yielding to the charm of her manner and the fascination of her double smiles. She has you on both sides. If you remove your head from one position you are immediately the victim of another pair of eyes, which fix you and, in fact, transfix you. We candidly admit that we were fascinated, and that we immediately lost sight of the phenomenon and became overpowered by the influence of this dual brain. The young lady will shortly hold *levees* in London, and the public of Liverpool may hope to see her by-and-by. The eminent medical men of the United States testify that this remarkable freak of nature is united at the lateral posterior portion of the pelvis, while above that portion they are separated, have separate chests, two pair of fully developed arms, but only one trunk. With the double head they possess separate intellectual faculties as entirely distinct as in the brain power of two different individuals, while their faces indicate to a remarkable degree intelligence of a high order and great amiability.

Visit of Eminent Men in Liverpool to Millie Christine.

On the 4th of May a reception for medical men was held at the Washington Hotel, Liverpool, and was attended by the following eminent members of that faculty: Dr. Nevins, Dr. Bickersbeth, Dr. McGregor, Dr. Greegan, Dr. Slack, Dr. Gorst, Dr. Steele, Mr. T. Dickerton, F.R.C.S., etc.; Mr. Edgar Browne, M.R.C.S.; Mr. Jas. Pen Harris, Mr. W. H. Manifold, etc. Having had an opportunity of explaining the bond of union, these eminent men were unanimously of the opinion that Millie Christine is the most extraordinary phenomenon the world has ever seen.

The Two-Headed Girl

Laughable Account of the Two-Headed Girl by a Western Editor.

"Girls in this city are divided into two classes—single-headed girls and double-headed ditto. The single-headed ones are certainly the most numerous, but the double-headed ones appear to be the most attractive. This is evident from the fact, that while we can see a single-headed girl almost any time, we have to pay in order to be introduced to the maid with the duplex cranium. We say 'maid' because the last double-headed girl we saw was not married. There was one man who courted her successfully, as he thought, for a time, but before popping the question he kissed one face first, and could never get the consent of the other head. She is now waiting till a two-headed man comes along, and is gay with hope.

"This duplex girl, however, must be in every way a desirable match. Though the assurance given that she eats with both heads may tell against her with parsimonious wooers, yet the fact that she buys dresses for one only must be an immense advantage. The same with her talking. The two-headed girl must be extremely circumspect, not only in her walk, but in her conversation. As she can never have a secret, she can have no opportunity to go around telling it. Neither will any one ever tell a secret to one head for fear that the other would split upon it.

"The fact of having two tongues should not militate against her, as, if she had only one, she would probably keep it going all the time, while, if she uses two, the one deadens the sound of the other. Whichever way we look at the two-headed girl we see her to advantage, though we don't mean to say the least that should be understood to disparage a girl because she happens to be born with only one head."

After an absence of eight years Christine Millie returned to her native land on October 1st, 1878. Her tour abroad was a continued ovation of success. She visited the principal cities and towns in England, France, Germany, Belgium, Italy, Hungary, Austria, Holland and Russia. At every point the young lady was commanded to appear before the nobility and rulers of these great countries. Kingly presents and valuable jewels were given as tokens of appreciation not only of her as a remarkable curiosity, but of her graceful bearing, her contented disposition and of her artistic musical abilities. Before she had landed, upon her arrival, a representative of the *New York Herald* greeted her, and the next morning that journal gave forth to the whole United States the return of one of its children, who had fully established herself to be the greatest curiosity of the greatest country in the world. Since her return she has exhibited to thousands in the cities of Boston, Philadelphia and New York. While in Philadelphia she again appeared before the professors and students of the Jefferson Medical College. Professor Pancoast for the second time examined her. A portion of his lecture is extracted from the *Philadelphia Evening Telegraph*.

This afternoon, at 1 o'clock, Millie and Christine were given a scientific examination by Professor W. H. Pancoast, at his clinic, at the Jefferson Medical College Hospital. The well-like room was crowded, and Professor Pancoast busy removing a cancer from a patient when the reporter arrived. During the operation Baron Littlefinger and Count Rosebud, two most intelligent dwarfs—perfect little men in figure—were present, and appeared interested spectators of the operation. In introducing Millie and Christine, the Professor said that he considered them the most interesting personages that have ever come under the notice of scientific men, far more interesting than the Siamese Twins. In the midst of his discourse the young ladies entered, clad in green silk on their two bodies, pretty little bronze boots on the four feet, white kids on their four hands. They moved forward like an expanded V, with a crab-like movement that was not ungraceful. Born back-to-back, the Professor explained that the natural desire of each to walk face forward had twisted them in their present position. Separate entities, separate individualities, each can pursue separate lines of thought and conversation independent of the other. From habit their appetites call for food and drink at the same time. All the ills of flesh are not, however, necessarily theirs in common. One may have the toothache and the other be free from any ache. But in the examination conducted to-day the Professor discovered a remarkable development of sensibility since his previous examination eight years ago. Touching them on any extreme of the body, on any foot for example, both in common were conscious of the touch. Christine has been and is now the larger and stronger of the two. As children they used to have little struggles and quarrels for supremacy, but, as they could not get away from each other, they early concluded that the best way to get along in their novel path through life was to yield to each other. Their present happiness and affection for each other is an example for couples who are yoked together in marital bonds. Sometimes Christine rolls over Millie in bed without awakening her. Both can sleep separately. They can stand and walk on their outside legs, but they prefer to walk on all fours. Millie cannot lift up Christine's legs, or Christine Millie's legs. Since the Hungarian sisters, there has been no similar case reported reaching adult life for 170 years.[14] The bond of union between these, which is just above the bones of the spine, is chiefly cartilaginous, but the spines are so closely approximated that there is an osseous union between them. To the question by Professor Pancoast, whether either was engaged to

14. Helen and Judith of Szony; see earlier in this chapter, 60–61n4.

be married, each denied the soft impeachment with decision, though the Professor explained that physically there are no serious objections to the marriage of Her or Them; but morally there was a most decided one.[15] During the Professor's lecture the Misses Christine Millie and Millie Christine appeared very much interested in the diagnosis of their singular condition, and evidenced their superior intelligence by their apt and ready answers.

While abroad Millie Christine made herself mistress of the French, German, Italian and Spanish languages. Always industrious, she makes her entire wardrobe, even to her dresses, for exhibition purposes. She dresses herself without trouble. Having lived thus long together, they express no desire to be parted and hope to leave this world as they came into it—together.

15. This is an interesting place to capitalize "Her or Them"—when discussing the possible marriage and, by implication, sexuality of the twins. The punctuation stresses the significance of individuality in relation to one's sexual activities.

CERTIFICATES
OF EMINENT MEDICAL MEN

Hundreds of certificates might be given, but the following are sufficient:

1,100 WALNUT STREET, PHILADELPHIA, PA., Jan., 1871.

I have examined Millie Christine and consider her a more interesting anatomical curiosity than the Siamese Twins, on whose bodies I made (assisted by a colleague) a post-mortem examination. I consider the union of the Carolina Twin more curious even than the famous Hungarian Sisters, who were born October 26th, 1701. Millie Christine is joined by the sacrum and coccyx. The lower part of the spinal cords are united together. There are separate bladders, but one common vagina, one uterus to be recognized, and one perfect anus. The bond of the union at this date measures 26 inches in circumference.

WM. H. PANCOAST, M.D., etc.

1,117 SPRUCE STREET, PHILADELPHIA, PA., Jan. 20th, 1872.

I have had the opportunity (in conjunction with Professors Gross and Pancoast) of examining very carefully the celebrated Carolina Twin. She and they are simply wonderful in their anatomical construction—far more so than the Hungarian Sisters or the Siamese Twins. Intellectually they are separate and distinct, sexually but one. Rectum and vagina in common and possessing but one uterus.

T. H. ANDREWS, M.D.

NEW YORK CITY, August 5th, 1871.

The undersigned were among those who were invited to visit Millie Christine to-day, heartily concurring in all former medical reports relative to she and they being both two and yet but one person, stamping her as the world's greatest and most interesting personage:

Dr. ANDERSON,	Dr. E. B. BELDEN,
Dr. DAVIDSON,	Dr. WOOSTER,
Dr. BRUCE,	Dr. BEACH,
Dr. CROMPTON,	Dr. C. H. BROWN,
Dr. CHADSEY,	Dr. J. C. BOULLE,
Dr. BARKER,	Dr. I. C. McCOY,
Dr. COOPER,	Dr. S. W. DAVID,
University Medical College,	
Prof. CARMICHAEL,	Dr. DEMAREST.

Lancet, Medical Journal of England.

The following prominent scientific men of Great Britain are among the few who vouch for the genuineness of the marvelous Two-Headed Nightingale:

SIR JAMES PAGET, Bart, Pres. R.C.S., F.R.S., &c.
SIR W. W. GULL, Bart, M.D., F.R.C., &c.
SIR W. FERGUSON, Bart, M.D., F.R.C.S., &c.
SIR HENRY THOMPSON, F.R.C.S., M.D.
HENRY FEE, F.R.C.S., &c.

And leading surgeons and medical men of Russia, Austria, Switzerland, Germany, Spain, France, Italy and Belgium fully concur and endorse the statements above given.

15 SOUTH CHARLOOT ST., 11th Jan., 1856.

I have this day examined Millie Christine, and find that the band of union is between 15 and 17 inches in circumference, involving at least the bones of the sacrum and coccyx immovable, uniting the sacral nerves and spinal cord, so as to constitute one individual, or two girls in one nervous system. I also find both heads sprightly and intelligent, and deem her a much greater curiosity than the Siamese Twins.

(Signed.) JOHN LEZARS,
Professor of Surgery to the Royal College of Surgery, and
Senior Operating Surgeon in the Royal Infirmary of Edinburgh.

NEW ORLEANS, 10th Feb., 1858.

I have this day examined the "Two-Headed Girl," and find her to be a very remarkable anatomical curiosity. The spines are united, having rectum and vagina in common.

I fully concur in the above opinion.

J. C. NOTT, M.D.
Thos. Hunt, M.D.

ST. LOUIS, Mo., May 28th, 1858.

We, the undersigned, having made a critical examination of the *lusus naturae* known as the "Two-Headed Girl," now being exhibited in our city by Mr. Vestal, would beg leave to state that this wonder, as regards the pelvic arrangements is in our opinion, one; in all other particulars double.

JOHN B. McDOWELL, M.D.,   WM. CARR LANE, M.D.,
B. F. EDWARDS, M.D.,   J. M. SCOTT, M.D.

ST. JOSEPH, Mo., July 13th, 1858.

The undersigned, physicians of St. Joseph, having been invited to see the *lusus naturae* now on exhibition in the city, fully concur in the statement that it is the greatest wonder of the age, having two heads, four legs, four arms and but one body, and one consolidated pelvis, and perfect sympathy of desire.

W. I. HEDDEW, M.D.,   Q. B. KNODE, M.D.,
J. H. CRAND, M.D.,   C. CATLETT, M.D.,
J. A. CHAMBERS, M.D.

ROYAL GUEST.

THE FAMOUS

Two-Headed Nightingale.

Four Times by Command before the Royal Family. Thrice before the Prince and Princess of Wales and also before all the Crowned Heads of Europe.

A ROYAL GUEST.—By Royal Command, Mdlle. Millie Christine, the marvelous "Two-headed Nightingale," visited her Majesty the Queen at Buckingham Palace.—*London Times.*

Mdlle. Millie Christine, the famous "Two-headed Nightingale," had the honor of appearing (by command) before H. R. H. the Princess of Wales, at Marlborough House.—*Pall Mall Gazette.*

H.R.H. the Prince of Wales, accompanied by Prince John of Glucksburg and Mr. Paget, attended by Col. Keppel and H.I.H. the Grand Duke Wladimar of Russia and Suite, attended by Col. Ellis, paid a visit to the exhibition of the "Two-headed Nightingale" at Willis's Rooms.—*Morning Post.*

So much pleased was Her Royal Highness the Princess of Wales with the "Two-headed Nightingale," on her departure for the continent, she left orders that a couple of brooches should be presented to the two-in-one young ladies.—*The Standard.*

They have been well educated, and appear happy, lively, and good tempered.—*London Times.*

The "Two-headed Nightingale" sings popular duets very sweetly and cleverly.—*Daily Telegraph.*

Her care will no doubt be regarded with great interest.—*London Daily News.*

The Carolina Twin, Christine Millie, is the owner of a most valuable brooch, presented to her by H.M. Queen Victoria.

MILLIE CHRISTINE A ROYAL FAVORITE.—Piccadilly Hall was closed last night, for Millie and Chrissie were commanded to appear at Marlborough House—her third time there.—*London Times.*

MUSICAL ENTERTAINMENT

BY

MILLIE CHRISTINE,

THE

TWO-HEADED NIGHTINGALE

Selections from the following, and many other songs, will be sung as Duets by Millie Christine, at each reception.

O'ER THE WAVES WE FLOAT.

Words by J. E. Carpenter.   *Music by Stephen Glover.*

O'er the waves we float, we float,
Fairies two, in our fairy boat,
Fanned by the breezes, rocked by the tide,
In our nautilus barque we glide, we glide.
When the strong cordage snaps in the gale,
Safe o'er the surges we sail, we sail;
In the bright calm we rest on the deep,
And, lulled by the zephyrs, we sleep, we sleep.

Cast by the winds from shore to shore,
A moment you view us, and then no more.
The nautilus shell, by human eyes,
Is seen on the waters, that sink and rise,
Over the billows away and away;
Ours is the freedom that knows no decay.
Braving the tempest, and stemming the tide,
In safety forever, we glide, we glide.

"As for Millie Chrissy, the two-headed girl, she is a perfect little gem or gems, or a gem and a half, we don't know which. She sings with one or two voices very sweetly, and in dancing we never saw any one more graceful. We expected to see a monstrosity, but were agreeably disappointed; on the contrary, we found her pleasing in appearance, agreeable in her manners, and endowed with good conversational powers. Great care and attention must have been bestowed upon her education."—*New York Times*.

"Take the children and go to Odd Fellow's Hall, and see the wonderful two-headed girl combination while you have an opportunity, and you will thank us for the advice."—*Washington Republican*.

WHIP-POOR-WILL'S SONG.
A BALLAD.

Composed by H. Millard.

Oh, meet me when daylight is fading,
    And is darkening into the night,
When song-birds are singing their vespers,
    And the day has far vanished from sight;
And then I will tell you, darling,
    All the love I have cherished so long,
If you will but meet me at evening,
    When you hear the first whip-poor-will's song.

CHORUS.
Oh meet me, oh meet me,
    When you hear the first whip-poor-will's song.

'Tis said that, whatever sweet feelings
    May be throbbing within a fond heart,
When listening to whip-poor-will's singing,
    For a twelvemonth will never depart;
So then we will meet in the woodland,
    Far away from the hurrying throng,
And whisper our love to each other,
    When we hear the first whip-poor-will's song.

Whip-poor-will, &c.

And in the long years of the future,
    Though our duties may part us awhile,
And on the return of this evening,
    We be severed by many a mile;
Yet deep in our bosoms we'll cherish
    The affection, so fervent and strong,
We pledge to each other this evening,
    When we heard the first whip-poor-will's song.

Whip-poor-will, &c.

"There are a lot of people in England, as elsewhere, always ready to strain at the smallest gnat and swallow the biggest camel, who will doubtless put this young lady down as outside the pale of ordinary humanity; if this prejudice should carry any so far as to lead them to avoid her, they alone will be the losers."—*Liverpool Leader.*

"This wonderful exhibition is of the most chaste character, and we can safely recommend it to fathers, mothers, sons and daughters."—*Boston Transcript.*

PUT ME IN MY LITTLE BED.

Words by Dexter Smith.   *Music by C. A. White.*

Oh, birdie, I am tired now;
    I do not care to hear you sing;
You've sung your happy songs all day,
    Now put your head beneath your wing.
I'm sleepy, too, as I can be;
    And, sister, when my prayer is said
I want to lay me down to root,
    So put me in my little bed.

CHORUS.
    Come, sister, come,
    Kiss me good-night,
    For I my evening prayer have said,
    I'm tired now, and sleepy too,
    Come put me in my little bed.

Oh, sister, what did mother say
    When she was called to heaven away?
She told me always to be good,
    And never, never, go astray;
I can't forget the day she died,
    She placed her hand upon my head,
She whispered softly, "Keep my child,"
    And then they told me she was dead.

        Come, sister, come, &c.

Dear sister, come and hear my prayer,
    Now, ere I lay me down to sleep
Within my Heavenly Father's care,
    While angels bright their vigils keep.
And let me ask of Him above

To keep my soul in paths of right,
Oh! let me thank Him for His love,
Ere I shall say my last "good-night."

Come, sister, come, &c.

"Millie Christine dances very gracefully, and appears to have no difficulty in moving about, and in no way differs in appearance from two animated and engaging young mulatto ladies, who, for sport, have agreed to pass an hour tied together nearly back to back."—*Liverpool Daily Post.*

"Each head is said to possess separate intellectual faculties, as entirely different as the brain power of two individuals, and the volitions of the will are independent, but very much in harmony with each other."—*Liverpool Daily Mercury.*

LITTLE FOOTSTEPS.

Song and Chorus by J. A. Barney.

Little footsteps, soft and gentle,
  Gliding by our cottage door,
How I love to hear their trample,
  As I heard in days of yore.
Tiny feet that traveled lightly
  In this weary world of woe,
Now silent in yonder churchyard,
  Neath the dismal grave below.

CHORUS.
  Little footsteps, soft and gentle,
  Gliding by our cottage door.

She sleeps the sleep that knows no waking,
  By the golden river's shore;
And my heart it yearns with sadness,
  When I pass that cottage door.
Sweetly, now, the angels carol
  Tidings from our loved one, far,
That she still does hover o'er us,
  And will be our guiding star.

CHORUS.
She sleeps the sleep that knows no waking, &c.

Little footsteps now will journey
   In the world of sin no more;
Ne'er they'll press the sandbanks lightly,
   By the golden river's shore.
Mother, weep not; father, grieve not,
   Try to smooth your trouble o'er.
For I'll think of her as sleeping,
   Not as dead, but gone before.

CHORUS.
Little footsteps now will journey, etc.

"All the intelligent men who saw her at the Washington Hotel, the other day, can bear witness to the marvelous intelligence which predominates in both brains."—*Liverpool Leader*.

"The exceedingly merry and amiable disposition of the mysterious pair deprives the exhibition altogether of that painful element which was present even in the case of those practical philosophers, the Siamese twins."—*Liverpool Daily Post*.

"As to the young lady herself—for we have surgical authority for saying so—she has bodily only one person, though possessed of two hands, two pairs of shoulders, four arms, and two pairs of legs, amalgamated curiously with one trunk."—*Liverpool Daily Courier*.

UNDER THE DAISIES.

A Ballad, by H. Millard.

I've just been learning the lesson of life,
   The sad, sad lesson of loving,
And all of its powers, of pleasure or pain,
   Been slowly and sadly proving;
And all that's left of the bright, bright dream,
   With its thousand brilliant phases,
Is a handful of dust, in a coffin hid,
   A coffin under the daisies.
     The beautiful, beautiful daisies,
     The snowy, snowy daisies.

And thus, forever, throughout the wide world
   Is love a sorrow proving;
There are still many sorrowful things in life,
   But the saddest of all is loving.

The life of some is worse than death,
    For fate a high wall oft raises,
And far better with two hearts estranged,
    Is a low grave starred with daisies.
      The beautiful, beautiful daisies,
      The snowy, snowy daisies.

And so 'tis better we lived as we did,
    The summer of love together,
And that one of us tired, and laid down to rest,
    Ere the coming of wintry weather.
For the saddest of love is love grown cold,
    And 'tis one of its surest phases,
So I bless my lot, though with breaking heart,
    For that grave enstarred with daisies.
      The beautiful, beautiful daisies.
      The snowy, snowy daisies.

"There was no difficulty made in exhibiting the upper portion of the dorsal connection, and it was done without any infringement of modesty." — *Liverpool Mercury.*

"All who met Millie Christine yesterday must have felt interested in her fortune, and well disposed to meet her again." — *Liverpool Daily Post.*

"The two-headed girl would be a good juror — she could look at both sides of the case at the same time." — *Cincinnati Enquirer.*

"Their reception at the Masonic Temple has been attended by thousands of our best citizens." — *Baltimore American.*

MOTHER WOULD COMFORT ME.

Words and Music by C. C. Sawyer.

Wounded and sorrowful, far from my home,
Sick among strangers, uncared for, unknown,
Even the birds, that used sweetly to sing,
Are silent, and swiftly have taken the wing.
No one but mother can cheer me to-day,
No one for me could so fervently pray.
None to console me, no kind friend is near;
Mother would comfort me if she were here.

CHORUS.

Gently her hand o'er my forehead she'd press,
Trying to free me from pain and distress;

Kindly she'd say to me, "Be of good cheer,
Mother will comfort you; mother is here."

If she were with me, I soon would forget
My pain and my sorrow; no more would I fret;
One kiss from her lips, or one look from her eye,
Would make me contented, and willing to die!
Gently her hand o'er my forehead she'd press,
Trying to free me from pain and distress;
Kindly she'd say to me, "Be of good cheer;
Mother will comfort you, mother is here!"

CHORUS.—Gently her hand, &c.

Cheerfully, faithfully, mother would stay.
Always beside me, by night and by day;
If I should murmur, or wish to complain,
Her gentle voice would soon calm me again.
Sweetly a mother's love shines like a star,
Brightest in darkness, when daylight's afar;
In clouds or in sunshine, pleasure or pain,
Mother's affection is ever the same.

CHORUS.—Gently her hand, &c.

"She has you on both sides; if you remove your head from one position, you are immediately the victim of another pair of eyes, which fix you; in fact, transfix you."—*Liverpool Leader.*

WATCHING THE DAYLIGHT FADE.

Christine.　Where shall we wander at evening,
　　　　Seeking retirement's shade,
　　On its seclusion reposing,
　　　　Watching the daylight fade?

Millie.　Down by the brook we'll wander alone,
　　　　Naught but the sky above,
　　There, while we hear the breezes moan,
　　　　We'll sing the songs we love.

Both.　There will we wander together,
　　　　Chasing our cares away,
　　Down by the banks of the river,
　　　　Cheerfully singing our lay.

Millie.　Come we alone to seek delight,

Both.   La, la, la; la, la, la; la, la, la; la, la, la, la;
            Cheerfully watch the coming of night,
               La, la, la; la, la, la; la, la, la; la, la, la, la;
                 Come we alone to seek delight, &c.

Both.   See, the sun is slowly retiring,
                Evening's dark veil is spreading so fast;
            See, the stars are faintly peeping,
                Now the time of day is past.
                   See, the sun is slowly retiring, &c.

Christine.   Here will we wander together,
                Seeking retirement's shade,
            On its seclusion reposing,
                Watching the daylight fade.

Millie.   Here, by the brook, we'll wander alone,
                Naught but the sky above,
            Here, while we hear the breezes moan,
                We'll sing the songs we love.

Both.   Here will we wander together,
                Chasing our cares away,
            Down by the side of the river,
                Joyfully singing our lay.

FROM OUR MERRY SWISS HOME.

DUET.

From our merry Swiss home we come, we come;
Our hearts are light and free;
With a smile we greet every eye we meet,
Two merry hearts are we.
    The live-long day we chant our lay,
    La, la, la, la, la, la, la, la, la, la, la, la, la;
    Two merry hearts, two merry hearts,
    Two merry hearts are we, are we,
    Two merry hearts are we, are we.
    Two merry hearts are we.

SOLO.

When the advent of morning appears in the sky,
    We rise from one peaceful repose,
To the valley, the meadow, the mountain we hie,

To call each fair flow'ret that grows.
    CHORUS.—From our merry, &c.

SOLO, SECOND VOICE.

Though humble our cot on the mountain may be,
    A life of contentment we live;
We sigh not for wealth, from its cares we are free,
    For wealth cannot happiness give.
    CHORUS.—From our merry, &c.

THE DEAR, DEAR FRIENDS AT HOME.

Written and Composed by Professor W. Wilson,
expressly for Miss Millie Christine.

What cheers us when we are far away
From home and all we love;
When storm and danger hedge us round,
And all is dark above?
When lightnings flash and thunders roar
O'er ocean's seething foam?
It is the thought that heaven hears
The prayers of friends at home.

CHORUS.

The dear, dear friends at home,
The dear, dear friends at home,
Kind heaven will surely hear the prayers
Of our dear friends at home.
Our father, with his silvery hair,
Our mother, kind and fond,
Our sisters, and our brothers dear,
The same kind thoughts respond.
The wind blows fair, our vessel sails
Right gaily o'er the foam,
And soon again we hope to greet,
The dear old friends at home.

CHORUS.—The dear, dear, &c.

Warbling Waters.

Where the warbling waters flow,
And the zephyrs gently blow;
Where the warbling waters flow,
And the zephyrs gently blow.

The fairies dwell; the fairies dwell
In grassy dell, in grassy dell,
Where the forest flowers grow,
And the zephyrs gently blow,
Where the forest flowers grow,
And the zephyrs gently blow.

Solo, 1st Voice —And a joyous home is theirs,
For it knows not mortal care,

Solo, 2d Voice —And its only tear
Is the dewdrop clear
That the bending lily bears.

Duet —And its only tear is the dewdrop clear
That the bending lily bears;
And its only tear is the dewdrop clear
That the bending lily bears,
That the bending lily bears,
That the bending lily bears.

Strangers Yet.

Strangers yet, after years of life together,
After fair and stormy weather;
After travels in far lands;
After touch of wedded hands,
Why thus joined, why ever met, if they must be strangers yet.
Strangers yet, strangers yet.

After childhood winning way; after care and blame and praise;
Counsel asked and wisdom given—after mutual prayers to heaven;
Child and parent scarce regret, when they part are strangers yet.
Strangers yet, strangers yet.

Will it evermore be thus, spirits still impervious?
Shall we never fairly stand, soul to soul, as hand to hand?

Are the bounds eternal set, to retain us strangers yet?
Strangers yet, strangers yet.

Wandering in the May-Time.

Wandering in the May-time, sweet it is to rove,
Just before the hay-time, through the leafy grove;
When the grass is bending, wave-like in the breeze,
And the white-thorns sending perfumes from the trees,
And the white-thorns sending perfumes from the trees.

Solo.—*First Voice.*
Spring she is a maiden, waiting to be wooed,
Hiding blossoms laden in her solitude;
Coy she is, and meeker than the summer fair,
But for those who seek her, gifts she has more rare,
But for those who seek her, gifts she has more rare.
(Repeat 1st verse.)

Solo.—*Second Voice.*
Yes, her sweets will rifle all her brightest flowers—
Of her wealth a trifle, they shall soon be ours;
When the birds are singing welcome to the May,
When the flowers are springing, we'll be there to-day.

Duet.
Just, just before the hay-time, birds begin to sing,
Wandering in the May-time, welcome to the Spring;
Just before the hay-time, sweet it is to rove,
Wandering in the May-time, through the leafy grove,
Wandering in the May-time, through the leafy grove.

Just before the hay-time, sweet it is to rove,
Wandering in the May-time, through the leafy grove;
Wandering in the May-time, wandering in the May-time,
Through, through, through the leafy grove.

Among the millions of human beings inhabiting the globe there is but
one two-header. Every one should see her, talk to her, hear her sing and
see her dance.

THE WONDERS OF THE WORLD.

The Pyramids first, which in Egypt are reared;[16]
Then Babylon's Gardens and Ramparts appeared:
Next Mausola's Tomb of affection and gilt,
With the famed Diana in Ephesus built,
The Colossus of Rhodes made in brass for the sun,
And Jupiter's Statue, by Phidias done.
Some the Tower of Pharos place next, we are told,
Some the Palace of Cyrus, cemented with gold.
Last—but not least—is MILLIE CHRISTINE.
The Two-headed Nightingale, alive to be seen.
Who will sing, who will dance, who will walk on two feet
And delight all beholders whoe'er she may meet.

MISS MILLIE CHRISTINE, *the eighth*, has spent nearly eight years in Europe, during which time she visited all the principal towns and cities of England, Russia, Germany, Austria, Hungary, Italy, Belgium, Holland and France, and in all those countries was honored by command from the Royalty to visit them. MISS MILLIE CHRISTINE speaks English, French and German.

16. The seven wonders of the ancient world referred to include the Great Pyramid of Giza, the Hanging Gardens of Babylon, the Mausoleum of Maussollos at Halicamassus, the Temple of Artemis at Ephesus, the Colossus of Rhodes, the status of Zeus at Olympia, and the Lighthouse of Alexandria; the list here also includes the Palace of Cyrus. Of all these "wonders," only the Great Pyramid of Giza still stands.

The Carolina Twins

William H. Pancoast, M.D.

Pancoast's article appeared in 1871 in *The Photographic Review of Medicine and Surgery*; the following information was included after his byline: Demonstrator of Anatomy in the Jefferson Medical College, Surgeon to the Philadelphia Hospital, and Surgeon to Charity Hospital.

Species 1st.—Pygopagus symmetros.

Derivation.—πυγη, the nates,[1] παγω, I fasten. συν, with, μετρειν, to measure.

Definition.—Two individuals more or less complete, separated as low as the pelvis, by the lateral or posterior portions of which they are united; genitals double. In the higher degrees there are two umbilical cords, which are normally attached respectively to each abdomen. Vital organs independent in the type.

Author note: A word of caution in relation to this article: while I have made every attempt to verify the accuracy of my translation of Pancoast's terms to better communicate to a contemporary reader, there is a very real danger that in doing so, one will see or suggest a kind of foreshadowing of future events and understandings in a mistranslation of scientific writing from the past. Readers are advised then to keep this in mind as they work through the material. I want to thank Dr. L. Lewis Wall for his crucial observation on this issue.

1. Latin for "buttocks."

Genus 1st.—Pygopagus.

Order 1st.—Terata catadidyma.

Derivation.—τερας, τερατος, a monster; κατα, down, διδυμος, a twin.

Definition.—Duplicity, with more or less separation of the cerebro-spinal axis, from above downwards, under the general head of diploter-atology or diploterography, the description and diagnosis of special forms of double monsters.

Under this heading, as the proper place in the classification of a compound monster of duplex development, as so admirably set forth in the excellent article by Dr. G. I. Fisher, of Sing Sing, New York, in the Transactions of the State Medical Society of New York, I would report my observations upon the "Carolina twins," or the "double-headed girl," as they have been called.

This case of pygopagus symmetros came under my professional care, January 18, 1871, while it was on exhibition in this city, in conse-quence of an abscess forming near the genitals, as stated by Mrs. Smith, who is the guardian of the twins. In the course of their treatment, I was enabled to make the following observations and to have them con-firmed by my medical friends whom I had the opportunity of inviting to be present. After great persuasion and with the kind assistance of my friend Dr. F. F. Maury (owing to the modesty of the twins and the natu-ral reluctance of Mrs. Smith), the accompanying photograph of them was taken.[2] They clung to their raiment closely, as may be seen, and it was only by earnest entreaty that they were willing to compromise by retaining the drapery as photographed. The expression of their counte-nances shows their displeasure, as their features ordinarily express great amiability of character. This living example of pygopagus symmetros is named Millie and Chrissie Smith. They are negresses, twenty years of age, born of slave parents in Columbus County, North Carolina, July 11, 1851. The parents are still living. The mother is now forty-nine years old and the father fifty-five years. They have had fourteen children, the twins being the ninth birth. The mother can assign no cause for the monstrosity, nor did she ever see the Siamese twins. Dr. P. C. Gooch, in *The Stethoscope* of July, 1852, describes the mother as a very stout negress of thirty-two years of age, very fat and of a large frame and pelvis. Her

2. See fig. 6 in the image gallery following this chapter.

labor in this case, he says, "was brief and easy. The larger twin was born first by a stomach presentation, and the second came by breech. The children were noted as being remarkably healthy and sprightly, perfectly formed, and united at the sacra.[3] The band of union seems to be chiefly cartilaginous, but the sacra are so closely approximated that some suppose there is osseous union of them." Dr. Gooch further says that when he first saw them "the elder one was in a tranquil sleep, but it was awakened by the action of the bowels, of the younger and smaller sister, who was then suffering from diarrhœa. When one has an evacuation of the bowels, they both strain." When I was called to see the twins, I found them very intelligent and agreeable, standing about four feet six inches in height, and so closely united that they were clothed in one dress large enough for them both, with sleeves for the four arms and a silken sash tied around their common waist. The frontal development of each was remarkably good, and though their complexion was of the dusky brown of the American negro, and their noses and lips possessed the characteristics of their race, yet the expression of their faces was so amiable and intelligent, and their manners so well bred, that they produced a most pleasing impression upon me. They sing duets and play upon the guitar very pleasantly, their voices being quite melodious. Though joined at the inferior posterior parts of their bodies by the contiguous sacra, and originally formed so as to be placed back to back, yet they have from their birth instinctively twisted themselves, as if the bond of union had yielded, and their spines have assumed a gibbous form under the exertion, permitting them to assume almost a lateral position, like an expanded V, thus facilitating their movements. They walk each partly sideways, the apex of the V advancing, their main support being from the outer limbs, steadied and guided by the weaker inside legs. Their movements are very graceful, and all the curves of their bodies yield harmoniously to their gliding step, as they walk to and fro, run with swiftness, or dance the schottische,[4] polka, or waltz.

They can either walk easily or stand upon the outer limbs, holding up the inside ones, using the outer limbs as in the case of a single individual. In walking and running they rest upon the outer limbs as they simultaneously swing forward the inner ones, and then, standing on the

---

3. A triangular bone composed of five fused vertebrae at the base of the spine above the coccyx that forms the posterior section of the pelvis.

4. A round dance like the polka.

inner ones, swing forward the outer ones. Owing to the obliquity of the junction, the inner limbs are somewhat shorter than the outer ones, and as they move, they step upon the ball and toes of the inner limbs, which adds much to the elasticity of their step. As they stand fronting me, Millie is on my left hand, and Chrissie on my right. Chrissie is larger and more developed than Millie, who was quite weakly as a child, but is now strong and hearty, owing to the support she has received from her connection with her more robust sister. Chrissie can now, as she has always been able to do, bend over and lift up Millie by the bond of union. This she was in the habit of doing as a part of the exhibition, but as Millie is now so strong and well developed, I advised them to avoid it as a practice, so as not to injure Chrissie's health. Millie, though the weaker physically, has the stronger will, and is the dominating spirit, usually controlling their joint movements, though from long habit one instinctively yields to the other's movements, thus preserving the necessary harmony. Mrs. Smith tells me that when they were little it was somewhat difficult for them to understand this, and individual desires sometimes led to little struggles and quarrels for supremacy. I noticed that what required only the exertions of one to perform, one alone did, as shutting the door or taking something from the mantel or table. But when their single plate was placed upon their dinner-table, then each used both hands to carry the viands to their respective mouths for transmission through each œsophagus to their separate stomachs, with evident satisfaction to each individual. Each brain acts separately, there are two intelligences, as shown by their conversing with each other, and they can carry on independent trains of thought, as is obvious from their talking at the same time with different persons upon different subjects. In consequence of habit, their functions generally work simultaneously. They are usually hungry at the same time, and generally desire the same food and drink, both drinking a great deal of water. Their habits are very much alike. They generally sleep and wake at nearly the same moment, though one can sleep independently of the other, and sometimes one turns over the other one in bed without awaking her. They defecate and urinate at the same time, though one may have a diarrhœa without the other suffering any pain, or one may be bilious without the other being so, as I found Millie so suffering on one occasion, while Chrissie was not. I ordered Millie a cathartic pill, thinking that she alone required it, but I was told that each had been given one, with the best effect, and I found Millie relieved of her headache.

I believe Millie could be sick at her stomach without Chrissie being so, and *vice versa*. It is reported that one suffered more in teething than the other, and that Millie had the diphtheria, but not Chrissie, and that they both had fever and ague at the same time. They menstruate regularly and naturally at the same time, and have done so since they were thirteen years old, there being no more blood on the napkin than is natural to a female of their age. Chrissie, on their left, is a little taller, stronger, and more robust than Millie, on their right. As far as can be recognized, there is no transposition of viscera.[5] The hearts are nearly in their respective places, and allowing for the curvature of their spines, there is but the slightest deviation of the respective apices to the median line. The heart and lung sounds are normal. The individuality of each twin was again shown on examining the pulse. On several occasions, Millie's pulse was found to be from ten to twelve beats quicker than Chrissie's. At one time Millie's pulse was ninety-six beats and Chrissie's eighty-four; on another occasion, Millie's was eighty while Chrissie's was sixty-eight.

When called to examine the so-called abscess, I caused them to lie down upon the bed. In lying upon their backs, Chrissie was upon my right and Millie on my left, both limbs on each side drawn up. They lifted up the inside limbs as far as they could, but I was obliged to push them gently still farther. I found only one vulva, deeply placed between the four limbs.

The above wood-cut,[6] drawn by the artist, Mr. Faber, from my description, represents the appearance they presented. Each lying upon her side, it shows how each vulva, commencing at the mons and running back between the limbs, meets the opposite vulva, thus making a common vulva joined at the fourchette. There is neither posterior commissure nor fossa navicularis.[7] Hence only one vagina, on each side of

---

5. Essentially, when the organs occur on the inverse side of the body than where they normally should; for M. H. Kaufman and other physicians and scientists today, the incidence of this kind of mirror-imaging plays a part in our understanding of how conjoined twinning occurs: "If fusion, rather than fission, accounted for all cases of conjoined twins, the incidence of mirror-imaging should be the same in all monoamniotic twins, whether they are conjoined or not. If the incidence of mirror-imaging is higher in conjoined twins than in separate twins, the fusion hypothesis cannot be correct" ("The Embryology of Conjoined Twins," *Child's Nervous System* 20, nos. 8–9 [August 2004]: 508).

6. Not reprinted in the current volume. See my introduction, 37–38n42.

7. Junctures and other areas of the external female genitalia. What follows are the details of Pancoast's findings of the women's genital anatomies including shared and separate sections.

which, at the right and left margin, juts out the meatus urinarius proper to each individual, then the vestibule between each meatus and clitoris. There are two urethræ, two vestibuli, two clitorides, two nymphæ, and two labiæ majoræ. The labiæ majoræ are continuous with each other. The vulva, as they lie, appears, as it were, crosswise, owing to their position, the limbs being firmly flexed upon each abdomen. About ½ inch below the middle of this common vulva is found the common anus, and in the same median line, and in a depression simulating the appearance of an imperfect anus, about 2 ½ inches above the vulva, was a fistulous opening which I had been called to see as an abscess. This had been annoying them for some months, occasionally closing up, then inflaming, opening, and discharging matter. Into this I could readily pass a good-sized probe; and I found it to lead upwards and backwards and inwards, as they lay, for some 3 ½ inches. On withdrawing the probe, which gave but very little pain, I noticed a marked fecal odor in the discharge upon it, although there was no odor perceptible otherwise. This sinus I concluded to be an opening into the common bowel, and judged it to be the result of an abortive effort of nature to make a second anus and rectum. On examining the vagina, which gave them more annoyance than pain, I found no hymen present, but the orifice naturally small and contracted, as that of an ordinary young unmarried woman. I readily passed my index finger up its whole length. I found only one vagina, and no bifurcation of it, only one womb, with an unusually long neck, around which the finger could be readily passed until it pressed against the *cul-de-sac* of the vagina, where I could still feel the body of the womb, but no apparent subdivision, though two distinct wombs might have coalesced above by their respective fundi. Dr. F. H. Ramsbotham, who examined them when five years old, in his report says: "There are two vaginæ, and without doubt two uteri" (Fisher); but there is now only one vagina; and the gentlemen who examined the twins with myself could clearly recognize only one uterus in the common vagina. The vulva, on each side, begins underneath at some little distance behind the symphysis pubis.[8] Each symphysis is natural, and separated from the other by the width of the two bodies between the thighs. I passed a metallic female catheter into each urethra, and could distinctly recognize a partition between the two bladders. I passed then two metallic catheters, one into each bladder; they did not touch each other, but pressed against the dividing partition.

8. A joint made of cartilage appearing between the right and left pubic bones, above the vulva in the female and the penis in the male.

On passing my finger into the rectum, I could not reach the point of bifurcation, nor feel the probe distinctly that I had passed into the sinus, but I could recognize perfectly the apex of a coccyx, thicker and stronger than natural, as if formed by the junction above of two, and on the lower side of the joined pelvis as they lay. There were four ischial tuberosities, two for each side, and in nearly their proper relations to the respective trochanters, but opposed somewhat obliquely, as can be readily understood from the twisting of the spinal columns above referred to.[9] The band of union, as shown in the photograph, I measured, and found it to be 26 inches in circumference. At five years of age, according to Dr. F. H. Ramsbotham, it was 16 inches in circumference. The distance between the top of the crest of one ilium to the other, at its greatest breadth on the back, was 14 ½ inches. There were two umbilici. To establish the accuracy of my examination, I invited upon one occasion Prof. Pancoast, Prof. Gross, Dr. Seavy, of Bangor, Maine, and Dr. T. H. Andrews; and upon another, Dr. R. J. Levis and Dr. S. H. Dickson, Jr. These gentlemen agreed with me that there was but one vagina, but one womb to be recognized, but one perfect anus, and that the parts are as I have described them. We also decided that the fistula communicated with the bowel; that the respective recti united at some point above, out of the reach of digital exploration; that the osseous junction was by the union of the sacra and coccyges; and also that the caudæ equinæ of each spinal cord were more or less united.[10] For on touching the left leg of Millie, the sensation and number of touches are recognized by Chrissie, but not the spot; and on touching the right leg of Chrissie similar efforts are produced.

In company with Dr. J. Murray Barton, I applied an æsthesiometer[11] on the inside of the leg, first of Chrissie, and then of Millie, and found the limit of tactile recognition to be about 2 ½ inches. On the 8th of March last I invited Dr. Wm. Pepper and Dr. R. M. Townsend to accompany me in my visit. We placed the pole of a Faradaic current[12] in the hand of Millie, another on the outside of the outer limb of Chrissie.

---

9. Ischial tuberosities and trochanters: parts of the pelvis.

10. Roots of nerves that extend beyond the first lumbar vertebra in the form of a horse tail.

11. Instrument that measures sensation on the skin and the distance between recognizable sensations.

12. A current responding to the reduction or oxidation of some chemical substance.

They both felt it. On placing one pole in Chrissie's left hand, and the other on the external popliteal nerve of Millie's outer left, the current produced powerful contractions of the peronei muscles of Millie's limb.[13] Chrissie also felt the current in her left arm. When one pole was placed on the external popliteal nerve of Millie's outside leg, and the other pole applied at the same point on Chrissie's outside leg, powerful contractions were simultaneously made by the peronei muscles of both outer limbs. The sensation was recognized from the points of application down to the ends of each one's toes. When the poles were applied to the middle line of the connecting band and the external popliteal nerve of Millie's outer leg, both felt the current, Chrissie feeling the current in Millie's leg, Millie's muscles contracting powerfully.

One pole being applied on each dorsal region, the current is at once recognized by both. One pole placed over Chrissie's dorsal region, another over the patellar plexus[14] of Millie's outer leg, a current is established that they both feel, and powerful contractions of the muscles of Millie's thigh are produced. We asked, one at a time, to try to lift up the leg or legs of the other, but this neither one could do; each one having complete control, however, over the limbs belonging to her trunk. I applied the point of a lead-pencil to the top of the band of union at the exact middle line, and each recognized the sensation; but removing the point on either side less than an inch, only the one touched recognized the sensation.

It is an interesting feature in this case, that it presents many points of similarity to that of the Hungarian sisters, born October 26, 1701, and that there is no similar case reported reaching adult life for one hundred and seventy years.[15] The Hungarian sisters were similarly united, a symmetrical pygopagus. A description of them is found in the Philosophical Transactions, vol. 1. page 311 (Torkos). On referring to it, we find that Helen, the stronger twin, was first delivered as far as the navel, Judith following in a reverse order. Dr. P. C. Gooch reports that the larger child of the Carolina twins (Chrissie) was born first by a stomach presentation, and the smaller (Millie) came by the breech. Judith, from an attack of paralysis, in her sixth year was much weaker than Helen. So

---

13. The popliteal nerve would be one of two branches of the sciatic nerve in the thigh; the peronei muscles are found in the fibula or outer portion of the leg.

14. A constellation of communicating nerves in the leg.

15. Helen and Judith; see current volume, 60–61n4.

Millie was much weaker than Chrissie in her childhood, but has increased and grown stronger since.

Menstruation with the Hungarian sisters occurred at the age of sixteen years, was continued regularly, although one was unwell a week sooner than the other. The Carolina twins also menstruate regularly, and at the same time, as I am informed. With the Hungarians one suffered from a slight indisposition independent of the other; it is the same with the Carolina twins. The Hungarians were intelligent; so are the Carolina twins. The Hungarians could not walk side by side; when one went forwards, the other went backwards. When one stopped, she raised her sister off from the ground, which Helen often performed, being the stronger. They had no sensibility in common, except in the immediate vicinity of the line of junction. Millie and Chrissie cannot place themselves accurately side by side; there is a marked obliquity of position, for originally they were placed back to back.

Chrissie, being the stronger, can readily lift up Millie on her back by the band of union. The sensibility is only common at the line of junction, or very near it, and in the two inner lower extremities. The vulva in both these cases is common to each twin, and hidden inferiorly between the four thighs. The urinary organs are separate in each case. The vagina bifurcated in the Hungarians; not so in the Carolina twins,—one womb only can be recognized in the latter. I cannot find mention of this point in the Hungarians, but, as there were two vaginæ, I presume there were two wombs. One rectum in each case. The desire to defecate is simultaneous in both cases. But with the Hungarians it was not so with the inclination to urinate. They would even dispute about it sometimes, though generally amiable to each other. The Carolina twins micturate[16] simultaneously, it is reported; but I believe that the consentaneous micturition and defecation are the result of habit. For in the case of the Ischiopagus Tripus Asymmetros, Minnie and Mina, now on exhibition here, aged four months, having a common genitalia and anus, each one defecates separately, as can be seen by the reddening of the face and the straining of the abdominal muscles of one while the other is tranquil.[17]

16. To urinate or the desire to urinate.

17. Minnie and Mina Finley were born in Mount Gilead, Ohio, in 1870 and died when they were only thirteen months old. They were dicephalus twins (two heads, one torso, two legs, and anywhere from two to four arms), and a plaster cast of their bodies is housed in the Mütter Museum at the College of Physicians of Philadelphia, as is the cast of Chang and Eng Bunker.

In each case the temperaments are decidedly different, and the mental functions and nervous systems seem to be quite independent. In the case of the Hungarian sisters, one often slept while the other was awake; they were affected differently by hunger; one could read and write while the other was asleep. So also is it with the Carolina twins. The osseous union of the Hungarians was from the second vertebral elements of the sacra to the end of coccyges. The union is similar in the Carolina twins. In the case of the two Hungarians, the aortæ anastomosed[18] inferiorly at the point where the iliacs were given off. The ascending venæ cavæ[19] were connected correspondingly, thus establishing a large and direct communication between the two hearts, producing, of course, a great community of life and functions. So I believe it to be with the Carolina twins, and in each case there are two separate hearts.

Thus we find a great similarity in the organization, both physical and mental, of these two cases of remarkable twins. The Hungarians lived to the age of twenty-one years, and as in their case it was considered impossible to separate them with safety, so I believe it to be with these (Millie and Chrissie); and as the Carolina twins are united in life, so I believe they will be in death, and that the analogy to the Hungarian sisters will be carried out to the last. The union, arterial and nervous, is so intimate, that if either Millie or Chrissie shall die first, the other will succumb almost at the same moment, either from the impression upon the circulation or upon the nervous system. So was it with the Hungarian sisters. Judith died from an affection of the brain and lungs. Helen, who had previously enjoyed good health, was taken ill with a slight fever, soon after her sister's indisposition, and suddenly sank into a state of collapse, yet preserving her mental faculties; after a short struggle she became the victim of the malady of her sister, both expiring almost at the same moment.

Eccardus (de Sororibus Gemellis cohærint, 1709), among other questions in regard to the Hungarian sisters, discusses whether their condition would admit of or justify the solemn rite of matrimony.[20] He answers that physically there are no serious objections, but morally there

18. Anastomoses are networks or streams in the body that branch out and reconnect.

19. Superior and inferior vena cava; the veins that bring blood back to the heart for oxygenation.

20. There is record of a dissertation, "D. physica naturae phoenicem sistens," authored by Johann Ludwig Hannemann and Johannes Michael Eccardus, printed in

are insuperable ones, more particularly on account of the extreme liability of propagating monsters. I agree with him, in reference to the Carolina twins, that physically there are no serious objections, but that morally there are insuperable ones; but I do not believe with him that such marital union would necessarily produce monsters.[21]

The most interesting point in the consideration of these cases of duplex formations is, perhaps, in reference to their embryogeny. Where there is simply an outgrowth of some supernumerary part, or even where there is a secondary body more or less complete, but only one intelligence, the development of the monster might very readily be explained by some one of the various theories that have been suggested by different writers upon Teratology.[22] The most plausible theories are, that these duplex existences are due either to the accidental fusion of two embryos at some early period of their development, or to the existence of a double yolk, or to the proximity and relative position of the neural axes of two more or less complete primitive traces, developed in the vitelline membrane of a single ovum, as suggested by Dr. G. J. Fisher, or to a hypertrophic power or process of budding, or to the fissuration of the cerebro-spinal axis at an early period of fœtal life, as suggested by Dr. H. R. Storer. We must first, I think, explain the development of these duplex formations before we can again discuss the question whether the quality of monstrosity be original to the ovum or acquired by it. This discussion was carried on from 1724 to 1743, Messrs. Lémery and Winslow being the principal champions, and was only terminated by the death of Lémery.[23]

1710. According to *Anomalies and Curiosities of Medicine* by George M. Gould and Walter L. Pyle, written in 1896, "Eccardus, in a very interesting paper, discusses the physical, moral, and religious questions in reference to these wonderful sisters, such as the advisability of separation, the admissibility of matrimony, and, finally, whether on the last day they would rise as joined in life, or separated" (http://etext.lib.virginia.edu/toc/modeng/public/GouAnom.html; accessed August 23, 2008).

21. Some believed at the time that viewing external examples of such congenital abnormalities would in fact prompt their causation in a pregnant woman.

22. Pancoast here refers to the circumstance of the parasitic twin, where additional body parts are found but no secondary brain and independent being.

23. Pancoast here undertakes a literature review and a review of the theory of the origin of the conjoined twins. Interestingly enough, the debate he here describes—whether conjoined twins are the result of one ovum that has failed to separate completely or two ova that have somehow joined in utero—is one embryologists seem to be revisiting, albeit in very different terms. Generally, it is now believed that the vast

A double formation, from the head downwards, or from the coccyx upwards, might be well explained by Dr. H. R. Storer's theory of the fissuration of the cerebro-spinal axis, or by a fissuration of the primitive trace or groove, provided the duplex existence has not two brains or two intelligences.[24] In Freyling's case of the two united females (symmetrical

---

majority of conjoined twins result from an early but incomplete separation of the blastocyst into two parts, similar to the way "identical" twins form. The point where the separation is incomplete is where they are "conjoined." (There is one case in the decade prior to 2000 in which fusion is believed to have resulted in the conjoining. See Roberto Logroño et al., "Heteropagus Conjoined Twins Due to Fusion of Two Embryos: Report and Review," *American Journal of Medical Genetics* 73 [1997]: 239–43.) As Marion Walker and Samuel R. Browd note, "the exact nature of how conjoined twins develop remains unclear. Older theories suggested that conjoined twins develop as a result of the failed fusion of a single fertilized ovum, with the abnormality occurring near the 2nd week of gestation. A new hypothesis, presented by Spencer in 2000, suggests that cranial fusion occurs between two separate embryos prior to the end of the 4th week of gestation when the cranial neuropore remains open. Spencer discusses that fission of the developing embryo is unlikely to result in conjoined twins, but secondary fusion of two originally separate monovular embryonic discs could theoretically explain each of the eight types of conjoined twins discussed earlier" ("Craniopagus Twins: Embryology, Classification, Surgical Anatomy, and Separation," *Child's Nervous System* 20 [2004]: 554). M. H. Kaufman initially states in this same issue that while "conjoined twinning occurs by the incomplete splitting of the embryonic axis. . . . Fusion of monozygotic twins is no longer believed to be the basis of conjoined twinning" ("The Embryology of Conjoined Twins," *Child's Nervous System* 20 [2004]: 508). However, he specifies that "in the case of conjoined twinning, it would appear to be the *timing* of the twinning event that is of critical importance, rather than the fact that a twinning event per se has taken place" (513). Kaufman also revisits the fusion-fission debate, citing Spencer as well as others. James L. Stone and James T. Goodrich recast the debate in still different terms: "rather than 'fission' or 'fusion,' the defect leading to conjoined twins may well be a coalescence by overlapping of closely contiguous twin embryonic axis formative fields within a single embryonic disc. It is likely that future understanding of embryonic induction and organizational centres may radically change how we envision the initial development of this complex anomaly" ("The Craniopagus Malformation: Classification and Implications for Surgical Separation," *Brain* 129 [2006]: 1092). While Pancoast's terminology and general understanding is necessarily dated in his account, the general terms of the debate seem to have come around again. For more, see R. Spencer, "Theoretical and Analytical Embryology of Conjoined Twins. I. Embryogenesis," *Clinical Anatomy* 13 (2000): 36–53, and R. Spencer, "Theoretical and Analytical Embryology of Conjoined Twins. II. Adjustments to Union," *Clinical Anatomy* 13 (2000): 97–120.

24. The "primitive trace" is a term used by period physicians and scientists and refers to "a very transitory structure" in the development of the embryo "which marks the direction of the embryonic axis, and is gradually lost sight of as development

pygopagus) born in Carinola, Italy, A.D. 1700, and who died at the age of four months, after being separated, there were two intelligences. On the other hand, in the case of George Washington—, when the supernumerary body was cut from the cheek with the écraseur[25] by Professor Pancoast, no intelligence died out. George Washington—lived, and is living now. Here was one perfect cerebro-spinal system, in one complete body, united to an incomplete cerebro-spinal system in the imperfect body. The connection of the incomplete body with the complete was such that great fears were entertained lest the child, only seven months old, should succumb to the operation. In assisting in giving ether, I was ordered to cease administering it, lest the child should die; for here there was only one intelligence; there was none in the supernumerary body.

The theory of fissuration, or that of the fusion of two primitive traces, might well account for the development of this case (cephalopagus prosopodidymus), as they explain the hypertrophy,[26] or in a case of a single entity; but they do not seem to account for the existence of two entities, which would appear to involve the idea of two original germs. If the two primitive grooves represent two entities, then how are these two grooves developed? For any doctrine to explain satisfactorily these duplex formations ought to account for the highest as well as the lowest grades of union. Neither of these two theories would explain the development of the Carinola twins, the Hungarian sisters, the Siamese twins, the Carolina twins, or the case of Ischiopagus Tripus, Mina and Minnie, or any of the duplex formations possessing two intelligences, unless they can account for the development of the two intelligences. In conversation with the Siamese twins, with the Carolina twins, and in Mina and Minnie, I recognized two distinct intelligences. It is difficult to avoid the conclusion that such cases are due to the development of two entities at the earliest stage of embryogenesis, whether by the ordinary manner of fecundation[27] of the spermatozoa, or by the double-headed spermatozoon, the existence of which Dr. H. R. Storer says was demonstrated to him by

---

proceeds" (Henry Gray and Thomas Pickering Pick, *Anatomy: Descriptive and Surgical* [Boston: Lea Brothers and Co., 1897], 107). Today, "primitive streak" is the term most often used to describe this structure.

    25. A surgical instrument used instead of a knife to sever the base of a tumor; essentially a chain or a wire loop is gradually tightened to create the desired cut.

    26. An increase in the size of an organ due to an increase in the size of its cells.

    27. Fertilization.

Professor Salisbury, of Cleveland, Ohio.[28] If the bicephalous spermato-zoon be proved to exist ordinarily, it would be yet difficult to understand how it could impress the germinal vesicle in a manner to produce these duplex formations, although we know that the sperm cell makes a great impression upon the germinal vesicle. It might, possibly, have as much power in determining the sex and peculiarities of the embryo as the ovum itself, for we know that characteristics of the father are transmit-ted. But to effect the doubling of the embryo, and the formation of two primitive grooves, it would seem as if it should have the power of splitting the germinal cell in two, or that the germinal cell must possess the power of doubling itself, or that there should be two germinal cells or vesicles to be fecundated.

With the existence of two intelligences there exist, also, two entities, each one, it would seem probable, due to the development of a corre-sponding germinal vesicle, fecundated at the same time, or one soon after the other. That two or more ova can be impregnated about the same time in the human female we know, as in the case of twins or trip-lets. In the inferior animals—those that produce litters—we have sev-eral ova fecundated at the same connection, and each is produced perfect, as each ovum is kept separate from the other; but let any two fuse during any stage of their development, and we may have a duplex formation more or less complete. The law of homologous union which controls these duplex organizations, making them of the same sex, joined together at the same parts, bone to bone, organ to organ, blood-vessel to blood-vessel, is no argument against the fusion of two germinal cells; it only insists upon the explanation of this law.

There is no question but that the union of the entities composing these highest duplex organizations has taken place at a very early period of embryonic life. In examining the reports of such cases, not always minutely given, or of double monsters of any variety, there is not a single instance that I know of where there has been found a separate bag of waters for each individual composing the double monster, such as is almost always the case, I believe, with ordinary twins.[29] Cazeaux says

28. While there are indeed two-headed sperm, such entities would be unlikely to successfully compete with other sperm to complete conception; whatever the case, a two-headed sperm would not result in a two-headed embryo.

29. Kaufman offers a similar scenario in his diagram showing the variant amniotic environments in which twinning can occur; see Kaufman, "The Embryology of Con-joined Twins," 512.

(p. 866, Tarnier's edition) there are never two envelopes (amniotic) for a double monster.[30] They have been reported with two umbilical cords and two separate placentas, and with a single cord and single umbilicus and single placenta. Admitting the fact that the double monster has but a single chorion and a single amnion, it would seem, if we ventured upon the consideration of its development, to be necessary to consider the formation of these membranes and how there exists but these single ones.[31]

They are found in the ovum itself. The chorion, the most important of the two for us to consider in this relation, and which ultimately does so much to form the placenta, is gradually developed out of the external wall of the fecundated ovum (the vitelline membrane), within which is the vitellus or yolk containing the germinal vesicle (vesicular germinativa), and the yolk itself (Bischoff) is converted into a secondary vesicle, the blastodermic membrane, within the substance of which, about the tenth day, appears the rudimentary embryo.

The presence of spermatozoa, singly or in numbers, has been recognized so frequently in the interior of the ovum (Meissner, Wagner, Heal, Robin,—Cazeaux, Tarnier, p. 122) that, at least, the occasional entrance of a spermatozoon must be allowed even before the ovum may have entirely left its ovarian birthplace. The spermatozoon itself, developed in a cell in the spermatic (semniferous) tubules of the male, is here found to enter again into a cell, the ovum of the female. With its entrance the germinal spot disappears (Bischoff), and the spermatozoon, according to Tarnier, undergoes a retrograde metamorphosis, and is resolved into granulations, which are mingled with the vitellus or yolk. This vitellus or yolk is now, as we may consider, endowed with unusual power; it quickly arranges itself into a granular layer, lining the inner surface of the wall of the cell or elementary chorion, and quickly develops into the germinal membrane, in the substance of which begins the formation of the new being.

Wagner (Cazeaux, Tarnier's edition, p. 92) has sometimes met with two or even more germinal spots in the ova of the mammifera. Though the fact must necessarily be more difficult to detect in the human race, from the less frequent opportunities for examination, there cannot be

30. Pierre Cazeaux and Stéphane Tarnier, *The Theory and Practice of Obstetrics; including Diseases of Pregnancy and Parturition, Obstetrical Operations, Etc.*, 1886.

31. The chorion is a membrane that separates the developing fetus and the mother during pregnancy; the amnion is the sac that surrounds and protects the embryo.

sufficient grounds for denying the great probability of their existence in woman. If there exist two germinal spots or two germinal vesicles in one ovum (as can be illustrated by drawing two nucleated germinal vesicles, in the ordinary wood-cut, representing an ovum in a Grafian follicle, as figured in the text-books), we can readily admit that the spermatozoa, which enter in numbers, might effect a double conception in a single ovum, even if the existence of a bicephalous spermatozoon be not proved, and that there consequently would be but a single chorion and a single bag of waters. With this condition of development one could also understand that with a single chorion there might be one or two umbilical cords, and a single or double placenta, and yet, further, that the two embryos, formed from two germinal vesicles and developed on the same blastodermic membrane, could be united more or less completely, by a more or less adhesive junction or fusion of the two embryonic primitive grooves.

If we admit the possible fusion of two germinal vesicles, it does not seem improbable, also, that two or more fecundated ova may occasionally so coalesce as to cause a fusion of their membranes, and the union more or less complete of the corresponding primitive grooves. If this prove to be correct, we may then account, possibly, for the least complete union of the highest duplex organizations, as in the case of the Siamese Twins, Carolina Twins, Hungarian Twins, or in the closer union of Mina and Minnie, for a double body, with one umbilical cord and one placenta, or having two cords and two placentæ. At the same time, the existence of separate intelligences is recognized and explained, as the result of the fecundation and development of separate germinal vesicles.

For the lowest duplex organizations, with but one intelligence, we have only to admit, that if by the fusion of two germinal cells some one part is diminished, or is wanting in common, that it only requires a greater fusion of them to destroy a greater portion.

THE HISTORY

OF THE

CAROLINA TWINS.

SOLD BY THEIR AGENTS FOR THEIR (THE TWINS) SPECIAL BENEFIT, AT 25 CENTS.

SOLD BY THEIR AGENTS FOR THEIR (THE TWINS) SPECIAL BENEFIT, AT 25 CENTS.

S. Oliver Eng.

TOLD IN "THEIR OWN PECULIAR WAY"

BY "ONE OF THEM."

PUBLISHED AT THE

BUFFALO COURIER PRINTING HOUSE.

Figure 1 Cover, *The History of the Carolina Twins* (used with permission of Documenting the American South, the University of North Carolina at Chapel Hill Libraries)

Figure 2 "2 Headed Girl, Millie Chrissie" (courtesy of the Witte Museum, San Antonio, Texas)

Figure 3 "Millie-Christine" (courtesy of the Witte Museum, San Antonio, Texas)

Figure 4 "Millie Christine" (courtesy of the Witte Museum, San Antonio, Texas)

Figure 5 Millie-Christine McKoy (courtesy of the Witte Museum, San Antonio, Texas)

Figure 6 "Double headed Girl" from "The Carolina Twins" by William H. Pancoast, 1871 (courtesy of the North Carolina Collection, Wilson Library, the University of North Carolina at Chapel Hill)

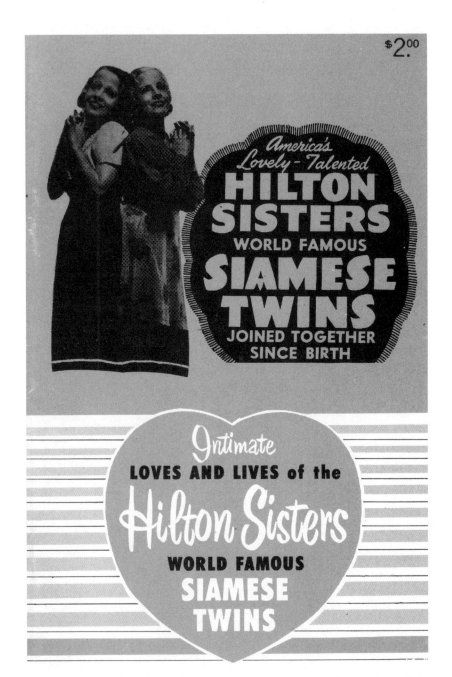

Figure 7 Cover, *Intimate Loves and Lives of the Hilton Sisters, World Famous Siamese Twins* (from the collection of Robert Bogdan)

Figure 8 Cover, *Souvenir and Life Story of San Antonio's Siamese Twins, Daisy and Violet Hilton* (from the editor's collection)

Their Life in Photographs

Its a funny thing, this world; here we have two bright little cherubs six months after they were born joined together in Old England.

Crossing the Atlantic Ocean at three and looking with wonder on their new home —America.

While young America was struggling with his A. B. C's. the Hilton Sisters were studying, practicing and preparing for real careers as musicians and entertainers.

The days of the street carnival—when the public looked on only in idle curiosity.

A proper home atmosphere—care and devotion, developed the sisters and the girls radiate happiness—Sweet sixteen around the corner.

SIX MONTHS

THREE YEARS

SIX YEARS

TEN YEARS

FIFTEEN YEARS

Figures 9a and 9b "Their Life in Photographs" from *Souvenir and Life Story of San*

Young ladies now—the Hilton Sisters dance, sing, swim, play the saxophone, piano and any string instrument.

They read good books, converse well with cultured people and enjoy all the good things in life that other girls enjoy.

Antonio's Siamese Twins, Daisy and Violet Hilton (from the editor's collection)

Figure 10 "Daisy and Violet—English Siamese Twins,"
studio portrait (from the editor's collection)

(*At right*) Figure 11 "Violet and Daisy, San Antonio Siamese Twins" (courtesy of the
Witte Museum, San Antonio, Texas)

Violet and *Daisy*
SAN ANTONIO SIAMESE TWINS

Figure 13 Daisy and Violet Hilton with saxophones and their dog (courtesy of the Witte Museum, San Antonio, Texas)

(*At left*) Figure 12 Daisy and Violet Hilton, publicity photo promoting a beauty pageant in Palisades Park, New Jersey, 1925 (courtesy of the Witte Museum, San Antonio, Texas)

Figure 14 Autographed still from *Chained for Life*, 1952, showing the Hamilton twins discussing the possibility of a surgical separation with their physicians (courtesy of the Academy of Motion Picture Arts and Sciences)

Intimate Loves and Lives of the Hilton Sisters, World Famous Siamese Twins

Originally appearing in six Sunday issues of the *American Weekly* in 1943 and billed as a "true and full double autobiography" as told to staff writer Ethelda Bedford, the memoir *Intimate Loves and Lives of the Hilton Sisters, World Famous Siamese Twins* was republished in 1953 in a booklet also containing the story for *Chained for Life*. "Wonder Book Co." in Hollywood is listed as the publisher but the text could easily have been self published.

Preface

The autobiography of the Hilton Sisters, famous San Antonio Siamese Twins, is an astounding story. Sold into virtual slavery at birth, exploited, mistreated and misunderstood, Daisy and Violet Hilton reveal in the pages that follow, the intimate and never-before-told story of their struggle for love and happiness.

The autobiography is true in every detail. The illustrations although borrowed from scenes of the motion picture entitled "Chained for Life," in which the Hilton Sisters play the leading role, nevertheless depict actual events of their lives.[1]

---

1. One still from *Chained for Life* that also appeared in the Hiltons' autobiography is included in the current volume. The other illustrations—a pencil sketch and several more stills from the film—do not appear here.

THE LOVES AND LIVES
OF THE HILTON SISTERS

By Daisy and Violet Hilton

THE eyes of a curious world have been focused on us almost from the moment of our birth.

You are undoubtedly wondering many things about our union as you read this—the story we never intended to tell. We have not told it before, so perhaps you, too, have imagined that, joined together as we are, there could be no such thing for either of us as a private life.

So much wonderment has centered around us, especially how two human beings can endure constant, continuous living together harmoniously. Yet, we two, without parents, without one intimate friend until we were 24 years old, have found a fascinating and interesting life.

Joined in the fashion called "Siamese" because the first known twins with a similar indivisible bodily bridge were born in Siam, we are believed to share identical thrills, pains and even diseases. The truth is that we are as different in our reactions as day and night.

I, Violet, often weep over something which makes my sister chuckle. I had whooping cough a year and a half before Daisy. We did not even catch the measles from each other! Yet—every breath, every second of the day and night, we are never parted. We will never be—in life, although the scientists often tried to persuade us to allow them to experiment in cutting us apart.

Because of our bond we register moods and movements of each other. We sense thoughts, feel currents and vibrations. But then, two good friends may have such experiences.

Sleeping, eating, walking, bathing and dressing, drinking and making love—we share our lives, just as amiably as we shared our childhood toys, without quarreling.

We have known the full scale emotions—even those that burn and bless and mature the hearts of women. Yet, we have never been jealous of each other.

We never consult or advise. We simply tell each other our wishes.

For instance, I, Daisy, may want to go shopping when my sister, Violet, has a headache.

I, Violet, tell Daisy that at a certain time the following day I'll go shopping with her. Having once given her my word, nothing will stop me—at least, nothing ever has.

We never coddle, pet or obviously humor each other. Our companionship would be endangered and neither of us wants to become a martyr.

We have loved, hated, dreamed and hoped and wept. We have been engaged secretly to prominent, handsome men other women admired. We have both been married.

Our marriages were headlined throughout the nation. Listen—I, Violet, will tell you the weird story of heartbreak which lay hidden behind the bold-faced type as it printed the sensational news that 21 states had refused to issue a marriage license to dark-haired Maurice Lambert, the popular bandleader, and me.

I have a right to love and marriage, just as my sister has. We have always longed to have homes and husbands and simple lives others experience.

When James Walker Moore, my six-feet-two dancing partner, and I said our vows, more than 100,000 persons attended the wedding.

I looked out over the crowd and pulled my wedding veil over my face to hide my excited tears—but Daisy was convulsed with mirth.

It was six years later when I, Daisy, married the wavy-haired, blue-eyed dancer, Harold Estep, son of a well-known Philadelphia family. Surely no girl was ever more serious and in love—but my sister, Violet, who of course was with me through it all, was analytical, friendly but unusually silent.

Yet we never quarreled through these emotional trials. It is as though some Power, greater and stronger than ourselves, has given us this inner harmony to compensate for our being forced to live constantly as an entity. And that harmony has been with us through the years—a harmony that has amazed many who have known us.

Here we are carefully, factually setting down the tangibles and intangibles we have learned about human relationships. About each other, too. Loving each other, bound by physical and spiritual ties, we spare each other nothing, except advice and domination. And we do not magnify or minimize our weaknesses and strengths. No facets of our characters are hidden, or can be, from each other. And yet we have worked out successfully a way to live our separate and very private lives.

"Do you really like—or hate—each other through your inescapable moments of intimate knowledge?" many have asked us. "Who makes the decisions? Who determines your joint activities?" And a million other questions, equally poignant. In almost all human relationships, friendship, love, marriage, even business, one person rules. In our relations, neither dominates.

While you expect us to be similar in tastes it may surprise you to learn that we even have different circles of friends.

Even our thoughts are bent on foreign tracks. They are as different as the types of our blood, which the Red Cross in Pittsburgh recently discovered when we became donors to the bank, are unlike and run in separate streams.

I, Daisy, am blond and green-eyed. I weigh 93 pounds, wear size 11 dresses and 1 ½ shoes. I'm five feet tall. I like show business. I live in my mind. I am impulsive and talkative and quick-motioned.

I, Violet, have dark hair and hazel eyes. I've never weighed more than 89 pounds. My shoes are size 1. I'm 4 feet, 11 inches tall. I've always longed to become a nurse. I live in my heart. I'm not a talker and I seldom do anything on impulse.

You can see that together we have contrast and balance.

It may seem odd, but we can remember when we were so very young. Even back in the days when we were turned loose on the floor to crawl. We seemed to move without much effort, because we propelled each other.

There seemed only a short time until we gained speed and direction.

Then, something happened! We discovered to our dismay that we could not pass when the leg of the bed, or table, was between us! We gave up trying that and began building block houses—but invariably one of us would move and knock down the other's blocks!

It was at this time, we believe, our thought processes began to function. We tried and tried again and again to pass the table leg and the bedpost and then to build houses—always with the same disastrous results. One of us would have to be allowed to build her house alone while the other remained motionless. Which one? Why, the one who wanted more to build.

The thought did not take such clear form until later years, but we soon stopped weeping because we had to give in now and then or give up. Our physical bond was not going to be our cross—we both decided on that—our decision was aided by the realization that it was nice never to be alone and lonesome. There was always a playmate there.

Walking came easy. We balanced each other. We learned to listen early. We learned to say a little, although we talked before other children our age.

There was a speech repeated to us daily, over and over again like a phonograph record. It was spoken by a big, curly-haired woman who bathed, dressed and fed us. She never petted or kissed us, or even smiled. She just talked:

"Your mother gave you to me. You are not my children. Your mother gave you to me." The speech grew longer as we grew older: "I'm not your mother. Your mother was afraid when you were born and gave you to me when you were two weeks old. You must always do just as I say."

This woman was Mrs. Mary Williams, the midwife who attended our coming into the world. She kept us clean and fed and taught us to rely on each other. We were taught to call her Auntie, and each of her five husbands was Sir.

Auntie had a daughter, a big girl, named Edith, but we were unable ever to learn from them much about our parents. Mother, they said, was named Kate. She was young and pretty and she married a Captain Hilton. He married mother in Texas. She ran away from him after we were born. We were unable even to learn our father's first name, Auntie and Edith couldn't remember. However, Auntie remembered to tell us later that our father had died in action during World War I.

Auntie was a tall woman with a pretty, oval face, framed with well-tended hair. About her waist was always a wide leather belt, fastened with a large metal buckle. And it took only a little jerk to release the buckle. Her temper was something that her daughter or husbands could not control—and when we displeased her she whipped our backs and shoulders with the buckle end of that same wide belt.

"She'll never hit your faces, girls," Auntie's third husband, Sir Green, whispered to us one day. "The public will not be so glad to pay to look at little Siamese twins with scarred faces."

Our awareness became accentuated. We were very knowing and we developed opinions although we were treated like animals, living in a cage. We were kept in one room, regularly whipped, scolded and trained. We were never permitted to play with other children, and when we looked over the sill of our window and saw little girls walking alone we felt quite sorry for them because they were not as we were.

We were always being looked at—on stages, in large and small theatres. It was a frequent occurrence to awaken and find a row of doctors and scientists surrounding our bed.

How we loathed the sight of a hospital and the very bedside tone of a medical man's voice! We were punched and pinched and probed until we were almost crazy—and we always screamed and scratched and kicked.

When the doctors and scientists left, Auntie would often whip us with the belt and call us ungrateful brats.

Then we came to wonder—what if Auntie were offered some fabulous price by the doctors and scientists? Would she stop showing us on the stages and let the doctors have us—to punch and pinch and take pictures of always?

We would lie awake, crying silently, holding hands, wondering.

"I will never leave you, even though they say that they can cut us apart," I, Daisy, whispered to Violet.

"I never want to be away from you," I, Violet, whispered back. "We can hold our breaths until we die."

We didn't hold our breaths, however. But our little pact and promises gave us a peculiar kind of confidence.

Then one morning, as we pretended to be sleeping, we overheard Auntie talking with a doctor.

"The cartilage, muscles and bone could be severed," he said. "It will be a worthwhile and interesting experiment to separate the nerves of the spinal column—you see, there has never been a set of Siamese twins operated on while they were living and science is deeply interested in making the experiment."

We lay there listening, straining to hear what Auntie would reply— and our hearts turned over.

"Siamese Twins" . . . "cut apart" . . . "doctor" are the first words we seemed to remember. They stood for fear and created our longing [to][2] remain joined by our birth-bond of flesh and bone.

2. In the original of the text, poor page trimming cut words off at the ends of specific lines of text; all of the words or parts of words contained in the brackets indicate a best guess of the probable missing text; where there is no partial word on which to base such a guess, I have indicated this with a question mark.

Our earliest memories center about a doctor pleading with Auntie to permit him to cut [us] apart. His voice was a cold, sharp blade through our hearts. To this day it symbolizes the aggregate of doctors' voices, begging to experiment with [us].

We hoped then that our mother would come back to help us. Eventually we were told [that] she had signed away all rights to us and [agreed] that if she ever interfered with our care she [would] pay Auntie the midwife to whom she gave us [at] the age of two weeks, ten shillings ($2.50) [a] week.

"Doctor, the girls belong to me," was Auntie's frequent remark. "I'm going to keep them [the] way they are!"

Hundreds of doctors have tried various persuasions throughout our lifetime. Even to[day?] medical men argue that we belong to science [and] should submit to the experiment of separation. (Recently, when a Siamese twin died, doctors separated him from his living brother— with[out] success. The living boy died during the experiment.)

Auntie was too eager for profit to let us become the object of experiments. So she set about making us "the smartest Siamese twins alive!"

At an early age, we were taught to recite, [read] and sing. We spoke plainly, perhaps because [we] got so much practice from talking to each other and because we were never permitted to be with other children. We copied the speech of grown-ups.

However, today we probably talk to each other less than ordinary twins living in the same house. We have been forced to do this because we would destroy each other's privacy.

As strongly as we have fought against being separated, we have determined to live harmoniously in our bond—and yet, be able to have our private lives. In order to do this, there are many rules we are forced to follow. Among them [are] not to seek advice from each other, not to advise, ever, and not to speak aloud our thoughts.

These rules were really our early habits. They began so soon we were unaware of their formation. Yet, it seems oddly pathetic to us that [so] many persons, when there are five or six in a family, fret against having to adjust to one another! You see, we have learned by experience that there is no adjustment in human relations that cannot be made—and made happily.

Our earliest lessons in getting along were taught to us in the tiny cabin of a ship, where Auntie, her daughter, Edith, and Auntie's husband crowded in with us. In the close quarters Auntie and Sir (Auntie's husband) quarreled frequently. He wanted us to be taken into the air. He thought we should go to religious services. She argued that people would not pay to look at us if they could see us for nothing.

Auntie won. We could have been unhappy too, only we did not hold grudges. The grudges that Sir held against the dominating woman made him ill! We decided early that a grudge was the lowest form of emotion. Each of us has to endure slights.

Our early thought development was remarkably adult. Our voices strong; I, Violet, liked low tones; I, Daisy, chose a higher pitch. We harmonized—in many ways which made living together more satisfactory. Mental as well as physical resistance by either of us would prove fatal—the other can retaliate with the same policy too easily.

We liked the vibration of the violin as it traveled over our connecting bridge. The piano was too detached. However, I, Violet, studied hard to accompany Daisy's violin.

When I, Violet, awoke with measles one morning Daisy sensed my discomfort, but for ten days she did not catch the disease. We consider this another proof that our blood streams probably are different. (Perhaps we are joined, as the doctors say, just as Eng and Chang and Rose and Josefa Blazek and other known Siamese twins. Doctors claim they could cut and tie up the blood vessels and outside nerves and saw the bone of the bridge which joins us. The separation of the spinal cord, which is one, would mean the great experiment, as the fluid which bathes the cord might escape during the operation. This would mean death.)

It was ten days later that I, Daisy, contracted the disease. (I, Violet, had whooping cough a year and a half before my sister, who was stricken with appendicitis and I felt no twinge of pain. I had pleurisy when Daisy suffered pneumonia.) We have never caught a disease from each other.

Daisy came down with measles after Auntie put us in a home with other children who had measles and mumps. We rallied nicely in the novel experience of being with other children.

"Some day I'm going to have yellow hair just like this doll's," I, Daisy, cried. Now I am proud of my bleached curls, which I dress my self. Violet prefers her natural black tresses.

We did not know how to play with children. I, Violet, was fascinated by the mechanical toys. I climbed and swung on bureau knobs. I, Daisy, amused the children by making faces at myself in the mirror. I never liked to climb. Violet never seemed to like dolls.

Even during illness we have never been bored by the presence of each other.

When Auntie discovered that we could stand in a chair, rock until it turned over and flip in the air without falling, she added dancing lessons to our long days of study.

We had new dancing partners and Violet's was a youngster who'd taught us the Black Bottom. Today the world knows him as Bob Hope.[3]

It was amazing how much training was crammed into our early lives. In preparation for our debut in Berlin, our first appearance in a theatre we had endurance tests. I, Violet, played "The Princess Waltz" two and a half hours without a mistake. I, Daisy, played my violin and directed an orchestra of 14.

The theatre thundered with applause our opening night and as we came off the stage Auntie and Edith rushed us into the dressing room in the midst of the cheering. They refused to open the door to the knocks from backstage folks.

"Won't you let the girls come out to a little supper with us?" Vivian Duncan[4] asked one night. Vivian succeeded in coming to our room for a few minutes, and Sophie Tucker[5] and Harry Houdini[6] were among the few who seemed to sense our need for friends.

---

3. According to Dean Jensen, the twins picked up two new dance partners when they switched to the Orpheum circuit of vaudeville theatres—two comedians who called themselves "The Dancemedians." Bob Hope, then Leslie Townes Hope, was one of these, and Jensen quotes him as saying that, "at first it was a funny sensation to dance with a Siamese twin. . . . But they were wonderful girls, and it got to be very enjoyable in an unusual sort of way" (*The Lives and Loves of Daisy and Violet Hilton: A True Story of Conjoined Twins* [Berkeley, CA: Ten Speed Press, 2006], 130).

4. Vivan and her sister Rosetta Duncan were major vaudeville stars in the 1920s and capitalized on their success with a musical written for them based—more than loosely—on *Uncle Tom's Cabin* entitled *Topsy and Eva;* Rosetta played Topsy in blackface.

5. An immensely popular singer and comedian, Sophie Tucker began her career singing largely African American–influenced and/or composed songs in blackface; she eventually dropped the makeup, but her show numbers continued to draw heavily from an African American musical tradition. Her stage work influenced such later entertainers as Mae West and Bette Midler, and she was elected president of the American Federation of Actors in 1938.

6. Harry Houdini (born Ehrich Weiss) was a legendary magician who gained greatest fame for his feats of incredible escape; at the end of his life, his evening performances were entitled "3 Shows in One: Magic, Escapes, and Fraud Mediums Exposed," highlighting his campaign to debunk spiritualists. He died in 1926.

"Read all the newspapers you can," Harry Houdini whispered to me, Daisy, one night as he passed me in the wings—as if he knew that we had never been permitted to have a newspaper. After that we hoarded every news sheet we could. We read the sensational trials and began to look forward to the day when we'd become 18 and could get legal aid to straighten out our affairs.

Our lives were spent in study and practice. Years went by, somehow. Then we were in the United States, in San Antonio, Texas, making our debut in the Temple Theatre.

We had become strangely wise and filled with unvoiced thoughts. I, Violet, had a quarter hidden in my shoe. A stagehand had slipped it to me in St. Louis. I, Daisy, had fifty cents. And for seven years these were our only pieces of money—yet we were making thousands.

We were not allowed to have friends, but Edith, Auntie's daughter, received her beau[7] in our crowded room while we were appearing with a circus in Australia. He was the balloon man, and sold candy, too, on the grounds. We thought that even when he begged Auntie to let him marry Edith his eyes were cruel.

"We need a man to travel with us—will you give up your balloon concession?" Auntie who was nearing 60 and had lost her fifth husband asked.

Edith and this new Sir (as we called him) were married, and when Auntie developed an infected leg Sir helped with our bookings and travel. He told us how a brute had raised him in Perth and whipped him when he did not obey. We took this to mean that he approved of Auntie's thrashing us with her belt buckle.

In Birmingham, Alabama, Auntie died, and as we looked at her, our first corpse, and you might say, our first friend, the cunning and shrewdness seemed out of her face. I, Daisy, did not care that she was dead.

"Why cry?" I asked Violet. "We have hated her forever!"

"I'm afraid without her," I, Violet, answered. "Now Sir will boss us."

"Let's run away!" we whispered.

We had gone to the funeral parlor with the quarter and half-dollar in our shoes.

"We'll never have a chance like this again!" Violet urged.

Edith was crying beside her mother's casket.

7. Myer Myers.

"Let's run!" I, Daisy, said. Naturally, Violet came with me. But I had gone only a few steps when Violet lagged. I felt a sudden alarm tremble through her.

Sir clutched my hand and we stopped.

"Don't touch me," I, Violet, cried. He clamped his fingers around our arms, and without a word, he led us back to our seats.

The funeral services were over and after a while we were back in our room, with Edith and Sir. The tension was electric as we sat waiting for them to speak.

I, Violet, cried. I, Daisy, laughed in their sullen, suspicious faces.

Our emotional reactions are not usually the same. Perhaps laughter and tears both serve to release tension. I, Daisy, felt equal to any ordeal. I, Violet, felt that I could not compete with the possessiveness I read in the faces opposite us.

"Tell them, Sir!" Edith said after what seemed hours.

"You girls belong to us now! You'll do just as we say. See here—Auntie left you to us—you and her jewelry and furniture are ours! Do you understand?" He waved a paper in our faces.

Willed as an old ring or chair! It couldn't be! While I, Daisy, protested, I, Violet, kept crying. It couldn't be . . . yet, it was. We had to work as hard—and the only privacy we were to have was in our minds. Our new owners slept in the same room with us. We were never out of their sight.

Theatrical lights over the world soon blazed with our names. Our work as musicians, dancers and singers stood out. But at 18, stage fame did not answer the wish in our hearts[.] I, Daisy, was in love. I wanted to get married. I, Violet, wanted to become a nurse. I was in love, too, but the man of my dreams was married. We had new adjustments to make.

But at 18 and with the world at our feet—we had never had a date, never held hands with a man or been kissed!

"Why can't we go out and have some fun? Other girls our age do. We've never smoked a cigarette, tasted a cocktail—had our hair cut. We—."

"You are not other girls! You are Siamese twins!" was always the answer from both Edith and Sir.

In the wings of the theatres, across footlights, men looked at us—not as unusual performers, but in the way they look at girls they long to know. Romantic interest had overcome the scientific lure. Charm was in the air. We sensed it—and naturally we fretted because our guardians herded us into the dressing rooms and back to our hotel.

Our need to let down and get our minds off work was met with inevitable cups of hot chocolate each night. We had no haven of refuge and we had to do as Harry Houdini once said to us:

"Live in your minds, girls." He told us that as we stood beside him in the wings one night in a Detroit theatre. "It is your only hope for private lives. Just recognize no handicap!"

During the ten years following the death of Auntie, the midwife to whom our mother had given us, our hearts were scarred. Auntie had willed us to her daughter, Edith, and her husband, Sir, the former circus balloon salesman. But our minds grew strong and our Siamese bond of flesh and bone became one of real understanding between us. Our desire to harmonize with each other was, indeed, our real salvation.

So much happened during those sad years, when the audiences of the world believed us cheerful and carefree. We had learned, you see, to put our worries aside and in no way ever inflict them on each other. Therefore, as we danced, played and sang, only pleasure and the feeling of well-being ever was projected by us over the footlights of theatres.

It wasn't easy to laugh while our hearts ached and yearned for freedom and love.

Notes, gifts, love letters were sent to us in the most sophisticated cities, in little towns. Under the management of Edith and Sir we played India, Egypt, the great cities of Europe and every theatre of any size in the United States and throughout Central America.

"Big-time!" Sir would say. "You should be grateful and willing to do as I tell you!"

Big-time. The largest booking agencies handled our act. The social and handsome William Oliver, of Kansas City, traveled three weeks ahead of us as advance man—having our pictures on billboards and stories about us in all the newspapers when we reached the cities in which we played.

"Bill," as we called him, was one of the few men Sir ever allowed in our presence, and then we saw him only seldom and briefly. He was gay and in love with his wife. He called her Mildred and showed us pictures of her.

"I often tell her about you," Bill would say. "Autograph a picture for me to send her."

If we could only have foreseen what the autographed picture was going to bring about in our lives! But we were too unsuspecting and not even Edith and Sir seemed to think anything about the sentence which I, Daisy, penned, and both of us signed:

"To our pal, Bill, with love and best wishes from your pals, Daisy and Violet Hilton."

"With love" didn't mean that we loved Bill Oliver. It was just the way we had observed other showfolk autograph pictures. We soon forgot about Bill and never once saw or met his wife.

We were big-time: 46 weeks on the Marcus Loew circuit at $2,500 a week. Our salary jumped then to $3,000. Then followed 44 weeks on the Orpheum circuit at $3,850 a week! We signed contracts which Sir never read to us. All our activities were in his hands . . . and we learned that he had himself named our legal guardian.

What's more, we understood that if we ever ran out on him, if we ever refused to perform at his command, we would be put in an institution.

We lived constantly in fear—and at 18 we still were forced to share the same bedroom with our managers, so that at no time could we run away—or plot together.

"I can get rid of you," I, Daisy would say to my sister. I could—mentally. Just as she could dismiss me—mentally. This irked our managers. But it was our only protection from each other, as well as from our keepers and their constant vigil. By saying it aloud to each other, we let them know that we could dismiss them from our consciousness, too. We could adjust, even to them.

"The Hilton sisters are attractive young ladies now. Couldn't they be allowed to look like that instead of kids?" wrote a critic when we appeared at Loew's State in Newark, N.J.

I, Daisy, just happened to read the remark in a newspaper we had read during our bath. I showed it to Edith and that day we visited our first beauty parlor, had our hair cut and marcelled.[8]

As we waited in the wings that night for our turn Don Galvan, the headlined guitarist, looked at me while he played, and every word of his song seemed meant for me.

Now my heart hammered the way Violet's did the night the famous bandleader, Blue Steel, dedicated his song, "Darling," to her.

Don Galvan bowed off the stage and stood beside me. Our hands clasped for a throbbing second—and I heard my sister gasp for me. The surge of emotion swept through both of us as Edith elbowed Don away from me.

---

8. Deeply curled with a curling iron.

Sir kicked the bunch of yellow roses which Don left at our dressing room door. He would not permit us to pick them up. At the hotel that night I recalled Auntie's punishments. Visions of the leather strap came to me as Sir came over to us.

Remembering the clasp of Don's hand, hearing his song in my heart, for the first time I was not afraid. I turned my back to Sir. Auntie had always strapped our backs, never once hit our faces.

"Go on!" I said. "You won't kill us. You wouldn't destroy your meal tickets!"

His black eyes turned to flames. We had never talked back to Auntie. We had been too frightened of her heavy strap. Her whippings had come to be a part of our lives. We had accepted them along with our daily irritations, struggles and monotonies for love of each other. We tried, within our minds, to turn each quarrel and bickering and nagging incident into some kind of lesson for our own harmony. Now, a new fight had begun in our souls.

"We've made thousands for you—but we never received a dollar of our earnings! You still keep us caged up like animals in a circus! But tonight is different—listen, Sir, we are 18 years old. Don't you strike either of us or we'll yell like wildcats! And get us a separate room. We're grown ladies and you should be ashamed to force us to share your and Edith's room!"

So that night Sir's bluff did not work. Edith passed the cups of hot chocolate without a word.

This firm stand and the reaction to it gave us some spiritual courage. After all, they depended on our well-being more than we did on theirs.

Then we were in San Antonio, Tex., living in a $75,000 home—a showplace on Vance–Jackson Road. The furnishings and grounds were ornate. Stained glass windows. Tile roof. A swimming pool, greenhouse. Lloyd Wright, the architect who designed the famous Tokyo Hotel, had drawn the plans.[9] And while the five acres of surrounding gardens were landscaped and strewn with lights so that a night lawn party could be given—we were never permitted even to entertain any of our friends there.

9. Frank Lloyd Wright, famed architect and designer, lived from 1867 to 1959; the Tokyo Imperial Hotel was originally built in 1890, redone by Wright in 1923, and demolished, after the building and grounds had decayed, in 1976.

We could never enjoy the magnificent and splendid estate, let alone call it our own home.

During our rest periods, the servants were fired and we did the cleaning . . ."You need exercise!" we were told coldly.

We had made only one demand of Sir: "Buy us diamond bracelets. Not with small stones—big ones."

It was the plea we made in the presence of the beloved Daddy Morris, of the William Morris Agency, our bookers, before Bill Oliver and before any friend of Sir. Other stage stars had jewels, and this seemed reasonable for us—because in that way we could really get possession of something we could use for money. He never had given us cash.

We got the bracelets. We sneaked newspapers. We had a room and bath to ourselves. But now we were 23 years old and we had never had a date. I, Daisy, was in love with Don.

We had appeared on several bills with him, and although Edith and Sir guarded us too closely for conversation, I always thought Don told me with his songs and his brown eyes that he loved me.

Blue Steel had worked on the bill with us several times. He would arrange for his band to play either before or following our act, so that he could play "Darling." "Dedicated to a darling, Violet Hilton," he would announce. Then he would play "You Can Take My Heart."

Just then there seemed only one person in all Texas we wanted to see—in a copy of *Variety* we read that Don was booked there and was stopping at the St. Anthony Hotel. We were reading the sneaked paper in the greenroom when Sir burst in. He was excited; Edith was calming him.

"Just look at this!" Sir flung a newspaper down on the table in front of us. "What have you done? Bill Oliver's wife has named you in her divorce suit. You've alienated her husband's affections and she wants a quarter of a million dollars!"

"We don't love Bill Oliver! You know that!" I, Daisy, cried.

"Why did you write 'love' on that picture you autographed for him to send his wife?"

We were too stunned to reply.

Sir put us in the car and drove to the office of a lawyer—Martin J. Arnold, who kept his eyes squinted at the bright Texas sunshine all the while Sir was telling him why we had come to engage his services.

"The girls have got to fight this," Sir kept saying. We were told what

the complaint charged; that Bill was reported to have admitted friendship with us and that we both loved him. It was even claimed that
we were jealous of each other—that despite our physical condition we
would go for weeks without speaking a word to each other.

We tried to speak. Again and again we tried. Then, I, Daisy, pulled
up from my chair and Violet balanced me, giving me all her strength, it
seemed, as I raised my voice so all could hear.

"There is something very wrong! My sister and I have had only business relations with Bill Oliver—never have been with him or anyone
else alone. We've never been alone in our 23 years!"

For the first time the lawyer spoke. He looked at Sir but his words
were to us: "A woman who has never seen the twins dares to say they
have compromised her husband?"

"Read her complaint!" Sir said.

"Leave us alone," Mr. Arnold said in his deep drawl. "Close the
door as you go into the other room. I want to ask the girls about this
without your being present!"

"You can't send me out. I'm their guardian!"

"They are over 21, aren't they? They don't need a guardian. Now,
will you leave us?"

Reluctantly, Sir closed the door behind him.

We sensed that we had reached a momentous period in our life. We
were confused, of course by the unwarranted charges made against us.
But I, Daisy, seemed to have found courage in the kindly appearance
and soft voice of the Texas lawyer who, I felt, would give us protection.

"Is there any truth in what Mrs. Oliver claims?" the lawyer asked in
his kindly drawl.

"Not a word!" we cried together.

"You are two frightened girls. Isn't something else wrong? Do you
want to tell me?"

"We're practically slaves!"

"Slavery hasn't been practiced in this country since the War
between the States."

"Then help us get free." We produced the pathetic pieces of silver
from our shoes. In our great moment of opportunity we had left our
bracelets at home. "Please, Mr. Arnold, please help us. We're afraid!"

One of us is usually cautious; the other impulsive. We seldom wish
to talk about the same subject at the same time, but if this happens, one
always gives the other the floor.

That day in the law office of Martin J. Arnold, in San Antonio, Tex., we both were talkative.

"No one will believe our story," I, Violet, usually the cautious one, ventured to say. "We've been lonely—rich girls who were really paupers, living in practical 'slavery.' The public doesn't know all this and if we tell a judge he might send us to an institution."

"I'm all for the trial," I, Daisy, declared.

"Just talk to me," said the lawyer in his easy drawl. "Walk up and down the floor if that will help."

"We're Siamese twins who want to live and die joined just as we were born. Neither is a parasite on the body or mind of the other. We want to live as other human beings live, when they're over 21, to work and earn—yet Edith and Sir completely dominate us. We've done nothing but work during all our lives."

For 45 minutes we talked out our hearts—while outside Sir waited. Lawyer Arnold had asked him to leave us; for us to explain why Mildred Oliver, in her divorce suit against our former advance man, William, had claimed we were in love with her husband and asked that we pay her $250,000 for alleged alienation of his affections.

Sir left us reluctantly and it took only a second for the attorney to toss aside Mrs. Oliver's absurd claim. Then we told him about ourselves, sketching in our story from birth, as best we could.

"What became of all the money you've earned? What about the beautiful home you have on Vance-Jackson Road?" the lawyer asked.

We told him. And as we talked a sudden sob broke through the tension. It came from behind a screen where the attorney's secretary, Lucile Stotzer, a pretty brown-haired woman, had been taking down every word we said.

Mr. Arnold asked her to come out and meet us—and it was a strange experience for us to see a stranger crying over our predicament—something we had never done ourselves. We have never known self-pity.

"We have no money now, Mr. Arnold, but we need help."

"I'll help you. From now on you're my clients. You don't have to go home with this man."

We were supposed to go to a music lesson directly from his office, so we made a plan which would throw Sir off our trail.

As soon as he left us at the music teacher's door and drove the car around the corner, we phoned Mr. Arnold's secretary. Sir was to call for us in an hour, he had said. Could she pick us up and take us to a hotel before that time?

A taxi soon pulled up to the curb. Lucile Stotzer was in it, beckoning for us to come out. We stood in the door a moment, looking in both directions, making sure that Sir was not watching. Then we kissed the teacher and ran out—to begin what was indeed to become a new life for us!

In the suite at the St. Anthony Hotel we found flowers, candy, a radio, magazines and newspapers already provided for us.

"Girls, you're Mr. Arnold's guests—order anything you like," said Lucile. "Telephone your friends—see if you can't enjoy yourselves."

It was like a dream during the next few days while we waited for our trial to begin. For the first time we could order something on a menu which we wanted. We had dresses sent up—and selected no two alike—and all the silly hats we wanted. We could dress and act our age, and no longer be made up as children with bows in our hair. We got permanents and pinned up our hair.

I, Violet, had always wanted to drink a cocktail. I, Daisy, wanted to smoke a cigarette. We did.

We actually seemed to grow in stature during our frequent interviews with our lawyer. And between interviews we added daydreams to the other pleasant indulgences. What a unique sensation it was to telephone a man!

I, Violet, long-distanced Blue Steel, whose band, I learned from *Variety,* was playing the Peabody Hotel in Memphis, Tenn.

Then, I, Daisy, telephoned Don Galvan.

"I'm here alone," I said and told him the hotel room number. It was perhaps the first time I ever spoke of being "alone"—of course a Siamese twin could never be alone. However, it did not seem strange to Don.

"Daisy! I've hoped so long that you would break away from Sir," he said. "I knew you'd call me if you ever had the chance!"

A little later Don was at our door. We went to let him in and a thrill ran through us. This was our first date.

Then Don stood there looking at me, Daisy, and forgetting that Violet was with us, too. He was even better looking than I had remembered. His dark eyes glistened and his teeth flashed white against his Spanish complexion.

I, Violet, could not will myself to be immune to my sister's emotion, then. Although we both soon acquired the ability to blank out the other in romantic moments. This was, however, our first reality of romance and it intoxicated both of us. I was as anxious for my sister to experience her first kiss as she could be.

There seemed no words adequate to span the years that Don, I thought, had looked at us and sent thought messages to us across stages and from the wings of the theatres in which we had played.

We, always guarded from men, had no way of learning to say certain little niceties expected at sentimental moments. Till now, you might say, our private lives had been barren of adventures which might have profited us now.

There was a nervous ecstasy about Don—a wordlessness. Then he held out his arms—"Daisy—"

We were never to forget that Don's lips then pressed against Daisy's forehead! My first kiss—but it was as real is it was disappointing. I was to learn that it held all the romance I wanted it to hold, but that Don was old-world and did not believe that a man should kiss his lady-love otherwise before they were engaged.

I, Violet, used to say: "Gee, Daisy, I'm tired of waiting for Don to kiss you!"

"Siamese twin-slaves! Poor little rich girls without spending money! No friends! Twenty-three years old and never a beau! Earned thousands and never collected a dollar . . ."

So went the story unfolded in the San Antonio court. And every day we sat there, with Judge W. W. McCrory listening and shaking his gray head as if in disbelief—and with Edith crying. Her husband, Sir, glared at us like a hypnotist.

When Edith's mother died she willed us to Edith and her husband, and now in court we learned that our own mother, a frightened young girl in Brighton, England, gave us to the midwife soon after our birth.

Edith told how she, as a girl, had helped her mother care for us. She told how it hurt us when we learned that our mother had signed our lives away—and then how we had been willed to Edith and her husband, along with other possessions.

We wanted freedom—an accounting of our money and a receiver appointed to manage our property. We wanted the contracts broken which we had been induced to sign, making Sir our manager, compelling us to work for him for $500 a week, which we had never collected. Most of all we wanted an injunction preventing Sir and Edith from ever interfering with our lives again!

Judge McCrory listened to first one of us, then the other.

All this time Martin J. Arnold, our lawyer and friend, seemed to be our shield, protecting us from the influence of Sir, who sat there gripping the arms of his chair.

Mr. Arnold knew our whole story by heart. He knew, too, that the only happiness we had ever known was during the few days we had been his guests while he was preparing the case for our trial. He had given us courage to run away and fight for our freedom.

What had Sir done with our money? We calculated that we had earned more than $2,000,000. When asked, he looked at Attorney Arnold and said he had banked it.

"It was being kept in the family," he declared.

"In other words you made it a family affair?"

"Yes, it was a family affair until you stepped in and corrupted it!" Sir retorted.

The courtroom was filled with hisses.

Questioned about his conduct toward us, Sir straightened in his chair. Why, he had always treated us in a gentlemanly manner, he said.

"Once I raised my hand as if to hit Daisy, but my wife interceded. The girls had rushed at me and had torn the shirt off my back, beating me about the body before my wife could stop them."

The crowd applauded and cheered and ignored for whole minutes the hammering of Judge McCrory's gavel.

Wasn't it generous of our manager to give us those diamond bracelets? Was it! Our attorney showed that while Sir claimed to have paid $7,000 of our money for them, actually only $4,000 had been paid. This was brought out in testimony.

Where was our fortune? What had really become of it?

"What bank do you do business with?" Attorney Arnold asked.

"I don't know," Sir answered flatly.

The packed courtroom resounded with boos.

But Attorney Arnold tracked down a receipt for $36,000, which we had been induced to sign when guardianship proceedings were completed. It was said to have been paid us, but we had never received even a dollar of that sum from him for spending money.

"Isn't it a fact that the twins signed the receipt but never received the money?" Arnold asked.

"I don't know. They were paid through my bookkeeper in New York."

"Don't you know where that $36,000 went?" Arnold pressed.

"I offered it to them and they refused to take it from me. I wouldn't throw it into the gutter. I kept it," he said.

Contracts were produced which called for 40 weeks of appearances at $3,000 a week. So many profitable contracts, so many weeks of appearances. We signed our names on so many dotted lines.

During my (Violet's) time on the witness stand, I looked at Sir and said: "The contracts we signed were always covered, except for the dotted line. When we hesitated to sign, Sir would rave and ask us if we thought he was a thief and if we didn't trust him, and if we were afraid—so we always signed."

No one could forget Edith as she had sat in the witness chair choking and crying so she could barely talk. Looking at the judge she said through sobs:

"The girls don't seem to be making any allowance for the time I have spent with them, constantly caring for them and attending to their wants. I have spent the best part of my life in their interest—and now they ignore me. Why, they didn't even send me a card while they've been away from us!"

When I, Violet, was asked by Judge McCrory about our earnings I recalled that until 1925 we did not attempt to keep track, but from that period until the time we had run away to start court proceedings (Dec. 1930) we had made $2,500 and $3,000 a week.

In 1929 we became legally of age. We asked Sir then where he had placed our earnings. He said he had invested them in a trust. I testified how from the time we had reached our majority we were kept under even a stricter guard, as if we might in some way learn of our legal right to liberty.

No, we knew nothing about guardianship proceedings in 1927. Then Attorney Arnold said: "I'm going to file proceedings to have the final report of guardianship proceedings set aside on grounds of absolute fraud!"

As I, Violet, did most of the talking, I was stimulated and strengthened by my twin's concentration. My answers came clearly and quickly. When I hesitated only slightly Daisy would prompt me by the movement of her arm against mine, or shrug her shoulder. There are, you see, many times when being a Siamese twin has its peculiar advantages.

I said we were never paid the $36,000 which Sir said a bookkeeper paid us. I told how we longed to run away but were afraid because we had so often been threatened with being deported to England or put in an institution if we did.

Photographers and newsreel men and reporters crowded around us, and there were hundreds of well-wishers when the testimony was finished. They followed us to our hotel and crowded outside our room, so we asked our attorney if we could not move into a small apartment somewhere until a decision had been reached.

The night when Lucile Stotzer, Mr. Arnold's secretary, went with us to the little apartment she had selected for us, we found that the electricity had not been turned on, although Lucile had arranged everything before our arrival.

"Wait—I'll find a match," I, Daisy, cried. Having learned to smoke, I had them in my handbag.

Before I could strike the match, Lucile cried: "Don't! I smell gas. The place is filled with gas—we might all be killed!"

We ran out into the hall and she called the superintendent. He came with a flashlight; and then we learned that the jets of the kitchen stove were turned on full force. The discovery was very upsetting to both of us.

By the time we reached the hotel again, the crowd seemed off our trail—that is, the actual crowd was off, but there was a reporter waiting in the lobby who ran up to us as soon as we entered.

"I've been trying to find you," he said breathlessly, "I've just got word from my office that your lives are in danger. A tip came to the city editor—someone called and said, 'The Siamese twins may be killed tonight.'"

This information scared us no little and set us thinking. But we were sure that no matter how many enemies we might have made, none of them would want to go to the extreme of killing us.

Finally we dismissed the reporter's story from our minds. We ascribed it to someone's fertile imagination.

Attorney Arnold arrived shortly afterward and with him were five plainclothesmen who kept constant guard of our suite until Judge McCrory's decision came through.

One day in court Sir was ordered to produce bonds and books about which we had testified. Joe Freeman, one of the leading business men in Texas, who formerly had a seat on the New York Stock Exchange, was named as our receiver.

Judge McCrory looked at us, then out over the waiting crowd and said something we were never to forget:

"Jack Dempsey[10] was nothing but a ham-and-egger until Jack

10. One of the most popular boxers of all time, Jack Dempsey held the world heavyweight title from 1919 to 1926. Kearns was his manager and a successful promoter of other professional fighters as well.

Kearns took hold of him and developed him into a world champion. The Hilton twins would not be where they are today had this defendant not managed their affairs and proved a good promoter."

But we had never longed for fame. We did not want promotion and management. We only wanted liberty, freedom to live as we wanted to live—to live as other girls our age lived.

The Judge ordered Sir never to interfere with our lives again. We were given $67,000 in bonds, $12,000 in cash and $20,000 in personal effects. Sir was no longer our guardian and manager. All contracts existing between him and us were dissolved! Of all this our freedom was the most important and that part of the court decision which gave that freedom rang loudest in our hearts.

We did not care that the palatial home and grounds in San Antonio was given to Edith and Sir; other properties, too. Perhaps they had earned them.

We cried and laughed. So many persons rushed up to shake our hands and cry "Bless you!" that court attendants had to hold them away.

It was a dramatic climax to the unusual life we had lived for so many years.

Our new life began almost immediately. We went to shows, night clubs, dinner parties. Attorney and Mrs. Arnold threw open their beautiful home in our honor, invited our show business friends to a dinner and musical. Don Galvan brought his celebrated guitar. He won everybody with his singing.

We drank wine and smoked. Two young men begged us to dance. The "don'ts" of our childhood were all "dos" now, and we reveled in it.

It seemed as though we had been transported into another world. We looked forward to a future promising real happiness.

It was not long before Don asked me, Daisy, to marry him—but even as he asked me he took the cigarette from my hand, pushed my wine glass aside. Even he would suppress me!

"Marry me, Daisy, and forget about show business. Come to Mexico and live with my family."

Give up my little pet habits! Give up show business . . .

Wherever I went, Violet, my twin, must go. She must share my life. Should she be subjected to such restraint?

After all, we have just succeeded in getting freedom. Why should I submit both of us to another life of censorship in which we couldn't be ourselves?

I asked for a little more time to think.

Just before the trial was open Don called one night and there was a new seriousness about him. "You'll soon be free of Sir," he said, "then we can be married?"

We stepped back a little. I, Daisy, felt my sister start. But I thought that he couldn't very well ask her consent to marry me. Yet—I wondered if she should not be consulted, since she [w]ould share every moment of my life with my husband.

Actually confronted with this odd situation, [it] was very different from what I had imagined. [W/C?]ould either of us marry?[11] Could any man adjust himself to our lives?

Don had conducted himself well, but now there were lights of unrest in his dark eyes.

"Don—have you thought this out? Violet, my twin, will be with us every minute."

"I've thought it out, Daisy," Don said. "I'm sure I can make allowances for Violet." His voice was confident.

"How?" we both asked.

"This way: You will be my wife for six months of the year. Then, for the other six months you may go wherever Violet wants to go. And if she should get married then, naturally, you must spend six months with her and her husband."

We were not prepared for such an arrangement and for a few minutes we were silent. Then, I, Daisy, spoke:

"Don, I know now that I would not like a separation from the man I married. And I would never want to be separated from my twin. I couldn't bear to be separated from either of you."

Suddenly we all began to laugh.

This was what it felt like to be happy. And for the next few hours we three began making all kinds of plans—in all of which Violet shared enthusiastically.

Yet in this, my most gleeful moment, I, Daisy, realized that my sister loved in a different way from me. She loved Blue Steel, who belonged to someone else. Yet, she seemed happy to go on being content just to hear his voice over the phone and over the radio.

---

11. Context here suggests that the twins would ask if they ever *would* or *could* get married as opposed to Myers's question in *Souvenir and Life Story of San Antonio's Siamese Twins* of whether they ever *should*.

Love was nothing that belonged to her—not something or someone she needed with her, as I did. To her, love meant letting go. And here is a true-love code, perhaps, though one which never could be mine.

Marriage, with its legendary love and romance, became our most serious thought. Despite the fact that we are Siamese twins, we seemed to attract many admirers.

It gave us grave moments and much wonderment when our suitors were embarrassed by the inevitable presence of a third person. However, few were discouraged in their ardor. Some schemed ways to talk to one of us alone—over the telephone. The shyer men wrote and wired.

I, Daisy, worried because Violet still carried a torch for Blue Steel, the musician, and listened nightly to his broadcast.

I, Violet, knew Daisy was worrying about me. I felt hopeless about Blue.

So I tried to forget him. And, to my great relief and Daisy's, I got a crush on Harry Mason, handsome English welterweight champion.

Harry dimmed my torch for Blue, although he did not quite put it out. One thing—he had no objections to my being a Siamese twin. In fact, he liked Daisy. But she was interested in Don Galvan, the guitarist.

Yes, I, Daisy, liked Don very well. The trouble was he said that, if we married, we'd all have to live with his family in Mexico.

I used to go on dates with Violet and Harry and never hear a word they said. Then suddenly I decided I'd have to give Don up. At that time, Violet planned to marry Harry, who wanted her to travel with him in England. How could we both be happy?

But I wasn't the extra girl on Violet's and Harry's dates very long. Jack Lewis, the dark-haired band leader, entered my life—and I almost forgot Don. Also, he brought brown-eyed Maurice Lambert, another band leader, to meet Violet. We had a gay foursome, and it wasn't long before Violet broke her engagement with the ring champ and began wearing Maurice's diamond.

However, after a while, I realized that too many of my conversations with Jack took place over the phone. And when he asked me over the wire to marry him, I knew that his shyness made him unsuitable for the husband of a Siamese twin.

And when I did break my engagement to Jack, Maurice became upset. Fearful that Violet would throw him over, he raced to City Hall, New York, to get a marriage license.

"What? You want to marry a Siamese twin?" the clerk asked. "That's impossible! You'll be marrying two girls instead of one! That's bigamy!"

Maurice was not to be discouraged. He applied for a marriage license in 21 states—all of which refused him for the same reason: "contrary to public policy on the grounds of morality and decency." Poor Violet!

Indeed, I, Violet, felt deserving of sympathy. "Is it fair?" I asked court clerks. "Just because an accident of birth made me a Siamese twin—is that any reason why I should be prohibited marriage, the natural desire of every woman?"

But, no matter what pleas and arguments were offered, marriage was not for us. Or so it seemed at that time.

Thus, the tempo of our life changed. We went to cities and towns where there was excitement in fashionable seasons.

We leased a swank apartment overlooking New York's Central Park, and entertained. We had a continuous round of beaux. Some were rich, some poor. We saw many men of various types. We talked them over, trying to weigh the question: "Can we be happy with them?" There was no adequate, satisfying answer.

One day after a late supper party we awakened in our canopied bed. Central Park was sunny and green, and the futility of our years of play swept through us.

"Let's go back to work!" we said.

We organized a troupe and fashioned a revue to our own liking. We played violin, piano, saxophone, did ballet and adagio dancing and took part in sketches.

Again we toured Europe and the United States. We eventually were able to immerse ourselves in our work.

Terry Turner, our ace press agent, a jovial, handsome Irishman, came to us with a gleam in his blue eyes, announcing:

"A wedding of one of you girls would be the greatest publicity stunt ever pulled off since September Morn!"

"That can't be, Terry," I, Violet, said. "Maurice Lambert tried to get a marriage license to marry me in 21 states—and he couldn't."

"That's right! But if I get a license, will you go through with the ceremony?" Terry challenged.

"I'll be the goat, if you can manage," I replied.

Terry's Irish eyes fastened intently on my dancing partner, James Walker Moore.

"Jim's it. He'll mean more publicity for the act. Are you game, Jim?" asked Terry.

Jim smiled good-naturedly and shrugged his willingness.

Not one of us had any idea that Terry could ever make his big idea come alive, and no more was said about it for several days. Then, things began to happen. They began with a page one announcement that I, Violet, would become the bride of Jim at the Texas Centennial.

Terry had secured the license for us! Texas was, it so happened, one of the states that Maurice had missed.

The ceremony was to take place right in the great Cotton Bowl, on the 50-yard line. Daisy was to be my maid of honor. And Joe Rogers, famous Broadway character and a close friend of Terry, was to give the bride away.

The wedding day arrived. We were all ready when Joe Rogers began to shake. He needed a drink, he said.

About 20 minutes later, he returned. He no longer shook, but his dress suit was ripped and dirty. His eye was blackened and his nose was a red smudge.

"I can't go through with it!" Joe cried humbly. "I got in an argument with the bartender. I guess you'll just have to give the bride away yourself, Terry."

Terry moaned. But not for long. His eyes lit on a tall, good-looking young guy, leaning on a broom. He was a janitor of the Cotton Bowl. Terry went over to him. "Rent a dress suit and be back here in 30 minutes!" he commanded. "You're going to be in a wedding!"

The janitor appeared shortly afterwards, as smart appearing as a movie star. The ceremony began. Cameras clicked. It was as Terry had said a great publicity stunt. Reporters rushed up to interview us, especially Daisy, "the extra girl on the honeymoon."

A crowd pursued us to the very door of our wedding suite, where Terry Turner and Jim's sweetheart and other members of our troupe were waiting—to join us in a laugh and a supper in celebration of a publicity stunt which won space on front pages from Texas to Maine.

We have never gone through the formalities of a divorce, but Jim, in the service now, knows that when he wants the ties, made only in the name of publicity, broken he will have our full cooperation.

As Terry figured, the stunt paid off. We went to Hollywood and made several films.

Life marched on swiftly then for us for about five years—until I, Daisy, fell in love with the singing, dancing master-of-ceremonies of our act. His name was Harold Estep, known professionally as Buddy Sawyer. He was eight years younger than I.

"I'm going to marry Buddy Sawyer," I told my sister when I had made up my mind. I sensed, when she said nothing, that she was a little startled.

Yes, I, Violet, was startled. But I did not argue with my sister about her choice. We had never argued. I felt then that her marriage with Buddy would not be right. I thought she had not weighed the idea well.

Buddy was pleasant to me, and he was most friendly when we all sat down to talk over our future life together.

The marriage took place a few days later on Sept. 17, 1941, in Elmira, N.Y. A crowd gathered despite our efforts to avoid publicity. And all that night and through every night and day for the following ten days we were pursued.

Then, one morning when we looked across at the twin bed where Buddy had been when we drowsed between the incessant phone calls from reporters, Buddy had disappeared.

I, the bride, who had not yet known a honeymoon, tried to believe that Buddy would come back. For a while I waited for him, although I knew he would not return. When I began divorce proceedings some time later, I read in a newspaper his reason for leaving me:

"Daisy is a lovely girl," he was quoted as saying. "But I guess I am not the type of fellow that should marry a Siamese twin. As a matter of fact, I am not even what you would call really gregarious. In the show business there are times when you get tired of seeing anybody—let alone twin brides."

The sad thing about love is, you get over it. However, it took long, weary months before I faced the fact that this was true. And that both our marriages were without anchorage.

We had to turn our thoughts again from emotion and think of the only thing we ever really were masters of—work.

We had lived a variety of lives, virtually as prisoners and as rich play-girls. We both had been married—unsuccessfully. So, romance had palled. We had known freedom, had celebrated it, and then had failed to enjoy it.

Work alone never had failed us. And it isn't strange that we again longed to return to it.

It was at this time that out of the blue a wire reached us from Pittsburgh. It was sent by Don D'Carlo, whom we knew as one of the best-liked theatrical agents and head of the D'Carlo Entertainment Service. His wire was like a beckoning hand of welcome from an intuitive and understanding friend. It read: "Will you accept headline booking at Don Metz Casino?"

We knew it would be fun to sing with the tuneful orchestra where the guests laughed and drank. We wasted no time in answering Don D'Carlo's wire.

It was wonderful to be part of a new world, the night club world. We had friends in and outside the theatrical profession and now we were to enter the night club sphere. And from our opening night till now, we have enjoyed our pleasantest years.

Yet we still long to find real romance and love equal to our own tolerance and forgiveness. We dream of having homes and families. (Doctors tell us there is no reason why we can't have children.)

Perhaps you have seen through this story that life has given us plenty of problems, and that we have adjusted ourselves to most of them. And somewhere still, we believe and hope we will find the right mates, to whose understanding and love we can entrust our private lives.

Souvenir and Life Story of San Antonio's Siamese Twins, Daisy and Violet Hilton

Myer Myers produced this souvenir show booklet in 1925. The text includes a centralized photo-montage of the Hiltons (see figs. 9a and 9b in the current volume's image gallery) as well as other tidbits for the curious.

LIFE STORY AND FACTS
of the
SAN ANTONIO SIAMESE
TWINS

IN the rise of the famous San Antonio's Siamese Twins,—the beautiful, cultured and lovable Hilton Sisters,—we have one of the marvels of the age.

These talented girls, Daisy and Violet Hilton, were born inseparably joined together, at Brighton, England, in 1909, the daughters of an English Army officer. Their mother died a year after their birth. Their father was killed in Belgium in 1914. They were adopted by their uncle and aunt, Mr. and Mrs. Myer Myers, who devote their entire time to the girls and their activities.

These beautiful girls are today numbered among the highest paid and most popular features in vaudeville and their climb from the pit of the street carnival where they began their careers to the pinnacle in the amusement world has been attended by the children's willingness to sacrifice, to work, to study and to aspire, that they are today standing with Helen of Troy as object lessons of what can be achieved when the human soul aspires to greatness and usefulness.

When these little ones were first exhibited with a street carnival they were kept on exhibition for the gaze of that element of our race which enjoys feeling sorry for freaks, and whose own common expression is, "Thank God, they're not me."

The next step that the Hilton Sisters were allowed to take naturally came with their advancing years, and was made possible when their press agent began to turn the attention of the public to the fact that the girls have a home development that is both interesting and instinctive.

The public was informed of the girl's interest and activities in the kitchen, how they love to sew, get meals, cook, sing, dance, swim, play the saxophones, and practice on the piano, romp, raise pets, play tennis, gold, handball, go to the theatre, the movies, read good books and converse with cultured people.

The girls then tried vaudeville where they were confronted with the rigid rules and they met with very indifferent success in their efforts to play even small time houses in the East.

But during all the days, weeks, months and years of striving they were studying, practicing and preparing for real careers.

Throughout their lives they have been taught not to disagree but to give in to each other, to reason together and to try to come to a common understanding.

Their minds are supplied with those things that stimulate the mind and body with high ideals and healthful thoughts. If a young unfortunate jazz-crazed girl kills her mother there is every effort made to keep this sordid story from lodging in the minds of these little innocent girls. But instead of rehearsing all these tales of woe that make such fat fodder for mental morons, these girls have their ideals stimulated by higher ideals and nobler aspirations.

In recent interviews with the girls and their guardians, Mr. and Mrs. Myers,—Aunt Lou as Mrs. Myers is affectionately called,—said, "We have tried to show the girls every care and devotion, and have been paid back with every ounce of love their little bodies hold." Then with a sort of hushed tone she said, "That in itself is enough."

The girls radiate happiness for they say, "We have all the good things in life that other girls enjoy, so what more could we ask. And we get all the joy that comes to those who really love to make other people happy and we get our greatest pleasure out of entertaining other people."

Now we must deal with the girls not as Siamese Twins, joined together at birth, but as artists who must sing and dance,—stars if you please.

In the methods used to elevate the Hilton Sisters to the pinnacle of fame and fortune there is an absolute similarity with the way Henry Ford raised the fliver[1] from a freak to where last year it earned

---

1. A fliver, or flivver, refers most commonly to the Ford Model T made by Henry Ford's Ford Motor Company from 1908 to 1927; it was also called the "Tin Lizzy." In 1926, Ford pioneered the "Sky Flivver," a plane he predicted would be the automobile of the sky but that in fact only flew once and crashed during that test flight, killing its pilot.

him, his wife and son, Edsel, $115,000,000.00 profit and won him the greatest popularity ever enjoyed by a rich man in the history of the world.

Psychologists will tell you that not over one-fifth of what anything costs is represented in actual value; four-fifths are in the mind; four-fifths have been created by mental processes. In the case of the Hilton Sisters it is more than nine-tenths created value.

It takes imagination and enthusiasm to create those intangible values and convert them into realities. That is showmanship in its highest sphere. It is salesmanship in its highest phase.

Mrs. Myers will tell you that she and her husband have tried to show the Hilton Twins every care and devotion, and that they have been paid back with every ounce of love that these little bodies hold. Those who will tell you that not only has this devotion been rewarded by a deep, abiding love that these little girls have for their adopted parents, but that while training and caring for these little girls who came into the world so handicapped for life's race, they have brought themselves to the same standard that they sought for the girls, and as a result Mr. and Mrs. Myers have found married life to be one of pleasure and understanding. They have found a unity in purpose in doing for the little twins that has smoothed the path of life over which they themselves are traveling.

They are as careful about their eating as most girls are about the brand of cosmetics they use. In fact they are strict vegetarians, and very much of their pep, vivaciousness and ambition to achieve is the natural result of their living clean lives, thinking wholesome thoughts and cultivating noble purposes.

What Are Siamese Twins?

How does science explain that Daisy and Violet Hilton were born joined together?

Twins are a common phenomena. Twins born joined together are not so common. There are perhaps a dozen such cases known to history, and they are termed "Siamese Twins," because the first widely known twins of this kind were born in Siam. They were the original Siamese Twins, Chang and Eng, and were brought to this country in 1829.

They lived to be 63 years old, and each married and were fathers of several children.

Probably the most interesting case of anomalous twins ever known—they are Daisy and Violet Hilton, called the San Antonio "Siamese Twins."

As much by their charm and beauty as by their talent, these girls have captured public interest and popularity. With the single exception of being born joined together and going through life that way, they are normal human beings, talented, vivacious and personable.

Everyone wonders what is the scientific explanation of "Siamese Twins." By what caprice of Nature are they born joined together?

The first question that naturally suggests itself is—are twins joined together separate individuals incompletely fused or are they an incompletely divided single individual? In other words, are they two persons partly joined or one person partly separated? Strange as it may seem, science believes that conjoined twins have a single origin.

Scientists who have studied the phenomena of twins believe in two kinds,—identical twins, who come from the same life germ, and unidentical twins, who come from separate life germs, being merely born together. "Siamese Twins" belong to the first class.[2]

Identical twins are always of the same sex, two girls or two boys. They look exactly alike, and throughout life their tastes, dispositions, talents are remarkably similar. Unidentical twins may be a girl and boy, having no more resemblance in appearance and ideas than any other brother and sister of the same age and brought up amid the same surroundings.

"Siamese Twins" are in no sense "freak" creatures. They are merely an unusual type of identical twins. Every pair of identical twins had a single germ origin and passed at some time through the same stages of connection as did twins who are born joined together. Only in normal cases the separation is complete before birth.

In Daisy and Violet Hilton the complete separation before birth was retarded in some way. They were born with a spinal and tissue juncture at the base of the spine, and after birth Nature makes no further separation.

---

2. In essence, this issue remains the question for embryologists studying conjoined twins today; see current volume, 108–9n23.

Although joined twins have a single life-germ origin, they really are two personalities. Though in the main the tastes and dispositions of the Hilton Sisters are similar, there are little differences which environment has brought about. But they are closer than any other pair of sisters or any other identical twins.

Are the "Siamese Twins" Exactly Alike in Looks and Actions?

People who see Daisy and Violet Hilton, the San Antonio "Siamese Twins," notice that these girls look exactly alike in face and figure. Of course, from across the footlights little dissimilarities might not be apparent, and one of the questions everyone asks is—"are the 'Siamese Twins' exactly alike in looks?"

The answer is that they are as nearly alike as it is possible for any two human beings to be. They are more alike than any other type of identical twins because besides having a common life-germ origin, they have necessarily passed through the same experiences and been exposed to the same influences since birth.

Other identical twins, not joined together, may look alike to the casual observer. But different paths in life have made some differences. One may have taken more exercise and become a trifle hardier; the other may have had a severe accidental sickness, and so on. But the "Siamese Twins" have passed through essentially the same environmental influences in life, and consequently there has been nothing in their experiences to cause them to differ.

The Hilton girls look exactly alike in every respect. The only difference discernible to the eye—an inconsequential one—is that Violet has a small mole on her cheek. The greatest and most surprising differentiation has been found to be in the fingerprints of the twins, which are distinctly individual. Science explains that it is in the different skin ridges of the foot and hand that heredity has apparently reached its limit. Here are two girls who came from an identical life-germ, were born joined together and have led the same lives, and yet their fingerprints differ in some respects. This is a big boost for the fingerprint theory, for if conjoined twins have different fingerprints it is practically certain that no other two persons will be alike.

Are the twins exactly alike in disposition and actions? If one wishes to eat dinner does the other have the same idea? If one likes pink dresses and jazz music does the other have the same tastes? In a general way the answer to this is "yes." But in many particular instances they vary in likes and ideas.

The reason they differ is easily solvable. No two people can have exactly the same experiences even though they may go through life joined together. And each different experience tends to make one slightly dissimilar in thought and action from the other. Daisy may have read a book that made a great impression on her, while Violet was sleeping. While walking along the street or riding in a train, one may be looking to the right and the other to the left. The sum of their varied experiences has resulted in a very slight difference in ideas and tastes.

But in the main—what one likes the other also cares for, and when a course of action suggests itself to one the other is agreeable. Agreeable, both from hereditary influence, and also from training,—for they have always been instructed to give in to the other, for quarrels would only be useless and embittering.

But remember these things,—one may be sleeping while the other lies awake thinking or reading; one may be eating dinner while the other sits talking; one can play the saxophone while the other plays another instrument, etc. They have two different nervous systems each capable of thinking individual thoughts, and two separate bodies (excepting the juncture), each capable of separate action within certain limitations. Nevertheless, the "Siamese Twins" are as nearly alike and have as like tastes as is possible for any two human beings.

What Is the Connection between the "Siamese Twins"?

Many persons who have seen the San Antonio "Siamese Twins" have noted the ease and uniformity of all their movements, even in such complex actions as dancing. Of course, having been joined together since birth the Hilton girls have fallen into an unconscious rhythm of movement,—when one steps one way the other automatically responds, in somewhat the same manner as we may walk down the street reading and yet keep putting one foot ahead of the other.

The twins do not move awkwardly or clumsily but as gracefully and in as uniform a fashion as if one mind directed their actions. People have wondered about this, whether one would pull the other around occasionally, and if so would there be any pain due to the pulling on the juncture which connects them. And this leads to the query—what actually is the connection between the "Siamese Twins"?

Daisy and Violet Hilton are held together by a tissue connection measuring about six inches in diameter. The back outline of each of the girls runs in the normal shape down to a point just above the base of the spine. Then it verges out into the connection. On the lower side of the connection the bodies resume the normal shape.

There is no bone matter in the connecting link. It is made up of skin and muscular tissue, nerve, arterial and spinal connections. Blood circulates between the twins, as though there were but one body, through the major artery which is in the juncture. There is also a nervous connection, which is not an immediate one, however.

There is perfect freedom of movement in regard to this strip. For instance one of the girls may lie down in bed while the other is sitting up. There is not now no matter in what position,—and there never has been since birth,—the slightest pain in the region about the connecting strip. It affords the girls neither the slightest discomfort in itself nor in relation to their movements.

Other "Siamese Twins" have not been so fortunate. The original Siamese Twins, Chang and Eng, were joined together by a strip located at the lower end of the breast bone, and they, too, could move with comparative ease and freedom. There have been other famous joined twins who were connected in most unusual places.

There were the Hindu sisters who were joined face to face, the connection being at the chest. The oldest known case of joined twins were the Biddenden Maids, born in the year 1100, and joined at two places—the hips and the shoulders.[3]

---

3. According to Alice Domurat Dreger, Mary Chulkhurst and Eliza Chulkhurst, the Biddenden Maids, "born in England in 1100, lived to the age of thirty-four. When one died, the survivor was offered separation surgery but refused, saying, 'As we came together we will go together'" (*One of Us: Conjoined Twins and the Future of the Normal* [Cambridge, MA: Harvard University Press, 2004], 46). Apparently, there is also doubt among teratologists regarding the probability that the Biddenden sisters were in fact joined at the shoulder; for more on this, see J. Bondeson, "The Biddenden Maids: A

Can One of the "Siamese Twins" Be Well When the Other Is Sick?

People have wondered about the San Antonio "Siamese Twins" in regard to such matters as sickness, ill humor, gladness and excitement. Is there a connection of mind as well as of matter that makes every alien influence on one body communicate itself to the other?

In practically all things that concern bodily effects, Daisy and Violet Hilton are as distinct as any other two people. The nervous connections in the strip between them are not immediate but casual; there is no absolute juncture of their spinal cords or central nervous systems.

For instance, if you prick your hand the stimulus of pain instantly travels to the brain. If Daisy Hilton pricks her hand the stimulus travels to her brain, but Violet may be totally unaware that anything has happened. This same rule applies to all senses, seeing, hearing, tasting, smelling and, with exceptions, to feeling.

The exceptions are in very unusual cases. It must not be forgotten that in the connecting link there are some nerves. And it seems that if one of the girls has a very prolonged nervous stimulus, such as a steady headache for hours and hours, this is gradually communicated to the other. Perhaps, the headache is not communicated through the nerves at all, but may be due to prolonged inactivity lying besides the sufferer or to suggestion. While certainty cannot be expressed as to this, the evidence seems to indicate that there is some nervous connection between the twins but that it is not a very immediate one.

That is why one can have a tooth extracted and the other not be concerned; one can have indigestion and the other who ate less for dinner will feel all right. In ordinary matters any mental or physical condition of one will not be communicated to the other.

However, it must be remembered that there is a major artery in the strip joining the two girls, and blood circulates freely between them. Consequently any contagious disease, or one which is caused by microorganisms in the blood is practically certain to affect both of the twins. This would include such diseases as the various fevers, — typhoid, malaria, etc., severe blood poisoning, diphtheria, etc. So far the twins have

Curious Chapter in the History of Conjoined Twins," *Journal of the Royal Society of Medicine* 85, no. 4 (April 1992): 220.

never had any serious sickness, so it cannot be said positively that a severe illness would be mutual. But their physiological makeup seems to indicate that this would be the case.

Is It Possible to Separate the "Siamese Twins" by Surgery?

After a person has finished meditating on the strange case of Daisy and Violet Hilton, twins born joined together, the invariable final question is "Can't they be separated? Can't they be cut apart by surgery?"

There has been a great deal of scientific study and argument on this point, and at the end of it all, the question is still unsettled. There have been but few precedents for such a surgical operation, and surgery is often too speculative to be used merely as an experiment. All of our present day operations are the results of numerous surgical experience of the past. Any new operation is inspired mostly by absolute necessity and not as an experimentation.

Authorities say there have been a very few "Siamese Twins" who were successfully cut apart. These cases were not only rare, but were performed on infants. In one so-called successful case one of the twins died. In all cases where a separation was effected, the connecting strip was of such a slight tissue-like character that it made the separation seem quite simple.

In the case of such "Siamese Twins" as Daisy and Violet Hilton, it appears very unlikely, if not impossible, that they could be separated by surgery without a fatal result to at least one of them. The connecting strip between the girls, it must be remembered, measures about six inches in diameter, and contains besides skin and muscle tissue a major artery and some nerve connections. Just how closely bound up with the spinal cords are these nerve connections is not known, and this makes an operation increasingly hazardous.

An operation, no matter how slight, results in a great shock and is a source of great distress to the patient. Consider what an effect such an operation as this particular one would have, both mentally and physically on these little girls. The worry before such an operation would agitate their nervous systems and stimulate their heart actions. And then there is a very real danger in cutting through a tissue which was present at birth and has become solidified through twenty-one years of growth.

It is no wonder both the twins view separation with horror. Consider how nervous the average individual is about having a tooth pulled, while the amputation of a leg or arm—even though necessary—is viewed with alarm and repugnance.

Meanwhile the Hilton twins are healthy and happy. There is no physical necessity for an operation, and the fearful dangers of it are to them more important than the prospect of being separated. There are chances they might both die, and even more chances that but one will survive, and the consequent opinion is that they do not want to be operated on or to be separated. And who can blame them?

They are not the first conjoined twins who have refused to be separated. The original Siamese Twins, Chang and Eng, would never consent to an operation. When they were sixty-three years old, and each the father of a large family, Chang became sick. One night he died, probably from cerebral clot, and when Eng awoke in the morning and found his brother dead he suffered a nervous shock which affected his heart, and he died shortly after.

Some remember the quite recent case of the Bohemian twin sisters, Rosa and Josefa Blazek.[4] One became sick from jaundice, and though doctors sought to induce the other to consent to a surgical separation she refused and they both died about the same time.

In all cases there seems to be a mental aversion to separation, a fear of such a condition, which is more potent than the fear of approaching death together. Never having known life one apart from the other they cannot quite imagine the condition, cannot conceive of themselves as separate individuals. And if the twins themselves do not want to be separated, there is little likelihood that this will ever be tried.

4. Rosa and Josepha Blazek were born on January 20, 1878, in what is today the Czech Republic; both died on March 30, 1922, Josepha dying first of an unclearly diagnosed illness and Rosa following twelve minutes later. Rosa became pregnant and delivered a little boy, Franz, in 1910, a source of heated public discussion. Rosa later married Franz Dvorak after a court settlement in which Dvorak was charged with bigamy; a soldier, Dvorak died in battle in 1817. Josepha was also engaged but her fiancé died before they were able to marry. Myers details a conversation the Hiltons have about the twins and their relationships at the end of *Souvenir and Life Story of San Antonio's Siamese Twins*. For an account of the Blazeks based on contemporary newspaper articles, see the "Phreeque" Web site by Elizabeth Anderson at http://phreeque.tripod.com/balzek_sisters.html (accessed February 25, 2008).

Siamese Twins Admit That Physical Bondage Has Variety of Limitations in Social Life

Twins Tell Why They Won't Wed

That the thoughts of girls, budding into womanhood, turn naturally to marriage, has been a theory of mankind since the dawn of the ages, and it has been a theory borne out by facts.

It is human nature, that's all. Hence, it is the most natural thing in the world that Violet and Daisy Hilton, the San Antonio "Siamese Twins" born joined together at the bases of their spines, should now begin to observe the marriage scene about them with eyes somewhat sophisticated, for the girls are past 20 years of age. Perhaps, too, their critical regard is sharpened by the fact that they are pretty, charming, lovable young women, cultured and vivacious, with an amiable graciousness that is magnetic. Men and women, youths and children are drawn to them.

There is always the possibility that one of these twins, who are separate individualities despite their legal status of a single being, will suddenly fall in love some day. In meeting them, talking with them, observing their charm, one is struck with this thought. And one cannot doubt that deep in their hearts these happy girls have also considered this contingency, no matter how vaguely.

One wonders what their ideas of marriage are, naturally, and it was to learn from the girls, just how much they have considered the marriage question and what conclusions they have arrived at that the interviewer, in an entirely informal fashion, brought up the subject during an afternoon when the twins were engaged in fancy work and brisk chatter with their devoted uncle and aunt and the visitor. The talk began with a friendly discussion of the young married folks that Violet and Daisy know in their home city of San Antonio, and it is immediately manifest that the observations let fall by these delightful twins are indicative of keen powers of analysis, if entirely unconscious.

For instance, hear Daisy: "The Wallaces are such a charming couple. Tom is a great, big dear, so direct and sincere and faithful. He reminds me of a loyal affectionate Newfoundland—that is where Molly is concerned. But once in a while I fear he becomes frightened at Molly's extravagances. After all Tom is only on a salary."

Violet joins in: "Molly is foolish at times, but she really has a lot of common sense, and she'll give heed to Tom when he talks to her seriously. You see, Tom loves to regard her as a child."

Just about what two fond and charitable women would say of married friends isn't it? And there you have a line on the keen observation facilities of the twins. Their comments are those of adults with experience. It would seem from them that the girls use their eyes wouldn't it? Of course, they draw their conclusions largely from what they have absorbed of the opinions of their elders, but that is true of all of us, isn't it?

The outstanding fact about Violet and Daisy is that they are normal girls, who, by the very nature of their physical tie, have had more time for study, reading and serious conversation with older people than have most other girls of their ages. So obvious is this rather mature mental state that people who come to see them, prepared to treat them as abnormal children, almost instantly drop that attitude in quick confusion, for the gaze of the twins' thoughtful, observing eyes is not that of artless children—not at all.

What is the conclusion Violet and Daisy have reached in regard to marriage in general? Let Violet talk: "I suppose we are old-fashioned for we were born in England, and we have the English family viewpoint still—at least, Daisy and I are told so. We do not care much for women in business, in offices. We believe in the so-called bromide[5] that 'woman's place is in the home' and, of course, we are 'kidded' a lot about it. Folks tell us we are funny, for they say: 'Aren't you in the show business?' But we come back with this: 'We are the exceptions that prove the rule,' and it seems to me we are right in saying that, for we must regard ourselves as exceptions to girls in everyday life. We cannot forget, although we do not ever regret, that we are the 'Hilton Sisters, the San Antonio Siamese twins, born joined together,' so we never dodge the issue in our discussions. We believe no good comes of ignoring facts. Why should it?

"So, whether our friends are amused or not, we believe that the career of every woman is marriage, or should be. It seems to us that Nature meant the race to go on, or men and women would not have been created in the first place. We seem to feel that a woman who puts marriage behind her for the sake of a business or artistic career is not doing her allotted task.

5. A common saying.

"We do not overlook ourselves. We have not had much time to think
of the scheme of life, of marriage, but we are not stupid and we have
considered ourselves. But we have never discussed marriage as applied
to ourselves.

"We have thought of it," continued Violet, "and we have talked it
over seriously and sensibly with each other time after time. We know
that we are regular, human, creatures, just like other girls, except for the
tie that binds us together through life. So far, we have been perfectly
happy together. We have never yet wished to be separated and we
would not wish to be now, even if the operation were possible,—even if
it were a very simple one. No, we are in contented agreement about
that. We feel that there is a closer spiritual cord between us than between other human beings, for we have never been angry at each other
and we have never had a misunderstanding, but we do get angry with
other people now and then.

"Daisy and I realize that love is a mighty force. We have read of it
since childhood. Almost every play or motion picture we see has love for
its central theme, and we have drawn our own conclusions as everyone
does, I suppose. We have thought of love coming to one of us some day
and we have solved the problem in advance. Perhaps, it is better to say
that it was solved for us at birth. At best, love can only complicate the
business of living for us, and possibly bring us unhappiness."

And then Violet, in answer to a question says, "Yes, we have heard
of one of the Blazek sisters, who were born joined together, and of her
child. Our way can't be their way. We can't be separated, no matter
how the future may force such a desire upon us, so there is no way for
either of us to find happiness that others find in marriage.

"In discussing marriage we feel that we are merely spectators and
should be permitted the license to talk freely of it without our own relation to it being brought in."

Personal Staff for Daisy and Violet Hilton

TOUR UNDER DIRECTION OF
MYER MYERS

CONTRACTING AGENT,
H. A. WILSON

COMPANY MANAGER,
BEN BENSON

PUBLICITY MANAGER,
W. L. OLIVER

ACCOMPANIST,
MARGARET MOORE

SECRETARY FOR HILTON SISTERS,
EDNA STOSELL

To Scientific Colleagues and
the Appreciative Public [6]

I n placing this booklet before the public the writers desire to thank numerous scientific colleagues and authorities for their courteous and valued coopera- tion in clinical research dealings with the anatomical problems relating to twin-born progeny.

This book is submitted to readers with a desire to demonstrate the fact that although the subjects of this narration are joined together by one cartilaginous connection, two distinctly different lives are involved by the one union. The temperament desires and accomplishments of the twins are those of two distinct personalities.

A prolonged research has conclusively proved that the birth-union of the two girls, Daisy and Violet, is the most remarkable, from a scientific viewpoint, that has come under the notice of the Scientific Research Society.

In penning the story of the twins we have endeavored to interest the reader with facts concerning their life, travels and experiences and trust that our efforts on their behalf will be rewarded.

Very gratefully yours

JOE M. LINOVER M.D.
MYER MYERS
WM. L. OLIVER

6. This section and the one that follows it, "Here and There with Daisy and Vio- let," both appear as a center insert to the original pamphlet—pages 7 through 11 of the overall 14 pages that comprise the booklet. (Pages 8 and 9 contain the photomontage, which is reproduced as figures 9a and 9b in the image gallery of the current volume.) I have included these sections after the initial "Life Story and Facts" segment to facilitate a clearer reading experience. Readers will note the hearkening back to the McKoys' "Certificates of Eminent Medical Men" in the section of the Hilton's show history called "To Scientific Colleagues and the Appreciative Public."

Here and There with Daisy and Violet

Why Shouldn't the Hilton Sisters
Be Born Joined Together?

Their grandmother was a twin. Their grandfather was a twin. Their grandmother was the mother of four sets of twins.

Their grandmother's first children were twins, one of these twins was the mother of Daisy and Violet Hilton.

Those who believe in heredity have a strong argument in the San Antonio Siamese Twins.

ঔয়

Siamese Twins Visit Governor at State Home.

Violet and Daisy Hilton, the famous Siamese twins performing at a local theatre this week, called upon the Gov. Fuller[7] this morning. They told the Governor of their trip through the country and their visit to 38 Governors previous to their call on him. Gov. Fuller told them that although he was very busy, he could always take time out to talk to such interesting girls.

—Eve. Globe, Boston, Mass.

ঔয়

Up and Down Broadway.

Going the Rounds

Unless I am mistaken—and I probably am—the Siamese Twins Daisy and Violet Hilton, were recently standing on Broadway at 47th

---

7. Alvan Tufts Fuller was the founder and owner of the Packard Motor Car Co. and was elected governor of Massachusetts in 1924. He was reelected for a second term and did not receive pay for his public service employment while in office.

Street talking with some of the larks of Tinpan Alley when a cop came along and told them to break it up.

"Who are you talking to?" Daisy is reported to have answered the cop instead of asking, "To whom are you speaking?"

"Both of you. And don't give me any of your mug," he answered.

"That's different," said Violet and they hopped into a taxi.

—New York Eve-World.

No. 74,129 of the Siamese Twin Yarns.

The Siamese Twins were leaving the Pennsylvania Station the other day to fulfill their engagement in St. Louis. As they stood by the gate a crowd gathered and a policeman unaware of the fact that they were born joined together, began pushing the people away.

"Can't you see what you're doin'?" he said. "Here's so many of vuh that you gut these girls standing on each other."

—New York Eve-World.

Twin Beds for Twins Just Simply Can't Do? as This Hotel Finds.

Daisy and Violet Hilton, famous "Siamese" twins featured in vaudeville, just naturally had to have the room with a double bed they asked for yesterday at the Hotel Shelbourne at Brighton Beach. The hotel clerk, who did not recognize them, just as naturally did not see how he was going to give them such a room when there was not a vacant one in the Hotel.

Daisy and Violet seemed to the clerk to be two as pleasant ladies as ever he had met, but nevertheless stubborn, for they would have nothing to do with the two single rooms he offered them. The single rooms, they admitted might have all the attractions he said they had. Undoubtedly the view of the sea was magnificent, the rooms were every bit as comfortable and they were separated by only a few feet.

But even only a few feet, the twins said, was too much, for they had been together all their lives and could not be parted now. So the kind of a room they had to have was found, as often it has been done before, when the twins were recognized by a guest of the hotel.

—Telegraph.

ᵭᵽ

Twins See Show on One Ticket.

Being Siamese twins has some few advantages. Last night Walter Duggan, manager of the Selwyn Theater,[8] was called upon to decide whether the Hilton Sisters, Siamese twins and headliners in vaudeville, should buy two seats or one to see "Gentlemen Prefer Blondes." Mr. Duggan was ready to arbitrate when the pair showed him that they only occupy one seat. The twins witnessed the performance for $3.30 instead of $6.60.

ᵭᵽ

Famous Twins Solve Missing Pencil.

Milton B. Runkle, who has the display of demolished stills on the Wortham midway at the Fair, is the great jester. But unlike many others who promote fun at the expense of some one else, Milton can be the butt of the joke and appreciate it, that is why he is welcome everywhere with everybody in the Big Wortham show family.[9]

Saturday Milton was greatly absorbed with his thoughts. Then something worth noting down came to him. He felt for his gold pencil. It was gone.

---

8. A theater in Chicago built in 1918.

9. Clarence Wortham ran his railroad carnivals from the early twentieth century until 1922 when he died. The Hiltons appeared in Wortham World's Greatest Shows in 1916 almost immediately upon their arrival in the United States. See Dean Jensen, *The Lives and Loves of Daisy and Violet Hilton: A True Story of Conjoined Twins* (Berkeley, CA: Ten Speed Press, 2006), particularly 69–80.

Milton fled to his own office, but the pencil was not there. He sped to the office wagon of the shows, but did not find the pencil. He tried to remember everyplace he had been in the morning. From one to the other he rushed, telling his tale of woe at each step and getting no line on the pencil.

He had looped the loop from the cook house to the wild west show and was on the return trip when he met Violet and Daisy Hilton the grown-together girls who were visiting on the lot. Runkle rushed up and asked the twins if they had seen his gold pencil.

The girls looked at him and laughed. Then they asked the question. "If every animal according to size used his ears as a common carrier would an elephant walk around with a bale of hay?"

Runkle reached up and found his pencil. Being a great user of slang he blurted out, "And all these folks around this show have been stalling me all the time when they knew the write-stick was back of my ear."

Chained for Life

Robert De Seville, from a Story by Ross Frisco

The film was directed by Harry L. Fraser and produced by George Moskov, and the screenplay was written by Ross Frisco and Nat Tanchuck; additional dialogue was provided by Albert de Pina. This version of the screenplay appeared in the 1953 reprint of the Hiltons' autobiography *Intimate Loves and Lives of the Hilton Sisters.*

At every performance of the Hamilton Sisters, in fact, at every rehearsal even, Ted Hinkley, manager and cicerone[1] of the Siamese Twins, always sat in the fourth row, of the theatre they happened to be playing. He always wore a grey double-breasted suit, with a carnation in the lapel, and he always champed on an unlit cigar, as he sat there, in the same fourth row unnoticed in the welter of humanity that surged around him.

Leaning back against the upholstered seat, his soft hands folded across his paunch, no one would have suspected a curious and imaginative soul encased in all that lard. No one would have dreamt he could possibly be an instrument of fate. Yet he was.

<hr />

1. Someone who guides and informs tourists.

As the sole impresario[2] of the Hamilton Sisters, he built all their successes out of his own brain, and out of his own spectacular approach to life. Unaware of so doing, he was a weaver of destinies, a promoter of achievements—and sometimes an arranger of calamities. Had anyone confronted him with these facts, he would have laughed raucously, for he never dramatized himself. On the contrary, it was his pride that he thought himself to be intensely practical, and his unvarying "Leave it to Hinkley" an index to that pride.

Everything about him was soft—his portly, paunchy figure; his mild blue eyes; his soft, moist hands—except a steel-trap mind forever in conflict with a rather generous and sentimental heart.

Ted Hinkley had lived a full life, but now in the decline of his years, he had only two real passions—money and "the girls," as he called them. If he ever had stopped to think about it, he would surely have tried to convince himself that he loved Dorothy and Vivian Hamilton the best.

However, in Ted, the two passions had merged, blended and become transmuted into a "way of life," so that whatever successes he promoted for the Siamese Twins, he tried to bring them about with the least possible concessions at the highest possible price. The result was an unending war with theatre managers—nonetheless deadly because it was carried on in an atmosphere of easy fellowship—who on their part, knew every trick of the trade.

The sums of money Ted Hinkley checked at the theatre box office every Saturday were as thrilling to him as the sum total of the artistry the Hamilton Sisters, Siamese Twins, had displayed throughout the week on the boards of the local theatre. Their success was his success. Their achievement, the child of his heart and brain. And their earnings, something he created for them, much as a fond father, who only keeps a minor part, preferring to indulge his beloved children. He was a cheerful man—a happy man. For he loved the color and tinsel of backstage; the flavor of greasepaint; the glaring lights. And somehow he identified himself with the achievement represented by the girls themselves, so that, when speaking of them, he would always refer to them in full as "the Hamilton Sisters, headliners!"

He had only one fear—the frightful specter of losing them as he had lost many years previously, two boys, also Siamese Twins, one of them

2. Producer; professional promoter.

had died, and the other had only survived a few days, the imperative operation.

But ordinarily such gloomy considerations were farthest from his mind. He liked best to let his thoughts dwell untrammeled on the factors that go into the making of a very successful act, on the elements that might be combined to produce a box office hit. And, as with all art forms, he knew that publicity had much to do with the shaping of the final achievements.

The links in the chain of destiny, which were to lead to the Hamilton Sisters' greatest success, and Hinkley himself to a pinnacle of publicity beyond his dreams, began to be forged one quiet summer morning in June, at a large sun-dazzled California city on the sea.

Ted had puzzled and worried over the slow, insidious decline of the Hamilton Sisters' act. Box office receipts were growing smaller; something of the zest and excitement had definitely dulled. And his dreams of at least reaching the big time—goal of all show people—had dulled too, receding into that shadowland of the entertainment world where so many headliners are consigned.

He perspired gently, as he walked leisuredly towards the Bijou Theatre, mulling over and over in his mind, the idea that had finally emerged from the involved recesses of his brain. "Would that lousy manager, Mackenzie, see its value? . . . Would that pimping sharp-shooter, Andre, go for it? . . . Would the girls agree? . . ."

When Ted arrived at the Bijou and walked down the dark aisle to the fourth row, the Hamilton Sisters were already rehearsing on the stage. He sidled quietly over to where the manager, Mackenzie, was sitting, took out a cigar and sat down without a word, champing on the unlit cigar, which he rolled from one corner of his mouth to the other. Mackenzie said nothing.

Dorothy and Vivian were swaying gracefully, now and then executing an intricate step in time, as they sang their new song, "Every Hour." As always, they were putting heart and soul into the number, despite the fact that this was only a rehearsal. He noted the filmy dresses they were wearing, and grimaced as he thought of Mable, the girls' personal maid, with whom he carried on a good-natured running battle. His experienced eye noted the backstage curtain was up, revealing the usual disarray of theatrical flats and props, the sprinkling of performers waiting for their turn; he was thinking only superficially, with the top of his mind, while his real concern was the idea he had conceived and which revolved over and over within him.

He heard soft footsteps on the aisle carpet, and turning his head saw Andre Pariseau had arrived, and at the same time he estimated the house capacity with a practiced eye. He had made his decision.

At that moment, a somewhat unsuccessful vaudevillian was sitting behind him and Mackenzie in the person of Andre; a heart-hungry girl on the stage, singing a banal and slightly suggestive ballad, was thinking to herself as she smiled: "How false . . . how unreal! Where does all this get us?" And the manager of the Bijou was thinking, "They're good, but what the hell, we've tried everything, and we still can't pack 'em in! Wonder how it feels to never know what it is to be alone?" And a girl, Renee, who served as shooting target for a man she loved against her will, knowing him to be what he really was, was crying in a cheap hotel room.

As Dorothy and Vivian reached the end of their routine, their pure, clear voices lifted higher and higher, soaring faultlessly over the stage. Hinkley could not help but smile, and he turned towards Mackenzie to comment. Mackenzie was smiling too, momentarily forgetting himself. He saw Hinkley's eyes on him and instantly, the smile was replaced by a slight frown. He knew Hinkley. As the act on the stage came to an end, Andre rose behind them, applauding noisily, as he shouted, "Bravo . . . Bravisimo!" He walked nonchalantly towards the stage and went up the steps where the girls were standing.

"Great! Ain't it, Mackenzie?" Hinkley asked in his soft voice, as he shifted the cigar to the other corner of his mouth. Mackenzie nodded reluctantly. "Well . . . it's a good routine Ted . . ."

He watched Andre Pariseau start a conceited pose, arching his chest, as he reached the Hamilton Sisters on the stage. He gave no indication of how pleased he felt inside at the girls' routine.

"Good routine!" Hinkley exploded in mock indignation. "Why, with that act and some smart publicity, your theatre won't have enough seats to hold the audience!"

"Look, Ted," Mackenzie said patiently, "I know you're after a percentage deal, but all you're offering me in exchange is conversation. As for the publicity—there isn't a trick we haven't tried before!"

"Except one, Mack . . . except one!" Hinkley smiled, rubbing his soft hands, feeling Mackenzie's interested stare. He too gazed at the stage where Andre had now changed his pose, and gazed at him coldly, dispassionately, much as an expert studies a horse, taking in the man's broad shoulders and flat belly, the almost classic profile and dark, wavy hair. And he nodded to himself in a mixture of paradoxical satisfaction and distaste.

"You were saying . . ." Mackenzie prompted. "What's this new angle we ain't tried before? . . ."

Hinkley removed the dead cigar from his mouth, and turned to Mackenzie, grinning. "I'll tell you in the office. That's why I sent for Andre."

They walked down the aisle and up the few short steps to the stage, as the orchestra blared discords from the pit, getting ready for another act. Andre was beaming—his brilliant smile flashed under the lights, despite the frown of annoyance on Vivian's face. Hinkley paused to get his breath and also to get the drift of the conversation. He wondered if Andre had ulterior motives, but it fitted in with his plans. Mackenzie paused too, as Andre was saying, "Each time I see you girls, you're more wonderful. It's unbelievable!"

"Each time I see you, I can't believe it either! After the riot in Memphis, when your mental act backfired, I really thought you'd given up your . . . er, career!" Vivian replied tartly. She nudged Dorothy and started to leave the stage, but Dorothy put her arm around her sister's waist and held her ground, smiling at Andre, who said nonchalantly,

"Oh, that! Just a mental lapse!" He grinned unabashed.

Hinkley felt he'd heard enough. "Come on, Andre, come into the office," he said a little more loudly than necessary, and together with Mackenzie, he walked away in the direction of the theatre's office. He could hear Andre's resonant voice saying to the girls in Italian, "*Sono como un angelo del cielo!*"[3] The rest was lost in the noise of flats and props being moved.

Hinkley followed Mackenzie down the musty aisle, carefully avoiding the busy stagehands, struggling with scenery and various props, and into an even mustier office decorated with faded posters of buxom lady acrobats in pink tights, and curling photographs of forgotten troupers. He waited until Mack sat down behind the battered desk, and sank into a chair next to it.

He had the feeling he was about to launch something big—bigger than anything he had attempted before. But long acquaintance with

3. Literally, "I am like an angel from heaven." While this could be a complimentary description of the listener's feelings on hearing the sisters sing, it could also simply be a mistranslation of the phrase, "sounds like an angel from heaven."

theatre managers had taught him the virtue of not seeming too eager, so now he crossed his hands across his ample paunch, and gazed boredly at the buxom beauties on the walls while Mackenzie fished in a desk drawer and brought out a bottle of whiskey and two clouded glasses. Mackenzie poured carefully, measuring out exact amounts in each glass, a half inch from the rim, and handed one to Hinkley.

"To old acquaintance!" he exclaimed, lifting his glass, and as Hinkley nodded, he drank it at one gulp. Hinkley followed suit and grimaced as he wiped his lips with the back of his hand.

A belch from the whiskey broke the silence, and Mack shifted in his swivel chair. He tried to look as uninterested as he could, but his words betrayed him.

"Well, Ted, get it off your chest! What's this idea you got now? Mind you, no percentage unless you put an SRO[4] sign on the box office!" He wanted to make that clear.

But Hinkley only smiled. He wasn't in a hurry at all. He was rolling the idea in his mind with gusto, savoring it to the full. Let him wait, he thought. And then a perverse thought struck him. "No hurry . . . maybe I'll save it for our next engagement, Mack. You ain't got too big a house anyway."

Mackenzie cleared his throat nervously. It must be good he thought. Never knew Ted to keep a publicity idea to himself. He brought out the whiskey bottle again and poured himself a glass then motioned towards Hinkley, reluctantly. But the latter shook his head. "Never drink even one during the day," he grinned, covering the glass with his hand. But today was sort of a special occasion. He waited until Mackenzie had downed his, then he sprang his trap with all the cunning the years had taught him.

"We been friends for a long time, Mack, so I thought I'd let you in on something solid. Like I said, it'll pack the house night after night . . . it'll put the Bijou on the map. You see," he paused and tapped his glass meditatively, "people're only interested in fundamentals—like love for instance—that's what makes a love story sure-fire! You lis'ning?"

Mackenzie was listening all right. Another belch broke the momentary stillness as he nodded.

"So, suppose one of the girls was to have a big romance? Fall in

4 Standing room only.

love and decide to get married, like anybody else? Can't you see the headlines? Siamese Twin announced forthcoming marriage! Figure it out, Mack!" He leaned back and waited for the full import of what he'd said to seep in.

Mackenzie's blue eyes had a glassy stare. He shook his head and his mouth opened, but no words came. Finally he gulped and exclaimed, "Holy Mother, are you serious?" Then, "But . . . how about the girls? Will they go for it?"

Hinkley was enjoying himself. "I'm their manager—just leave it to Hinkley." Before he could add anything else, the door opened and Andre Pariseau stepped in, glanced quickly from one face to the other, and deciding Mackenzie was the more important of the two, walked up to the desk in long, springy strides and grinned at the manager.

"Say, Mack," he began in his usual self-assured, cocky manner, "I happen to be a little short, and since I've been engaged, I'd like to . . . how about a . . . ."

But Mackenzie cut him short brusquely. "Sorry, Andre. You know our rules—no advances!" Then added contemptuously, "Besides, I didn't send for you!"

Andre's face underwent an instant transformation, as he inquired, "Then, who in hell did?"

"Me!" Hinkley tapped his chest with a pudgy forefinger, as he gave Andre a fishy look.

"Ah, then you can lend me a hundred till pay-day, can't you, Hinkley?" The scowl had melted into an ingratiating smile, as he stepped close to the manager-agent.

"How bad do you need it?" Hinkley asked silkily.

"Bad enough to ask *you*!"

Hinkley leisurely extracted a thick roll of bills from his pocket. "I'm not gonna lend it to you . . . This time, you're gonna work for it. In fact, an extra hundred every week, Andre!" He counted five twenty-dollar bills, and smilingly waved them under Andre's nose.

At sight of the money Andre tensed slightly. "What's the pitch?" he asked curiously.

"Romance!" Hinkley said softly. "Right up your alley. I've dreamed up a little publicity stunt for the girls—I need someone to play Romeo!"

"For a hundred a week?" Andre's eyes widened.

"And in advance!"

With a smile that Machiavelli would have envied, Andre extracted the bills from Hinkley's finger and pocketed them. He laughed. "Bring on Juliet!"

Two

When Dorothy and Vivian had showered and powdered after the hot, sweaty rehearsal at the Bijou, they sat on the fuchsia-colored bench before their dressing table. Dorothy's amber-colored hair drawn up high and glistening, from the nape of her neck, contrasted with the silver-and-green negligee she wore. Vivian as usual was draped in white satin, over which a cascade of dark ringlets fell in a soft cloud.

While she made up, Dorothy let her mind dwell on how Andre had looked at her, how he had smiled, and what he had said in Italian—something about angels—that morning on the stage. It seemed to her it had been going on for a long time, every time they were on the same bill. She could not remember everything, but his flashing, gay smile, and the meaning in his eyes was etched in her mind, and it gave her a feeling.

Relaxed and languid from the warm bath, she could feel the warm inner sides of her thighs pressing together under the silk. Her eyes were brilliant, and unconsciously, she was smiling, her small white teeth biting her lower lip. She wondered if Andre was as powerful as he looked.

Vivian glanced at her in the mirror, with slight surprise, then she smiled too. "Darling, you look . . . radiant! What's on your mind?"

Dorothy colored and veiled her eyes. "Nothing, silly!" She started applying lipstick, as her sister gazed at her dubiously. It occurred to Vivian that there was so much about her sister Dorothy she would never know. They were as one in so many respects. They knew a completion, an identification scarcely dreamed of by the majority of human beings—and that was their greatest compensation—that sense of completion. But there were times when another Dorothy, whom Vivian was never to know, seemed to peer through her eyes, and smile through her lips.

At that moment they heard the sharp voice of their personal maid, Mabel, saying sarcastically: "That door ain't got no usher, and you got hands, so knock before you come in! There's such a thing as privacy!"

And Hinkley's soft voice replying derisively, "From burlesque to privacy! That body beautiful of yours has been reflected from too many front row bald heads! All of a sudden it's Mabel, the modest maiden!"

"During my career," they could hear Mabel saying indignantly, "burlesque was an art! My act had dignity!"

"Dignity! One more bump, and *you* would've been outside the theatre! . . . where're the girls?"

"In there!" Then Mabel's voice rose higher, "Hey, girls, the ten percenter's here!"

Dorothy sighed. "They're at it again. We'd better go on out there . . ." They rose and went out into the small living room connected with their dressing room, a concession due them as headliners. As they emerged into the outer room, Mabel was pointing to Hinkley's cigar.

"Look, this ain't the wide open spaces, and that's no lily of the valley. Why don't you smoke a good cigar?"

"After today, Mabel . . . After today!" Hinkley answered unruffled, puffing luxuriously.

"What's it all about?" Vivian asked, looking first at Mabel and then at Hinkley.

Vivian, with the dark ringlets falling over the satin dressing gown, and the ivory face like a cameo.[5] Then she looked at Hinkley and saw the triumph written all over his face. Dorothy lifted her eyebrows.

"Girls," Hinkley blurted with suppressed excitement, from now on it's mink and Cadillacs! Just like I told you, leave it to Hinkley!"

"I hope you don't expect us to understand that," Dorothy said calmly. "What's happened?"

"The best!" Hinkley exclaimed with an expansive gesture. "After I got through with Mackenzie, he couldn't wait to say yes!"

"Yes, to what? Ted, you're talking in short-hand!"

"Don't tell me you've had another brain storm," Vivian interjected coldly. "Because if you have . . ."

"What do you mean? Did I ever tell you girls a story? Did I ever lie to you? . . . Did I ever . . . ," he asked with an injured air. Then as the girls stared at him silently, he faltered, "Well . . . it's nothing serious. Just a little publicity stunt."

Mabel who had been hanging the girls' costumes, gave a derisive snort. "Uh-oh! The last publicity stunt he pulled was when they buried that swami . . . If it hadn't been for the fire department, they'd never have dug him up!"

---

5. Some part of the original text seems to be lost here.

She flounced out of the small living room, and disappeared into the dressing room, her arms filled with several costumes.

"Why are you talking about burials?" Hinkley frowned. "This is an engagement. We're gonna get married!"

As if motivated by a single impulse the girls gazed at one another with startled faces. If Hinkley had purposely set out to shock them, he couldn't have been more successful. There was a moment of appalled silence, then:

"Ted, you must be out of your mind! Nothing serious, eh?" Dorothy exclaimed.

"Just a little publicity stunt!" Vivian mimicked. "I've heard enough!"

"Outa his mind!" Mabel sneered, entering the room. "For ten percent he'd bury his own mother in-law!"

Hinkley's expression underwent a sudden transformation. He managed to look hurt and outraged and misunderstood all at once. He gave a long melancholy sigh, and spread his hands in despair. "I'm sorry . . . Maybe I love you too much for my own good . . . you're right girls, calm yourselves, maybe I am outa my mind. My only thought was to get you into big time once and for all, to reach the goal we've struggled and fought and prayed for all these years! After all, it's for you . . . what do I care for myself? I'm an old man, girls!"

He saw their faces soften, their eyes grow liquid.

For once he felt a pang of regret in the cold and unfeeling organ that was his heart, at having to use such methods even for their own good.

Mabel watched him with the fixed intensity of a serpent mesmerizing a bird, but ironically, it was she who was mesmerized by the sheer gift of the man. It awed her. And for once in her turn, it rendered her speechless.

He turned as if to go, the cold cigar in his hand; he gazed at the cold ashes on its tip as if they were a symbol of his defeat.

"No one's really getting married," he said softly as a parting word. "And, good publicity never hurt an act!"

It was Dorothy who reacted first. She had a really brilliant mind which had enabled her to lead her own orchestra at one time, but she was forever being hamstrung by her generous, her warm and love-hungry emotional nature.

"Viv, maybe he's right after all," she said slowly. "We mustn't forget, this *is* show business!"

Vivian, whose mind was equally as good, and not the least trammeled by emotional complications, gazed at Ted dubiously. All the affection between them, all the years of struggle and achievement, all the give and takes of service and care and sharing which perforce had ruled their strange partnership, were not enough to balance against Hinkley's dangerous imagination.

"I don't know . . . ," she said slowly. "I knew you'd come up with some crazy idea, Ted . . . but . . . perhaps this one may have possibilities."

Ted Hinkley was a master showman, and he knew when not to press his advantage. He shrugged. He smiled wanly. "It's the one thing the world's interested in—love. I think," he said slowly, "it would be a sensation."

Dorothy smiled. "Well, which one of us is supposed to get married, Ted?" Then, without awaiting a reply, "And by the way, who's the groom?"

Hinkley hesitated, then said casually, "Andre!"

Dorothy's eyes flew wide; she felt as if a surging tide were rising within her and her breath quickened. She lowered her head to hide her confusion, and her eyes looked down the V of her negligee to where her virgin breasts rose and fell rhythmically.

"With millions of men in the world," Vivian protested, "why did you have to pick on that chiseller?"[6]

"Who else would do it?" Hinkley said mildly, spreading his hands in a questioning gesture.

"Well, count me out! I'm not the romantic type," Vivian said flatly in a cold voice. "What about his human target, won't she object?"

"You mean . . . Renee? She's got nothing to say about it. She has no claims!"

Dorothy raised her head and smiled at Hinkley, "I guess from here on, my love story begins!" Whether from her own surging blood, the excitement or all the romantic dreams which had awakened in the innermost recesses of her being, she would never know, but the fact was her voice was tremulous, ecstatic almost, with a lyrical quality which made Vivian turn her golden head to stare at her sister.

Hinkley sighed this time with relief and elation. It had been a strenuous morning. He mopped his forehead and clamped the dead cigar between his teeth, then said grinning, "Baby, leave it to Hinkley!"

6. Cheat or swindler.

He waved at the girls and left, walking as briskly as his pudgy figure permitted.

"Sure, you just leave it to Hinkley!" Mabel murmured as she glared at his retreating figure. "So if things blow up, I can always go back to Minsky's!"[7]

Dorothy and Vivian smiled quietly at each other. It was Mabel's unchanging refrain whenever anything annoyed her, forgetting she was long past the age when she had anything to offer Minsky's patrons. She babied them, was fiercely loyal and took all manner of liberties, but the girls loved her. And as the years went by, Mabel had become a permanent fixture in their lives, with all her jealousies against Hinkley, her domineering attitude, which really hid her deep, protective instinct. The girls knew Mabel loved them, and that in itself was enough.

Left alone the girls returned to their dressing-room and dressed for the afternoon. As a rule, they chattered a great deal, exchanging the eternal backstage gossip, and commenting on new numbers on the bill. But today they said little, immersed in their own thoughts, much as travelers venturing into unknown territory take refuge in silence.

Their faces, mirrored in the large glass over their dressing table, were pensive—faces that were so similar, and yet, so unlike—and somewhat troubled.

They had had many experiences in publicity before—some with happy ending, and some touched by the sordid and the tragic. They had long since learned how to inure themselves to the careless, unthinking cruelty of their public—just as they had learned how to achieve an identification with each other, which was their extension of being. They had known pain, and grief—even despair. But their courage and an infinite faith in that Kingdom which is not of this world.[8]

But there was another Kingdom where they spent the major part of their lives, and that was the theatre. And there, Ted Hinkley was the arbiter.

They wondered, in the simplicity of their limpid minds, whether Hinkley's publicity stunt would succeed. In the end, it was to succeed beyond their greatest expectations.

---

7. The four Minsky brothers—Abe, Billy, Herbert, and Morton—initiated and ran what became known as Minsky's Burlesque; the Minsky brothers managed their business against significant opposition from 1912 to 1937 in New York City.

8. Here too, something from the original text seems to be lost.

Already Ted Hinkley was beginning to set in motion a hurricane of publicity beyond even *his* gifted imagination.

That night Pariseau called Dorothy on the phone to tell her how happy he was over the publicity arrangements. Only he made it sound like it was something more than just a stunt. He spoke close to the phone so she could hear the cello undertones of his rich baritone, and the soughing of his breath when he laughed. Dorothy felt this was a new experience, and for the first time in her life, became unaware of her sister next to her.

Yes, she would indeed, she would love to. The Fireside Cafe would be wonderful, they had such heavenly music. Yes, she would be ready . . .

When she turned after replacing the receiver, she saw Vivian was staring at her. "That . . . that was Andre . . . Mr. Pariseau. He wants me . . . us to have dinner with him after the show tomorrow."

Vivian nodded, gazing at her sister curiously, until Dorothy colored and asked, "What're you staring at? Anything wrong with that?"

"No, nothing wrong!" Vivian said quietly.

"After all, we've got to make the publicity convincing—we must be seen in public together . . ."

"That's right!" Vivian replied even more quietly.

There was a feeling of tension between them, unspoken, intangible, and yet none the less real.

It was the first time they had failed in understanding, and felt as distant, as most human beings are from each other.

That night as they lay in bed, with the large neon sign across the street casting blue gleams through the open window of their suite, they lay awake, pretending to each other that they were asleep.

Vivian had a nameless feeling of foreboding she could not quite understand. The idea of a man like Andre Pariseau entering their lives, even for a publicity stunt, somehow revolted her. And Dorothy was acting strangely. No one knew better than she just how impressionable Dorothy could be. She shuddered. "You're a fool, Vivian," she told herself, and tried to banish from her mind the unwelcome thoughts. But the recollection of what Hinkley had told them later that afternoon, that Pariseau would have to be paid a hundred dollars a week for his role, came into her mind. If the papers found it out! Wasn't Ted walking into his own trap? A man like Pariseau would stop at nothing—not even blackmail!

But Dorothy on her own side of the bed was thinking far different thoughts. The blue glow from the neon sign penetrating through the open balcony window seemed to have an unearthly magic. She heard the sweet wailing of the music rising from the cocktail lounge below, and the flurries of laughter and distant voices as if she had entered an enchanted world. She felt as detached as if she were someone else—that someone else of her secret thoughts—and through it all, she could hear Andre's deep, rich voice, whispering to her, as she relived over and over the telephone conversation. Lying there on her back, her body relaxed and cool, feeling the caress of the sheets on her nude body, she let her hand slide over her breast, down her molded belly and thighs. She closed her eyes, but sleep was far away.

She thought of their childhood in Texas, in the long somnolent afternoons in San Antonio, and remembered Fiesta time, when the magnolias riotous with white blossoms raised white, waxy cups against a blue sky. She saw the blue dusk settling over the Alamo, and the young couples walking and laughing towards the Plaza in the springtime. She saw the girls and boys again, walking arm and arm, their faces glowing with a kind of excitement she had never known . . .

She sighed softly and smiled in the warm darkness, but her eyes were wet. There had been so much to learn, dear God, and so much one had to remember to forget!

She felt Vivian's arm slide under her neck, then the soft touch of Vivian's other hand brushing her cheek, and she turned impulsively and kissed her sister, without knowing why.

Below, in the garish cocktail lounge of their hotel, a high soprano voice continued to wail of unrequited love, while men and women who used that word to cover a multitude of sins played their little games for the night.

Three

When Dorothy and Vivian left their dressing room the following night after the last performance, and walked to the stage, the house was empty; the orchestra pit, dark and forlorn, yawned below in the semi-darkness. But the stage itself was filled with people. There were several men with cameras, and Hinkley was waiting for them in a new grey suit, painfully groomed. Mabel was standing by his side, dressed in her best black satin dress. And, leaning against a flat which had been left on stage, on which satyrs and nymphs frolicked in a mythological forest, Andre Pariseau was talking nonchalantly to reporters.

The moment they stepped on the stage, bedlam broke loose. They found themselves surrounded by reporters and photographers all talking at once; Andre took Dorothy's hand in his own possessively, and Hinkley was striving to be heard above the Babel of voices. Finally, some semblance of order was achieved, and they were posed against a part of the Grecian garden—the part without the nymphs and satyrs. Andre, looking very handsome and romantic, drew Dorothy's arm through his own, and smiled down at her in a perfect imitation of tenderness.

One of the photographers, from a leading daily, sighted through his camera and shouted, "A little more to the left, Miss Hamilton . . . and raise your chin—a trifle, just a trifle!" The bulb exploded in a burst of light. Another photographer, mimicking the first, said, "Just a trifle! Hell, what we want is a great big smile . . . You're very happy, aren't you, Miss Dorothy?" Dorothy's smile seemed to shatter in the coruscations of light as the bulb flashed. A member of one of the acts on the same bill wandered on stage, his shirttail out, buckling his belt, as he inquired, "What's going on here? What's this all about?"

Hinkley managed to grab him and motion for him to get back. "They're taking pitchers, can't you see? Dorothy's engaged to Pariseau . . . they're getting married!" The fat performer's mouth opened and his jaw hung slack. The bulbs kept popping as more and more pictures were taken. A lady reporter managed to ask a multitude of questions, without bothering to listen to the answers, most of which she had already resolved for her column. They were almost finished when a man came hurtling up the steps out of breath and slightly disheveled. He had an engaging grin as he blurted, "I'm from the *Times* . . . Am I late? That darned fire—just when I wanted to . . ." All the while he was trying to recover his breath and adjust the camera he was carrying at the same time. Finally he was ready, sighted and motioned for Andre to move nearer to Dorothy.

"Ready? Now, kiss your fiancée, Mr. Pariseau . . ."

As Andre leaned over and kissed Dorothy, the photographer shouted, "Still!" and again the brilliance of a flashing bulb bathed the stage in its ghastly glare.

After that, the reporters had a field day. The girls looked bewildered, despite their being used to newspapermen and their ways. The stage vibrated with excitement, and the word love was bandied about as if it were a commodity.

Finally Mabel could stand it no longer. "People talk too much!" She glared at Hinkley. "The girls're tired. How long are they gonna stand there and be psychoanalyzed, eh?"

"How should I know?" Hinkley shrugged eloquently.

"Well, if you don't, I do!" And with that, she resolutely barged into the encircling representatives of the fourth estate as if she were scattering ten-pins. She took Vivian's arm and began to steer the girls to their dressing room. The reporters followed, asking questions, wheedling, cajoling, until they got to their dressing room, where Mabel calmly closed the door in their faces. Slowly, they began to disperse. But one bright youngster wasn't quite through. Deliberately he banged on the door until Mabel, her nerves taut, was forced to open it. Before the reporter could say a word, Mabel said in a voice like a knife, "Lissen punk, you got your pint of blood. Now scram—and I mean scram, before I give ya a bath with the toilet water, and it ain't perfumed!" Her eyes blazed. She looked about ready to rend with tooth and claw. The young reporter retreated, grinning. He flung at her from a safe distance.

"You were a strip-tease queen, weren't you?"

"One more crack and I'll strip you . . . louse!" She closed the door with a bang.

The next morning Hinkley barged into their suite in such high spirits that even Mabel's barbs failed to daunt him. He carried a bundle of newspapers whose screaming headlines were a variation on the same theme, aptly headlined by the *Morning Times* in bold type reading:

Siamese Twin to Marry Vaudevillian

Beneath there was a two-column cut of Dorothy and Andre, with part of Vivian's face in the shot. Pariseau was bending down as he kissed Dorothy. Next to the cut, a two-column spread proclaimed:

> Dorothy Hamilton, blond and winsome half of the world-famous Siamese Twins, announced her forthcoming marriage to Andre Pariseau, vaudeville performer, whose daring sharp-shooting act is featured as Andre and Renee. Both the Hamilton Sisters and Andre Pariseau are currently appearing at the local Bijou theatre. The sensational announcement is expected to arouse interest throughout the world.

There was a great deal more, and in great detail. Ted Hinkley was flushed with excitement. The girls had never seen him like that before.

"See . . . see!" He kept exclaiming. "I told you!" "Don't you realize what this publicity means? Girls, the Bijou won't be able to hold 'em!"

They spread the papers on the floor, while Mabel made comments to herself. The reviewers of the theatre-world suddenly had remembered the Hamilton Sisters existed, and had resurrected all their clichés upon orders from their editors. The reporters had pulled out all their stops—one lady columnist who by-lined herself "Madame Cupid" had titled her interview: "Virgin Love!" And had taken it from there in a rapturous and somewhat torrid column in which the least she said was that "Dorothy was like a madonna!"

Dorothy was silent, slightly dazed, her soft blue eyes on the cut of Andre kissing her, as if she were reliving that, for her, memorable moment.

"I hope you know what you're doing, Ted!" Vivian remarked quietly.

"Why, whassa matter Viv? You don't seem enthusiastic!" Hinkley was genuinely surprised.

"I don't trust him," Vivian answered coldly. "That man's capable of anything. I hope you're not falling into a trap!" She turned away as Dorothy looked at her reproachfully.

"I'm paying him a hundred a week. If he gets out of line, his salary stops—that's all!" Hinkley said briefly.

"He might tell the newspapers this was just a publicity stunt," Vivian pointed out.

"He wouldn't dare!" Hinkley exclaimed. "He's got no proof. He'd only be making himself out a liar, and that guy's all vanity . . ."

"All vanity!" Mabel sniffed. "He's more'n that . . . every time I see him, he's got a new partner in his act—he'd be sensational at stud!"

"Mabel!" Vivian exclaimed, shocked. Hinkley only grinned and rolled the cigar in his mouth, pretending to be immersed in the newspaper headlines.

"Sorry girls! Sometimes I forget," Mabel said unabashed. "I guess it's Minsky's training!"

Dorothy raised her head; her cheeks were flushed and her blue gaze bright with anger. "What right have all of you to say such things about Andre? He's not here to defend himself . . . it's . . . it's horrible!" She started to get up from the settee upon which she and Vivian had been sitting and Vivian was forced to rise too.

"Dotty! What's wrong with you?" Vivian was pale. It seemed to her as if they had fallen into a torrent that was carrying them willy nilly into a whirlpool. Dorothy had never acted like this before. They had always shared their lives without quarreling. There had been many rules the girls had been forced to follow, but they learned that most of their problems could be settled amiably. Sleeping, eating, sharing their lives even to their most intimate moments, there had been no adjustment in their unique relationship which they had not been able to make.

But now Andre Pariseau had risen like a spectre between them!

"Please, dear . . . sit down!" Dorothy obeyed her sister's request, but there was a strange expression of rebellion on her usually candid features.

There was a loud knocking at the door, and Mabel went to open it. Framed in the doorway were the other performers on the same bill at the Bijou. The DiSantos and Margo; the Benedettes; the members of an acrobatic team they scarcely knew . . . They kept coming in, a gay, noisy group bringing flowers and boxes of candy and endless congratulations.[9]

Hinkley was beaming all over the place, as if it weren't just a publicity stunt to whet the jaded appetites of the public, as if a romance had really and truly blossomed in the arid soil of an incredible situation. And when more newspapermen from other cities and towns began to arrive, begging for interviews, demanding more pictures, his elation grew in direct ratio to the confusion and noise. The flash bulbs popped. A crowd had begun to gather in front of the hotel, and the manager called up wanting to know what to do about people in the asking for their suite number.

Hinkley answered. "Only the press . . . nobody but the press," he said importantly.

The Gypsy Dancers had brought a basket of Spanish wines, and the merry rattling of castanets was heard presently amid Oles and Bravos of

---

9. The film *Chained for Life* features a group of vaudeville performers including Paul Gordon, a trick bicyclist, and Whitey Roberts, a juggling cook, entertainers whose stock performances occur throughout the film. Tod Browning's *Freaks*, in which Daisy and Violet would also appear, similarly utilizes moments of freak performance by figures like Johnny Eck, "The Half Boy."

the "Flamenco" dance, accompanied by the nostalgic music of Spanish guitars and *Bandurrias*.[10] One of the dancers began to sing a love ballad in a husky contralto voice, dripping with emotion:

> The moon is weeping silver tears,
> Over the lonely promenade—
> And under the balconies flaming with roses,
> Are heard the notes of a serenade . . .

> Es uns cancion vie ja y olvidada,
> Llena de penal y de sollozos.
> Que exalta los celos y las punáladas,
> Y las vie jas rejas do los calabozos![11]

The girls sat on the settee in the midst of the tumult and the laughter, with the flash bulbs making a thunderstorm of bluish lightning, and the crowd swirling and eddying about them. As usual, Mabel stood guard, standing at their side, fending off reporters and interviewers—and now and then glaring at Hinkley who swam through the extraordinary confusion in a sort of wordless ecstasy.

One of the reporters was insistent, addressing Vivian and Dorothy, "How will your public react to this announcement, girls?" Then to Vivian, "What's your reaction to your sister's marriage?"

The girls glanced at each other not knowing what to say. Vivian looked at Mabel pleadingly.

"The public," Mabel intervened, "is unpredictable—one day it's love and kisses, and the next day, cat-calls and tomatoes! I know! Maybe this love affair will make the public take the girls to its heart—though personally, I've often wondered if the public has any . . ."

"Don't, don't write it like that!" Hinkley exclaimed apprehensively with a glare at Mabel. "What she means is the public's got a big heart, and Dorothy's romance and forthcoming marriage will touch them deeply!"

---

10. A Spanish stringed instrument.

11. The Spanish is obviously in error here; nevertheless, the text translates roughly as follows:

> It is an old and forgotten song,
> Full of pain and sorrow.
> That sings of jealousy and stabbing,
> And the old bars of prisons.

The song obviously foreshadows what will become of Andre, Vivian, and Dorothy.

"Yea," Mabel nodded, her expression bland for the kill. "We all hope to touch them . . . at the box office!"

The reporter laughed. He was an experienced man, and hoped for a by-line out of this interview. "I understand," he smiled. "You hope to touch those heartstrings of the public with the tenderness, the courage and daring of this supreme bid for that mainspring of the universe—Love!" He gave Mabel a derisive smile with a world of meaning in it, as he turned.

"Wow!" Mabel exclaimed with fervor. "I thought the mainspring of the universe had a dollar sign on it!"

"You're just shallow, that's what; you just ain't sympathetic!" Hinkley said disgustedly and turned away.

"Why, the old goat!" Mabel murmured to herself, as she stared at Hinkley's retreating figure. One of the guests approached with two glasses of wine and offered them to Dorothy and Vivian.

Another one came with a platter heaped with slices of hard Spanish mountain ham; anchovies in oil from Italy; hard-baked Sicilian bread slices, and olives big as plums. There was jack cheese, and small torts with pickled meat inside. The man held the platter with both hands so that the girls and Mabel could take their choice. They made a sandwich apiece, and munched on the olives.

It was all confused and impromptu, and noisy, but there was a genuine warmth, a camaraderie, an easy joy and laughter that lifted it out of the realm of the ordinary. They were show people. They had come to celebrate something which was an intimate part of their lives, like debts, and disappointments, and all the old familiar despairs. And in their simple spontaneity, they managed to make a huge success of the unplanned party.

Mackenzie, the manager of the Bijou, came in to offer his congratulations, tongue-in-cheek, but he knew it was a required gesture. So far the press had gone along in a magnificent fashion, but the least suspicion that it was merely a publicity stunt would immediately turn it against them. He found himself surrounded by reporters.

And finally, dressed in a pale tan gabardine suit that set off his splendid shoulders, Andre arrived. He was one of those men who have the knack of flaunting their sex like a beacon, and the [pantherish?] grace of his walk, the long, muscular thighs rippling under the thin material of his trousers, added to the effect.

As he ploughed gently but determinedly through the cluster of reporters, photographers and well-wishers, he smiled warmly, crinkling the long hazel eyes which at times were almost golden and at others a faint greenish hue, depending on his mood. He walked over to the girls and took Dorothy's hand in his with a gentleness, a tenderness that drew a gasp from one of the Spanish dancers, the tawny one with the large dark eyes, who had ceased swirling and stamping upon his entrance. She sighed enviously, turning to her companion. "If he touched me like that," she said huskily, "I'd melt like a candle!"

Some one brought Andre a chair, and he sat next to Dorothy, drawing her to him, so she could feel the line of his arm and the warm pressure of his shoulder, as he held her hand in his. He spoke to her low, with an intimate note in his voice, which only she could hear, so that he managed to isolate her from the swirling crowd and the noise and the music, leaving them alone as if no one else were present.

"Happy?" His voice caressed her, as did his eyes.

Dorothy nodded wordlessly.

"I'm glad. Dorothy . . . Dorothea . . ." He slid his arm under her neck so that her head rested on his shoulder, and ignored the outraged glance Vivian gave him. "So you don't think I'm as bad as people say I am?"

"Andre, I don't listen to people . . . I never judge."

"I know people will come and tell you things . . . it's their way. But just so you don't think I'm as bad as they say . . ."

"Andre, why do you keep talking about it? I always thought . . . well of you!"

"I'm glad. Ever since I first met you . . . I . . . well, I always hoped you might like me! I wish I could show you the real me—I mean sincerely, in my heart. I'm a lonely man . . . I don't know why. I wish I knew!" He turned so his face was close to her, and she could feel his warm breath on her cheek. "I wish you could know me as I really am!"

"It's important to you, Andre?" Dorothy's heart was in her eyes. His mouth came closer to hers, as he whispered, "More than anything in the world!"

A flash bulb popped, and she drew back. He tried again to recapture the moment and the mood, and bent towards her. "I've never lived the life I would have liked. Even in my work danger follows me—I must use live bullets in the cigarette act, and when I play the organ by firing bullets from my rifles . . . Funny, what I really want is peace and someone . . . someone . . ."

"Oh, Mr. Pariseau, tell me when you first fell in love!" gushed a female interviewer dressed in baby blue, with a flight of birds in her large floppy, pink hat. She clasped her hands as if thrilled to the marrow. A very ugly expression flashed in Andre's eyes, then it was gone.

Andre smiled graciously, then he bent down and kissed Dorothy's hand languorously. When he raised his head, he said softly, "I guess I have always been in love . . . the only difference is that now I've found my dream girl!"

"At a hundred a week!" Mabel murmured to herself.

After that, the enchanted island they had created out of their words and their thoughts, and the intimate isolation Andre had brought about with his magic, were gone, and the crowd engulfed them again.

Nothing would do but that the girls sing for them. They wanted to hear them, to take them to their hearts. And Vivian, whose throat was constricted with anguish, could only think inwardly, "Dear God!" Finally Dorothy sang alone, on Vivian's plea her throat hurt and had to save what voice she had left for that evening's performance.

Dorothy's Lyric Soprano soared faultlessly, as she sang "Un Bel Di Vedremo," from *Madame Butterfly*.[12] She sang it with all her heart, with her eyes lingering on Andre's hazel eyes, as if within them, she saw a vision of a bliss, a happiness she had never known before.

When she finished, flowers rained at her feet, and she found that her eyes were wet.

Four

It has been a fantastic week. The crowds seemed endless. While previously a certain percentage of the seats at the Bijou had been empty, now even the SRO sign had to be removed, and disappointed customers turned away. Packed houses became a commonplace. And in the elation

---

12. "Un bel de vidremo" or "One fine day we shall see," is the aria sung by the lead character in *Madame Butterfly* in which she imagines the day when her absent American husband will return to her. Unbeknownst to her, although suspected by her friends and acquaintances, Lieutenant B. F. Pinkerton has indeed forsaken his Japanese wife and married an American woman. At the end of the opera when Madame Butterfly realizes the truth, she kills herself. The opera was composed by Giacomo Puccini and first performed in 1904; today, it remains one of the most popular operas performed in the United States.

of their incredible success, Vivian lost some of her fears. She tried to convince herself, with a measure of success, that Dorothy wasn't really serious. That it was merely a passing reaction to a new experience in her life—perhaps a certain ego satisfaction which she had never had before. But that it would end, as it must. Anything else was unthinkable. And yet, deep in her subconscious the fear persisted—was it a fear? Perhaps a premonition of disaster which she strove to banish from her mind.

Only Mabel, saturnine and vinegarish as ever, could help her. Hinkley was riding a rose-colored cloud in which he dreamt of staggering percentages, and envisioned filling a theatre the size of the Hippodrome.[13] She tried to shrug off the unwelcome thoughts as she and Dorothy creamed their faces to remove the stage make-up, then began to get dressed, now that the last evening performance was over.

As they were almost finished, putting on the last touches to their street make-up, Mabel came in carrying their wraps, a green one for Dorothy, who was dressed in sapphire blue chiffon, and a black one for Vivian, who was all in white. Dorothy glanced at the wrap dubiously.

"No . . . I don't think I'll wear this one after all . . . Get my white fur-jacket, Mabel."

"What is this, a quick change act?" Mabel asked of the world in general and Dorothy in particular. "This is the fourth time I've had to go back to the wardrobe! Make up your mind!"

Dorothy scarcely paid attention as Mabel flounced out indignantly. She turned back to the mirror, touching up her hair here and there, turning her head to see her face from various angles, and using such care and artistry to apply the final touches to her make-up that Vivian could not help but look at her wonderingly.

"I think I'll go shopping tomorrow," Dorothy said absently. "I haven't a thing to wear!"

"Really! But Dotty . . . this is only the first time you've worn that dress!" Vivian pointed out. She eyed the expensive sapphire chiffon creation—it had cost a great deal, and the sapphires around Dorothy's throat, even more.

13. The Hippodrome Theatre in New York City housed performances from 1905 to 1939; at the time of its existence, it was the largest and most cutting-edge theatre of its time. Seating over 5,000 people, the stage could hold up to 1,000 performers at a time and full circuses were often staged there. A state-of-the-art theater, it also contained an 8,000-gallon water tank that could be raised and lowered by hydraulic lift for performances.

"You forget, Viv, I'm engaged," Dorothy smiled blithely. "I can't possibly be seen in . . . just anything!"

Vivian's mild surprise slowly turned into shocked amazement as the implications of her sister's words began to dawn on her. "Dotty," she said quietly, "this thing's getting to the point where it has to be faced. You're not taking your publicity seriously? I hope you're not falling for that sharp-shooter!"

Dorothy frowned impatiently. "Well, what if I do like him? He's shown me what living really means!"

"Fine! May I remind you it's costing us a hundred a week to keep you engaged?" "Oh, Viv," Dorothy answered wistfully, "it wasn't my idea in the first place. And anyway, why count the cost where the heart is involved!"

Vivian's face blanched, and she said slowly, "Dotty! You're in love with him!" She was very close to tears. All she had feared had come to pass.

"Yes . . . and he's in love with me!" Dorothy said very quietly indeed.

"But, Dotty, you . . . you don't know what you're saying. . . . you can't buy happiness, my dear!"

"Maybe you can't . . . if you're trading for even money, Viv. But I can afford to be short-changed . . . Don't forget, I'm thirty-five!"

The lipstick Vivian had been using clattered down on the dressing table and lay forgotten in the ensuing silence. Mabel returned with the white fur-jacket and stood waiting for them.

"Hurry up, Viv, we have a date!" Dorothy said with an attempt at gaiety, and she made a motion so that Vivian turned from the dressing table with her. "*You* have a date . . . ," Vivian said somberly.

"If I have a date, you have one too, my dear . . ."

"Yes," Vivian nodded, "with Hinkley!"

Mabel helped them with their wraps, her face a study in disapproval, but for once, she had nothing to say.

Dorothy was spectacular in sapphire chiffon and white luxurious furs when, with her arm around Vivian's waist, she entered their living room, and smiled at Andre, who rose from the settee. His black hair, she noted, had deep blue gleams—like her gown, and his eyes were golden as if the sunlight had concentrated in their depths. When he took her arm, he whispered a compliment in Dorothy's ear, and she could smell his masculine scent, mixed with the faint odor of tobacco and fainter still, cologne.

Outside, in front of their hotel, he helped them into the front seat of the car, as black and glistening as his hair, then went around to get in at the wheel. Vivian was silent, wondering where he had managed to get the car, and the expensive flannel dinner jacket he was wearing—a hundred a week was surely not enough . . .

And Dorothy was thinking, it was real, she wasn't dreaming. Pressed close to him as he drove to the Fireside Cafe, she could feel the hard muscled line of his body, all of it, down to her thigh, and feel the virility pulsing next to the warm softness of her own body, now suddenly so vibrantly alive!

When they arrived at the Fireside Cafe, the table had already been arranged for—the large one in front of the mammoth fireplace from which the famous cafe derived its name. It was pleasant in that corner, with the darting flames adding art to Dorothy's chiffon gown and the blue sapphires at her throat, while a strolling Gypsy guitarist played languorous music to accompany her songs. In the subdued light, her golden hair seemed flawless, as was the nacre of her skin. They sat so that they could be comfortable at the curving table, with Andre a little behind and to the side of Dorothy.

All eyes in the cafe had turned to them, and the whispered conversations blistered the silence like summer rain on placid waters.

They ordered "*Coq au champignon,*"[14] and a sparkling burgundy that shone like a shower of rubies as it bubbled to the glasses' rim. It was all unmarred and flawless, sitting there next to each other in the dim light, talking in the barest whispers, eating together. It exhilarated her so that she forgot her shyness, and something of wit and sparkle flowed into her answers, matching his, so that it was better than the food and the atmosphere—better even than the wine, and more exhilarating.

Vivian strove to hear what her sister and Andre were saying, but for all the success she had, they might as well have been speaking in another language.

Quite suddenly, the conversation changed pace between them. A serious note intruded, as Dorothy said, as if thinking aloud, "I can't quite believe it, Andre!"

"Why not?"

"This . . . this couldn't happen to me!"

---

14. Chicken cooked with mushrooms.

"With all the cities of the world you've seen? With all your fame, Dotty? You're a very great celebrity!"

"Nothing . . . nothing like this, Andre!"

"I'm the one who doesn't believe . . . after my years of loneliness, of hunger for some one to love! . . ."

"Have you ever been in love, Andre?"

He sighed. "Not until now . . ."

"Neither have I," Dorothy said quite truthfully. Then, "When I was a little girl, I used to dream dreams . . . But then . . . I guess I gave them up!"

"You gave up too soon," he smiled at her, and his smile was an adventure.

Vivian could stand it no longer. It seemed to her she had been sitting there for an eternity, as effectively isolated as if she had been on another planet, or they were.

"Well . . . Hinkley certainly's no fool," she said to divert the conversation. "His idea has really worked!"

"We're certainly packing them in," Andre agreed smugly.

"Who is *we?*" Vivian inquired icily.

"Why . . . Dorothy and I . . . and you too, of course!" Andre smiled blandly at Vivian.

"Where do you come in?" It seemed to Vivian that the man's effrontery was incredible.

"My dear, I am the groom!" He could be cruel.

"In this case, any man would do!" She could be cruel too, and at the moment she despised him.

"You forget," Andre said silkily, aware of her feelings, "that not every man has my charm—and that's what brings them in!"

"How dare you!" Vivian exclaimed, outraged, and she started to rise. But Dorothy held her.

"Viv, please!" Dorothy pleaded.

At that moment Ted Hinkley came dashing in, he ran down the marble stairs that led to the dining area, and came up to their table out of breath and bubbling with excitement. "Girls, it's unbelievable!" He fumbled in his coat pocket and took out three envelopes, which he brandished as he stood before the others. "Look! I just balanced the receipts!" He placed an envelope before Vivian, and another before Dorothy; on the face of each envelope was written, $1,542.73.

Andre, leaning over, stared at the figures. "Not bad at all!" he said, obviously impressed.

"Imagine what we woulda made if we'd packed in the crowds we turned away!" Hinkley bubbled. "It's terrific . . . colossal, girls!" Then he turned to Andre. "And, I'm raising your salary fifty percent, Andre!" He placed before him another envelope on which was written $150.00, and stood beaming as Andre picked it up.

Andre nodded in lieu of thanks, and Hinkley picked up a chair and sat next to Vivian, taking out of his pocket a box office list, which he started to check aloud, showing Vivian the various figures.

"So, you have separate payrolls?" Andre smiled at Dorothy, his eyes straying to the amount shown on the face of the envelope on the table.

"Did you really think that we are one?" Dorothy said gently, as she placed the envelope in her bag. "We have separate payrolls, separate accounts, and we have always led separate lives!"

Vivian heard her, dividing her attention between what Hinkley was showing her and her sister's conversation with Andre. She lowered her head in chagrin—it was the one thing she didn't want Andre to know. At her side, Hinkley was droning, " . . . And look at this, this was Monday, mind you! But wait . . . look, Tuesday, almost double! Ain't it terrific? And Saturday, we broke all records! If we'd only had Soldiers Field!"[15] Vivian nodded mechanically, but with every ounce of awareness, she was trying to hear what was going on between Dorothy and Andre.

Aware of the situation, Andre wrote on a corner of his napkin, "I love you!" so that Dorothy could see it, but no one else.

To Dorothy it seemed as if a great harmonic chord had welled up within her and became a symphony of all her forgotten dreams, which had now flowered into a great, unimaginable happiness. She smiled mistily at him, through a golden mist of her own, and pressed his hand convulsively in the simplest of caresses—yet it carried all the adoration in her heart.

Andre continued to write, "Will you marry me, my darling!"

This time she nodded wordlessly and closed her eyes, bright with the gathering tears. Andre bent over and kissed the golden-bright strand at the nape of her neck, her cheek, and finally her eyes, then he whispered wistfully in her ear so that none but Dorothy could hear.

"I wish I weren't so poor, so I could place on your finger the purest gem I can find . . ."

15. A stadium in Chicago that in 1954 held its record-breaking crowd of over 260,000 people. It initially seated almost 74,000.

Dorothy turned as far as the birth-bond would allow her and surreptitiously opened her handbag, took out the envelope and, extracting
all but a one-hundred dollar bill, turned the rest over to Andre, who
pocketed it swiftly and then kissed her openly on the cheek near the curve
of her lips. At that moment Vivian, desperate with anxiety, leaned forward to see their faces and saw Andre kissing Dorothy.

"If this is for publicity," she remarked, her voice dripping ice, "your
timing is off . . . I don't see any photographers around!"

"Vivian!" Dorothy interrupted in a voice filled with happiness.
"Andre has just proposed!"

"At the same price?" Vivian inquired with a bitterness which was an
index to her hurt. "Or do we get a discount, now that he may be in the
family?"

"Oh, no!" Andre said blandly, masking with a perfect smile the hot
rage within. "It'll cost more!"

"What!" Vivian was outraged.

"Didn't you hear Hinkley say he raised my salary fifty percent?"

They faced each other across the table, deadly enemies, each one
aware of the steel of the opponent, neither underestimating the
adversary.

Vivian turned to her sister, her face tragic. "Dorothy, you're not . . .
you can't be serious!" She was unprepared for the absolute conviction in
her sister's voice, as Dorothy said, "Oh, yes . . . we are getting married!"

Hinkley, who had been listening dazedly to this interchange, suddenly realized that it was real, that his stunt designed to increase attendance at the Bijou had ceased to be publicity and had become a reality. It
was more than he had dared expect, and his eternal battle between love
of the girls and love of money was suddenly won by the latter. He rose
trembling, the words bubbling up into his throat as he pawed the air for
an instant before he shouted:

"Hurrah! Congratulations! This is the greatest thing that coulda
happened! . . . Waiter," he shouted, "Waiter . . . champagne . . . a bottle
of Mums . . ."[16] Seeing no waiter near he left the table and scuttled
across the floor towards the stairway where the Maître D' was seating
newly arrived guests, and seeing a girl descending the marble stairs, he
bellowed exuberantly, "They're getting married!" Then he stopped

16. G. H. Mumm's: renowned French champagne.

short, as he realized the girl was Renee. The girl gazed with a world of grief in the direction of Dorothy and Andre, then she turned and re-traced her steps.

The solicitous Maître D' came over to Hinkley and took the order himself. "Immediately, sir . . . would you like a magnum?" But Hinkley's enthusiasm had cooled at the sight of Renee's tragic face. And besides, a magnum was too expensive. He shook his head and returned to the table. In his mind, he was already calculating the effect Dorothy's wedding to Andre would have on the morbid curiosity of the public. "If this lasts long enough," he thought aloud, "we . . . we can retire in two years!"

Somewhere in the dimly lighted Cafe, the Gypsy singer was playing a Spanish song in which the Moorish soul wept through a Spanish theme.

At the table, Vivian's hand trembled as she took the cigarette from her lips and ground it in the tray. Within, she wept too, but without tears.

Five

That night, with the awareness of undreamable success within his grasp, Andre was in a benign mood as he slowly unbuttoned his shirt, and lis-tened tolerantly to Renee, in their hotel room across from the suite oc-cupied by the Hamilton sisters.

Renee was far from sharing Andre's feelings. Her face stormy, she flung the newspaper she had been reading across the room; it landed face up at his feet. There was a cut of Dorothy and him, and the col-umns of publicity that had become commonplace. He bent down and picked up the newspaper, gazed at the photograph and then at Renee.

"Nice technique!" Renee flung sarcastically at Andre.

"My dear," Andre said smiling, "the true artist gives his all at every performance!" He held up the paper so that Renee could see the cut wherein he was kissing Dorothy. "This profile of me isn't bad at all!"

"Arrh! While you're making headlines, I'm getting the brush-off! The only time I see you now, since this thing started, is on the stage!" Renee blazed at him.

"You are fortunate . . . think of how many are turned away at the box office!"

"Tell it to Mackenzie." Renee was almost beside herself. "He might appreciate the big attraction!" She turned away from him, her eyes smarting with tears of rage and humiliation, her small fists clenching and unclenching. Andre gazed at her for a moment with a self-assured smile, then he again turned to the newspaper to admire the photo.

"He does," Andre said good-humoredly. "Haven't you seen our new billing? Andre and Renee . . . in the second spot!"

Renee turned and faced him. "With my name in fine print! But it's the Hamilton Sisters who're getting the percentage!"

"Percentages have a habit of seeking their own level. That, my dear, is the basic law of supply and demand!"

"What are you going to do, hypnotize her?" Renee inquired ironically.

"Charm is the word, Renee . . . Charm!" He arched his chest and flexed his biceps. "And as you can see from this photo, my subject is quite susceptible!"

Renee gazed at him in a white fury, goaded almost beyond endurance. "What am I supposed to do while you're teaching her economics—join a lonely hearts club?"

"I don't think you're eligible for membership . . . yet!" He added with implied threat. "I'm getting our percentage," he said, taking the roll of bills from his pocket and holding it up for Renee to see. "Now, be a good girl and leave me alone for a while . . ."

Renee gazed at him, quickly, obviously frightened by his implication, then at the roll of bills. Wordlessly, she walked out into the hallway, leaving Andre alone. He started taking off his shirt leisurely, and stripped to the waist he walked over to the open window, and gazed in the direction of Dorothy and Vivian's suite. He saw the Hamilton sisters in their pajamas also at their window, and Dorothy gazed at his magnificent torso, then smiled.

Vivian took one look and quickly shut the window, then pulled down the shade. The sight of the man, apparently nude, sickened her.

Andre smiled quietly to himself. He had seen the wide-eyed wonder in Dorothy's startled gaze, the shy sweetness of her smile. And besides, the triumph he had achieved over the enmity and opposition of Vivian was meat and drink to his ego. For years he had hoped and strived for an opportunity that would make him a headliner, and in the frail loveliness of the Siamese Twin, he had found it.

He went into the clothes closet and took out a guitar, then he stretched out on the couch and dialed the Hamilton Sisters' number.

Dorothy answered, and he said simply in his rich baritone voice with a world of tenderness in it, "This is for you!" Then he began to strum the guitar, plucking deep, resonant chords, and sang an Italian love song into the receiver. Renee came in quietly and lay down at his feet, watching him sing, watching the way he looked at her, as he sang at her with a slow smile. As she listened, she melted slowly, as all her animosity, her jealousy and rage evaporated under his spell.

Andre finished, laid down the instrument and bent forward. He grabbed Renee in his arms and kissed her brutally, audibly. From the receiver hanging off its cradle, came the sleepy, far-away voice of Dorothy saying happily, "Good night, darling!"

It was a long time before Dorothy managed to fall asleep; when she did, it was with Andre's kiss burning on her lips, and the melody echoing in her ears. Suddenly it seemed to her as if she were awake. She started to turn over on her left side, then remembered she couldn't, but it was too late, her body obediently had turned over. As the realization smote her, she involuntarily sat up, and looked down at herself in amazement, then at her sister on her own side of the bed. *They were no longer joined.*

She flung back the covers and stood up trembling, a wild joy surging through her. Still unbelieving, she walked around the bed and stared down at Vivian peacefully asleep. It was incredible . . . She walked over to the great French windows and flung them open, and stepped out into a moonlit garden. Deliriously, she danced among the flowers and shrubs, and then over to a tree whose leaves were silvered by the bright moonlight. She looked down at herself, still in negligee, the filmy stuff swirling in the soft night breeze, and at her body, free and untrammeled. And when she looked up, she saw Andre walking towards her with his arms outstretched. She ran to him, wild with joy, and heard him say "I love you!" He held her for a moment, then kissed her and began to spin and whirl her in a waltz around the flowers and the shrubs in the enchanted garden, feeling his heart beat against hers, feeling the warmth of his cheek, and his strong arms around her.

Suddenly she found herself at the very brink of a yawning black abyss, and she cried, "Andre!" But he was gone. Again she cried before the darkness engulfed her, "Andre . . . Andre!"

She found herself sitting up in bed crying hysterically, while Vivian, pale and shaken, was asking, "Dotty! What is it, darling?"

Dorothy gazed wildly about the room, as if she could not realize where she was, as if the reality were less vivid than the dream. Then she burst into bitter tears and buried her face in the pillow.

"Honey . . . what is wrong?" Vivian's anguished voice rose above her sobs. But Dorothy couldn't answer, until Vivian put her arms around her, crying too. Then Dorothy said brokenly, "I had a dream . . . I dreamt that I was free! I . . . I can't go on!" And there, on the shoulder of the one being that loved her more than anything in the world, Dorothy poured out the tide of her long inarticulate despair.

"Darling, don't cry: Don't you think I know how you feel? . . . I've wanted love too!"

Through her sobs, Dorothy said brokenly, "All our lives we've had to bury every normal emotion . . . I'm not a machine. I'm a woman . . . I should have the right to live like one!"

"My dear, we can't have everything! We've always said we were like other people . . . yet different. From the moment we started to crawl, when the leg of a table came between us and we couldn't pass . . . we knew!"

"Yes," Dorothy said somberly, "I remember! But we decided that our physical bond would never be our cross!"

"It hasn't been . . . until now. We've had so many compensations . . . We've been successful, we've reached the very top in show business . . . and there isn't a thing we can't have, Dotty . . ."

"Except happiness! We've fooled ourselves, Viv, that in bringing joy and pleasure to others, we were making ourselves happy!"

"Darling," Vivian said soothingly, "I've never stood in your way . . ."

"No, but . . . always together—on dates, parties, night-clubs! Now I know the only way I can be happy is to be alone with the man I love! I want to be free!"

"Free!" Vivian was aghast, realizing Dorothy's intentions. "But we've always been together . . . and we'll be that way forever!"

"No, not forever!" Dorothy exclaimed vehemently. "There must be a way . . . We'll find someone who can help!" Suddenly she remembered, "Viv, remember . . . Doctor Thompson? If anyone can, he . . ."

"Separation!" Vivian's voice was shocked. "No! We've been prodded and examined like guinea pigs . . . We've been sold and exhibited and looked upon as . . . as . . ." She couldn't bring herself to say it. And suddenly she was crying her own bitter despair which she had borne in silence. "No! This is my life too . . . I have a right to live it!"

"Yes, you have the right," Dorothy agreed, feeling a universe of pain, "but what good is it? Nothing you do has any meaning without love!"

"But how much can love demand from us," Vivian protested. "Remember the two brothers . . . when one of them died and the other had to be separated—he lived only a few days . . . We wouldn't have a chance!"

"I don't care," Dorothy wailed. "I'd rather be dead than go on like this!"

"You really love him so much!"

And as Dorothy nodded wordlessly, Vivian continued. "All right . . . let's see Doctor Thompson!" And as Dorothy again burst into bitter tears, Vivian compassionately took her in her arms.

Vivian held her until the sobs had run their course, until an eternity of time later Dorothy's rhythmic breathing told her that her sister was asleep. Held her as she held the sentence of being alive, while inexorably this tragic love drove them to a decision which might mean being alive no longer.

Vivian lay there in the darkness, holding Dorothy tight in her arms which had become numb; she didn't feel the pinpricking as her arms went to sleep. No feeling possessed her now, no mind, no body, no emotion of hate or pride, only a growing awareness that they were about to be destroyed. Death possessed her. And in that moment of final crisis, Vivian knew! With a flash of intuitive penetration, she saw in Andre Pariseau all the evil of life, personified in one being. She had carried the knowledge within herself without really being aware. But now, stripped bare to her yet living heart in the expectation of a futile death, the knowledge became a profound conviction.

She had made her decision. She had agreed to separation for the sake of Dorothy's happiness. But she knew there could be no happiness. She knew this was a threshold of pain to which she would have to bring her own private response, revealing what life had planted strongest in her, to save her and Dorothy when everything else had been stripped away.

She had made her decision!

Six

Dr. Thompson's voice was professionally impersonal as he pointed with a pencil to the X-Ray plate held in a frame on a portable illuminator.

The plate clearly revealed the union of bone and cartilage, and the shadowy outline of muscular tissue.

" . . . But of course," he was saying, "there is no clinical history of a set of Siamese Twins having ever been operated on while both were alive!" He turned to a tall, angular woman, a noted psychiatrist who was quite familiar with the history of the Hamilton Sisters.

"What is your opinion, Dr. Eckhart?" There was a brief silence while the psychiatrist consulted a sheaf of notes unhurriedly.

"I believe," Dr. Eckhart said in a well-modulated voice, "these two girls cannot live apart. Although they have two distinctly independent minds, they have been conditioned since birth to live as an entity. The psychic aspects are immeasurable. Even if physically the operation had a chance of success, in my opinion, the psychic and emotional factors involved are such, as to preclude their separation."

A nurse secretary took down in short hand the psychiatrist's statement, then having finished, she looked up at Dr. Thompson inquiringly. The latter nodded and she rose, walked over to the windows and rolled up the shades, flooding the room with sunlight; then she flicked off the light in the illuminator and rolled it out of sight. Doctor Thompson seemed to be pondering. He gazed at the other physicians he had called in consultation and saw in their faces the regret of the necessary decision in the negative. He sighed.

"When I examined the girls many years ago," he said reflectively, "the mere mention of 'Doctor' was enough to upset them . . . A great emotional stress has brought them here—Dorothy's desire to marry." He smiled ruefully and sighed again. "This will not be easy!" He turned to the nurse who had been waiting unobtrusively in the back ground and said, "Miss Manning, will you please ask the girls to step in?"

They could hear the nurse saying from the doorway to the Hamilton Sisters, "The Doctor will see you now." She held the door open for the girls, then went out, closing the door behind her.

Dorothy and Vivian came in and gazed apprehensively at the various faces, but Doctor Thompson greeted them warmly and had them sit on a couch near the door, facing the specialists. But for all of Doctor Thompson's efforts to lighten the atmosphere, there was an awkward pause—a feeling of failure in the air that was unexplainable.

Doctor Thompson decided to take the plunge. He saw it was the only way. "Girls," he smiled, "my colleagues and I have discussed the various aspects of your . . . er request, at great length. We want you to know how deeply we admire your courage . . ." He paused regretfully. "But I'm afraid that . . . there is very little hope."

Dorothy tried to mask the profound dismay mirrored on her face . . . she had steeled herself against just such a verdict, but she was unable to keep the heartbreak off her voice as she asked, "Then, there's nothing you can do?" Her exquisite face was pale, and violet shadows rimmed her eyes.

Doctor Thompson wordlessly spread out his hands in a gesture of helplessness. What could he do? What could he say? A world of sympathy was in his eyes.

It was then that Doctor Eckhart, the psychiatrist, took over. She knew there were all the elements of shock and hysteria in the situation, and she acted.

"My dear," she began in the modulated tones which were calm and unhurried and instinct with power. "As a woman, I understand thoroughly. What is in your heart is so simple—such an inalienable part of your birthright. There is nothing to stop you from getting married. No reason even why you shouldn't have children! All human beings seek completion—and most of us find it in the conjugal bond . . . My advice to you is, get married!"

They left Dr. Thompson's office dazedly. The echoes of Dr. Eckhart's advice rang like gongs in Dorothy's mind, as she clutched at that hope . . . any hope!

But was there hope in what lay ahead? From the depths of her renunciation, Vivian realized that her sacrifice was not to be necessary after all, that *another* bond, which was their completion, could not be dissolved. A crisis was past, but she wondered in silence if the next one would not be a greater one still. Marriage! If Dorothy wed Andre, what would it do to their lives?

They emerged from the elevator and walked to the sidewalk awash with moonlight, while above them, enormous clouds of pearl moved restlessly towards the sea. But neither Dorothy nor Vivian were aware of all that blue sky, all that sparkling sunlight, immersed as they were in their own private darkness, the clashing tension of their opposite hopes. Vivian was like a blue, golden hinge as they turned the corner searching for a taxi, and she was the first one who spoke.

"I guess there is nothing left . . . it's your happiness . . . Go ahead, Dorothy. Get married!"

ф

The weeks that ensued were even more hectic than the preceding ones. It seemed as if the sole topic of conversation throughout the city was Dorothy's forthcoming wedding. Columnists had advanced from embellished announcements to the level of conjecture. It became evident that literally nothing in the lives of the Hamilton Sisters was to be held sacred. Factions sprang up—some were for and some were against the marriage. But pro or con, all were prodigal with reams of words which appeared daily in the front pages of newspapers, tabloids and gossip columns. Offers poured in from other theatres across the nation—from as far even as England and France. A famous French house wanted to build a review around them with lurid African music, and make them Goddesses of the jungle. A more staid London impresario offered to provide a groom for Vivian and have a double marriage on the grounds of a palace—he didn't specify which one.

And meanwhile, the Bijou overflowed nightly. Hinkley poured over the box office figures with the loving interest of a mother eagle guarding her nest.

Dorothy had retained attorney Price to obtain their wedding license, and had ordered a fabulous trousseau, but as the days became weeks, and the weeks receded into the past, she became uneasy. Lawyer Price evaded explanations, but it seemed difficulties were in the way of obtaining the marriage license which they had thought would have been a mere formality.

Finally in desperation, they sent Hinkley to Price's office, and on the impulse decided to go themselves. Just before the girls arrived, Hinkley put in his appearance, and was closeted with Price for nearly half an hour.

Dorothy and Vivian, escorted by Andre, arrived and were ushered into the lawyer's private office. They found Price pacing up and down, exclaiming, "This is unheard of! If anyone would have told me, I wouldn't have believed it!"

"We got it?" Dorothy asked without preliminaries.

Price turned to her and smiled ruefully, "My dear," he said regretfully, "we got it all right . . . in the neck! That's why I sent for you . . ." He walked behind his desk and picked up a sheaf of telegrams.

"Twenty seven different states have denied you the right to marriage! . . ."

"But why?" Dorothy asked, bewildered. "I don't understand!" She glanced at Andre; he immediately hid the start of a faint smile.

"I'm baffled myself," Price shrugged. "They have given no reasons!"

"Oh, they said it was bigamy!" Hinkley blurted out before he realized what he was saying, then seeing the glare in Price's eyes, he mumbled, "I'm sorry!"

"How dare they!" Andre exclaimed, feeling perfectly safe under the circumstances. "I'll sue them for damages!"

"For what?" Price asked coldly.

"The . . . the insinuation . . . Me, a bigamist!"

Dorothy, on the verge of tears, closed her eyes. It seemed to her as if the entire universe was against her bid for happiness.

Price felt his heart go out to her, and he was far from being the type of man given to sentimentality.

"Look, Dorothy," he said in the kindest tones he had ever used. "Where there is a will, there is a way . . . I'm going to send you to a friend of mine—maybe he can see a way out. His name is Doctor Birnham!"[17]

"Another Doctor!" Dorothy wailed, shrinking.

"He's not that kind of a Doctor," Price smiled as he shook his head negatively. "Here's his address." He wrote quickly on a pad, tore off the sheet of paper and handed it to Dorothy. Then he saw them to the door, patting Dorothy's shoulder and saying comfortingly, "If anyone can possibly effect a miracle, he can! Don't worry, my dear, it's going to be all right." Hinkley stayed behind.

When they were gone, Price wiped his forehead, then turned to Hinkley. "Ted, you're a heel! Why'n hell did you have to start this mess?"

Ted Hinkley spread out his hands in a gesture of helplessness. The cold cigar in his mouth tasted bitter, and he threw it in the ashtray. He pursed his lips.

"I dunno!" he said finally. "All my life I've wanted the girls to hit big time . . . Always I've wanted them to have a chance for security . . . and that takes dough. I thought maybe, this would do it. Now . . . I dunno!"

"Now it's backfired right in your face!" Price said grimly. "That guy Andre's dangerous. You know that! Can't you see he doesn't give a damn for Dorothy? Why did you have to pick a rat like that?"

17. I selected "Birnham" as the standardized spelling of this character's name; at times, the name is spelled "Birnam" but it first appears as "Birnham."

Hinkley shrugged his shoulders. "It was just a publicity stunt to start with . . . Who else do you think I coulda got for a ratty part like this? I never thought it would go this far . . ."

"Why didn't you stop it when you saw it was getting serious?" Price asked relentlessly.

Hinkley only hung his head. What could he say? In the excitement and enthusiasm of success and easy money, all things had seemed possible—even desirable. But now, he realized that the toy was by way of becoming the master.

"Well," Price said with finality, "Don't be surprised if after the marriage—provided Birnham gets her a license—Andre Pariseau takes over. You've handled the girls for years without a contract, haven't you? See where that leaves you?"

"They wouldn't stand for anything like that," Hinkley said heatedly. "They love me . . . they're like my own children! They wouldn't know what to do without me!"

"No . . . But Pariseau would! And remember, he'll have certain rights as Dorothy's husband!"

And in his heart, for the first time in his life Ted Hinkley felt the clutch of an icy dread.

"And don't forget," Price added relentlessly, "that the honeymoon'll scarcely be over, before he's drinking champagne at her expense with some fancy whore! Just like any other pimp!"

Hinkley did not want to hear any more. He knew it was too late for vain regrets. He could only hope that it would turn out all right, now that Dorothy's happiness was at stake. He was a weary old man when he rose to leave, and forgot to shake hands with lawyer Price.

Once downstairs, he gulped in the fresh air of the brilliant afternoon, but the sun was too strong, and the bawdy blare of a jukebox moaning that a girl had fallen and had been abandoned to her fate made him grimace.

He decided grimly that if Andre Pariseau wanted a battle, he would get a good one—even if it was to be his last one, Ted thought. He marshaled in his mind the thousand and one stratagems and tricks that had served him in the past. "If he ever gets out of line," he murmured to himself, "he'll know he's had it!"

He took a taxi to the hotel where the girls were staying, although he hated to have to face Vivian now. He had an idea of how she must feel. It was a gigantic jest of fate. Here they had achieved fame beyond their wildest dreams; money was pouring in, in a never-ending stream—and yet, there was no happiness for anyone . . . save Andre. When he arrived at the hotel, the girls were not home.

Seven

Doctor Birnham had been in the service of the Lord more years than he cared to remember, but the passage of time failed to bother him, since "service" was his philosophy of life. He had acquired a profound insight into human beings and the poor passions of their hearts—as if to compensate in a measure for the loss of his physical sight.

He was a towering man, spare of frame, whose wavy silver hair contrasted with his deep blue eyes which seemed to be forever gazing at a distant vision. When Price telephoned him and explained the problem of the Hamilton Sisters, he had been silent for a long time, then he returned to the garden where he spent the major portion of his time.

It was there that Martha, his housekeeper, found him when the girls arrived, and she ushered them to the corner where Doctor Birnham, on his hands and knees, was digging a hole in the earth with a trowel. Near him, a double oleander bush was in bloom. He did not look up when he heard their footsteps, but waited until he heard Martha say, "This is Doctor Birnham. . . . Doctor, the Hamilton Sisters to see you!"

"I am happy to know you," he said in his slow, soft voice. Then he raised his head and smiled at them, much as a saint would give a silent benediction.

"Doctor, we were referred to you by Mr. Price . . . ," Dorothy began uncertainly.

"Yes . . . I hope you don't mind if we chat while I plant this bush." He indicated another plant near him, its roots wrapped in sacking. "You'll find a couple of chairs under the tree." Then to Martha, who stood next to the visitors, "Martha, why don't you fix us some tea?"

"Yes, Doctor," Martha said and withdrew.

The girls looked at the two chairs under the tree, then at the bench near where they were standing, and Vivian said, "Thank you, Doctor, but we'll sit on the bench."

"That old bench is rather shaky," the Reverend smiled. "I should fix it sometime, but the garden seems to take up all of my leisure hours . . . Of course, Martha objects—says I spend too much time with my flowers, and not enough on my sermons, . . . I'm afraid she's right . . ."

As Doctor Birnham spoke, the girls glanced around them at the beautifully kept garden, now riotous with a variety of blossoming plants and bushes. Dorothy's eyes widened as she saw the double oleander bush next to the kneeling Dr. Birnham. Vivian, attracted by her absorption in the bush, stared at it also, and saw that it was a *twin* bush growing from one stem, obviously having bloomed from one bud.

" . . . Though I must say," Dr. Birnham continued, "the congregation doesn't seem to suffer for it . . ."

"They're twins . . ." Dorothy said as if thinking aloud, turning to Vivian.

"Eh? Oh, yes . . . Sometimes nature permits twins to blossom from one bud." Dr. Birnham pointed out.

"Permits?" Dorothy's question was tinged with bitterness. "You make it sound as if nature were granting a favor!"

"No, my dear . . ." Dr. Birnham smiled as he began to untie a string. "Nature does not grant favors . . . What she does is with purpose and meaning. Every living creature is a part of her plan."

Dorothy gazed at him as if she couldn't believe her ears. "What purpose could she have," she said, indicating the oleander bush, "in creating this, when every other living thing is an entity by itself!"

Dr. Birnham, still struggling with the knotted string, smiled placidly to himself again. "God's mysterious ways are not always easy to understand! With patience . . ." He stopped trying to untie the string, and chuckled somewhat exasperatedly, "But I'm about to lose mine. This string simply will not untie . . ." Vivian took the string, untied it and handed it back to him.

"Thank you, my children . . . I understand your bitterness . . . You must free yourselves from all belief in limitations . . ."

"But the barriers raised before us are very real," Vivian replied.

The Reverend rose, placed his arms on either side of the girls and told them earnestly: "Faith can overcome these. You have been forced to live together constantly, bound by spiritual and physical ties—yet, I'm sure you've worked out a way to live separate and private lives."

"Mentally we do," Dorothy said slowly. "But it's almost impossible to convince people of that."

"That's why we came to you," Vivian interposed.

"I want to get married, but the officials of twenty-seven states have refused me a license," Dorothy said bitterly. "They claim it would be bigamy!"

"Bigotry! . . ." Dr. Birnham's voice was calm and soothing. "There can be no problem of moral or social wrong where there is no intent of immorality." Then he added with conviction, "You shall marry the man of your choice! I'm certain that in God's eyes your marriage will be hallowed."

Martha's voice, calling from the house, told them tea was ready, and Dr. Birnham answered: "We're coming!" Then to the girls, "Will you lead the way to the house? I don't have my eyes with me . . . my dog is in the hospital . . . Now, don't worry, I know all about your problem . . . I'll see that you get a license! . . ."

There was infinite conviction in his voice as he took Vivian's arm and followed the girls into the house, where Martha had prepared an old-fashioned tea, with English muffins and home-made jam. Slowly under the benign influence of the Reverend, the girls began to relax, feeling the tension and the stress leaving them, in that atmosphere of peace and understanding.

No one would ever know what strings Doctor Birnham was forced to pull, what influence he had brought to bear. But despite the extraordinary circumstances of what was certainly not an ordinary wedding, he succeeded where others had failed, and in the end, he presented Dorothy and the skeptical Andre with a marriage license. There are tears of grief and tears of happiness—he devoutly hoped that the tears in Dorothy's eyes when she saw the official document would be her last. Inwardly he had a premonition that this tall, dark man with the startling hazel eyes, whose description had been read to him, was not quite what he seemed.

Dr. Birnham could not see him, but he had the gift of keening in which human vibrations, however subtle, can be felt. And Andre's vibrations seemed to him to leave much to be desired. However, he gave them his blessings, and promised to marry them at the appointed time at his church.

When they had gone, Dr. Birnham turned to his housekeeper Martha, and said thoughtfully, "there are many ordinary love affairs, my dear. But ordinary people do not risk everything for love!"

Returning to the garden, he touched the double oleander bush caressingly, then with a sigh, he went about his chores.

Eight

Near the dressing table with its array of greasepaints and cosmetics, where he could see himself in the mirror, sat Andre, with the light of several unshaded bulbs shining on the array of pistols and rifles on a movable rack, nearby. Renee watched him as he shoved a ramrod with a bit of cloth at its end through one of the high-powered rifles.

He glanced at her, saw the brooding lock on her face, and could not resist the temptation of baiting her, as a sort of compensation to his ego. He extracted a folded document from the tight, highly ornamented hussar tunic he wore, and waved it at her.

"You see?" Andre grinned. "I told you . . . there it is!" The document unfolded as he waved it, and Renee could read the bold, black letters, which read: Marriage License.

"You're not going through with it!" Renee said grimly. He stared at her with an amused look.

"Who's going to stop me?"

"Me! Suppose I told them the truth, about us . . . it might spoil your marriage, Andre!"

Andre's smile was feral . . . as feline as his narrowed golden eyes. "You wouldn't dare . . . Accidents happen—I can miss! Don't forget, I use real bullets . . ."

Then seeing her reaction, his voice softened, as he continued, "Don't be foolish! Don't you want furs, jewels? I'm seeing to it that we get our share! You see where we're now, second spot on the bill . . . Give me time, and we'll be the headliners!" He smiled at her engagingly.

"Now, be a good girl and get dressed . . . and don't forget to be at our wedding after the show!" He put his gun aside, rose and, taking Renee gently by the arm, Andre ushered her out of his dressing room. He buttoned up his collar and straightened his tunic, then he walked over to the Hamilton Sister's[18] dressing room, knocked briefly and strode in with a happy smile.

Dorothy and Vivian were at their dressing table, and Mabel hovered hanging costumes and getting others ready for the next act. Dorothy turned her face slightly as Andre entered, but Vivian, after a glance in the mirror, continued applying her make-up as if he were not there.

"Darling," Andre bent over to kiss Dorothy's hair. "Everything's set! After the show, we'll be married!"

---

18. "Sister's" is singular in the original although of course this could be a typographical error; if not, it seems to underscore the desire to separate the girls from one another that Pariseau's character represents. The singular spelling appears again later in this section.

"I'm so happy!" Dorothy exclaimed fervently.

"Even the mayor's going to be present . . ."

Hinkley and Mackenzie came in beaming, Hinkley as usual carrying a bundle of newspapers, while Mackenzie was almost incoherent with the importance of the occasion.

"I raised the prices and they're still fighting to get in!" Mackenzie exclaimed. "You're going to have the biggest audience of any wedding in history!" he exaggerated, as he grinned at Dorothy.

"Audience," Dorothy asked wonderingly. "I . . . I thought we were going to be married by Doctor Birnham, at his church!" She gazed at Andre with a hurt look, and then at her sister Vivian, whose face was averted.

"Ridiculous!" Hinkley interposed. "This is the chance of a lifetime, Dotty! Have you any idea of the publicity we're getting? Every city official's here, including the Mayor . . . Look at this," he said, displaying a newspaper. "Look at the headlines. I wish this were Madison Square Garden!"

Vivian spoke for the first time, resentfully, "How is it we knew nothing about it?"

"We had no time for explanations," Andre explained in a conciliatory tone of voice. "After all, wasn't Dorothy anxious to get married?"

"Yes, but at least we could have been consulted!" Vivian persisted, gazing at Andre with hatred and scorn.

"What difference does it make where we are married, we're show people!" Andre said softly.

There was a knock at the door and the voice of the announcer saying: "Hamilton Sisters, on stage!"

"All right," said Mackenzie. "Let's leave them alone to get ready." The men left. Andre went back stage to watch the act which was finishing prior to the Hamilton Sister's number. A group of performers and stagehands surrounded Andre, congratulating him, slapping him on the back, and privately wondering what kind of a guy he was.

Andre nonchalantly displayed a large diamond ring on the little finger of his left hand. "See, five karats," he grinned. Then he pointed to the dial of his wristwatch. "Studded with real diamonds!" He turned back and watched the performers on the stage, while the men gazed at one another wordlessly. They had their answer.

Then it was Dorothy's and Vivian's turn on the stage. Mabel stood in the wings to hand them their props, as they danced and sang various numbers. Dorothy was radiant, her voice had an undertone of tenderness, and she gazed towards the wings where Andre stood smiling, as she sang their hit song, "Love Thief!"

To Vivian it was sheer torture. It seemed to her as if their routine would never end. And the prospect of Andre's inevitable nearness—of intimacy over which she had no control, terrified her. If only . . . dear God . . . if only it could remain Platonic . . . If only she could somehow blank out her mind so that she wouldn't be part of it! She almost sobbed through her song, as she executed the intricate steps of their routine, and the frozen smile on her face was like a caricature of the misery within.

They finished to the tumultuous applause to which they had now become accustomed. But tonight a new note seemed to have entered—the audience shouted and stamped and demanded encore after encore. Women in evening gowns, with jewels glittering here and there, were in the audience, and a sprinkling of men in tuxedos and some even in white ties.

At last they were able to leave the stage and the clamorous audience and go to their dressing room. But for Vivian there was no relief. She had to go through the ordeal of the wedding itself yet.

After the last act, Mackenzie stepped through the velvet curtains and held up his hand for silence, a fatuous smile on his perspiring face.

"Ladies and gentlemen . . ." He beamed. "This is a most unusual night in the history of the Bijou. Over two thousand guests will witness the marriage of Dorothy Hamilton, to Andre Pariseau. The number of social and civic leaders present is too numerous to mention, but whether you're a civic leader, social leader or just plain Jane and Joe, we are happy to have you with us tonight." He bowed and exited towards the wings, as the audience burst into frenzied applause.

The orchestra began to play the Wedding March from *Lohengrin*,[19] and finally the curtains opened slowly, revealing the garden setting on the stage. Dorothy, Vivian and Andre already were before the Justice of the Peace, while numerous members of the various acts on the bill were grouped about. The music became subdued, and the Justice of the Peace began to speak in a mumbling drone. The restless audience strove to hear his words in vain.

19. A romantic opera by Richard Wagner first performed in 1850; the Bridal Chorus or "Treulich geführt" ("Here Comes the Bride") appears in act 3, scene 1.

An overly stout matron, her ears glittering with diamonds, bent over and whispered to her companion, "What a strange marriage! Isn't he handsome? I just couldn't keep from attending!" She raised and adjusted opera glasses the better to see.

"What puzzles me," replied the other, "is how can they arrange to live together?"

"It's a new design for living, my dear . . . He must be a Frenchman!"

A gentleman back of them hissed loudly for them to quiet down and was rewarded by two pairs of frigid eyes.

On the stage, one of the feminine performers whispered to another, "I hope she'll be happy . . . Poor thing! She really deserves it!" The man next to her nodded sympathetically. "Did you see the five karat diamond she gave him?"

"And the bankroll he's sporting," a male voice said derisively. "He's sure made it pay!"

His wife gave him a sidelong glance. "I hope he's sincere. Men are such brutes! She deserves some love in her life, even if some of us haven't got it!" The man subsided as if he had been deflated.

The Justice of the Peace had got down to the part where who ever opposed the marriage was supposed to speak, or forever hold his or her peace. Renee in a corner near the wings was wordless and tearless as she watched the end of the ceremony.

And through the cloying scent of the banked flowers, the familiar music and the too familiar faces on the stage, Vivian felt like a stranger from a strange land who had strayed into some secret ritual in which she had no part. It was like a fantastic nightmare from which she was unable to awake. A nightmare through which the drone of the Justice of the Peace threaded like a ritual chant. She could only close her eyes and pray for strength, as she swayed slightly.

And then it was over, incredibly it was over! The pandemonium in the audience was matched on the stage in an unceasing salvo of sound. Colored balloons were released and serpentine and confetti swirled through the vitiated atmosphere, as the packed humanity roared its approval. They were surrounded by a tidal wave of people, as both men and women kissed the bride and even embraced Andre in the fashion of show people.

Flowers of all kinds and hues were strewn over the stage, the proscenium and the stairs leading to the milling audience. And rising in a crescendo of sound over the pandemonium, the orchestra began to play the triumphal March from *Aida*.[20]

After that, Vivian couldn't remember how they ever got to their suite at the hotel. It was planned they were not on a honeymoon until after their engagement ended.

Wearily they undressed with the aid of Mabel, who for once was strangely silent. Vivian donned her usual pair of white nylon pajamas, but Dorothy put on a filmy negligee, over which she threw an exquisite dressing gown, almost as filmy.

They sat on the settee in the living room, while Mabel made them some tea in the two burner electric appliances and brought it to them steaming, then stood by to see that they drank. Vivian sipped it with distaste, and but for her need for something warm that would stimulate her, she would have refused it. Her face was calm, but inwardly she was terrified, burning hot and cold by turns. Resolutely, she averted her mind from what the night might bring, clinging desperately to the one simple refrain which was at once the ultimate reason, and the life-saver to her sinking mind: "It's her happiness . . . It's Dorothy's happiness! Help me, dear God! . . ."

Dorothy picked up the novel she had been reading for several days as she awaited the arrival of Andre. He had gone to his own room. She wondered if he would come back. Her eyes did not see the print as with her mind's eye she remembered his wide shoulders and hard-muscled torso. Her gaze left the novel and wandered down her negligee, watching her breast rise and fall rhythmically. He had such white, strong teeth, she recalled. And there was a certain hardness to his hazel eyes at times . . .

Undoubtedly, he could be dominating . . . perhaps, brutal! She caught her breath and glanced down to where her breasts were trembling.

The tea burned a path down her body and out to where the rhinestone star glittered in the middle of her negligee. A long sigh escaped her. Somehow she couldn't quite bring herself to look at Vivian. Wonderful, wonderful Vivian. She owed all her happiness to her, Dorothy thought. But it was Andre who ruled her mind. She glanced towards the bedroom involuntarily, where twin beds close together had replaced the old double bed. A ruffled satin canopy, with a satin curtain along the

---

20. An opera by Giuseppe Verdi first performed in 1871.

middle, had been Mabel's idea. Dorothy felt Mabel's eye on her, and she felt as if she needed air.

Mabel went into the bedroom and then returned with her coat. She said, "Good night!" and started to walk to the door. Midway, she turned impulsively, ran to Dorothy and embraced. Then she turned away so that they could not see the tears in her eyes.

In the ensuing silence, they heard the doorbell ring, then the door opened, and Andre came into the living room in violet pajamas, with a black Chinese dressing gown over them.

Vivian felt every nerve in her body twang like a bowstring. She tried to avert her mind, to will herself to be oblivious of his purpose . . . of his presence even! But she was fascinated by his purposeful stride, the slow smile of anticipation which curved his lips so that his strong white teeth gleamed in the electric light. His muscular thighs stretched the violet pajama-trousers as he strode over to where she and Dorothy had risen from the settee at his entrance.

Andre stood for a moment, his hazel eyes golden with desire, then he silently opened his arms to Dorothy, they slid over her breasts, then he pulled her to him.

Dorothy felt herself engulfed in his embrace, with his nervous hands cupping her, his hot mouth on her lips. She could feel the long burning line where his body touched hers. Andre loomed over her all power and fire, commanding. He was huge. The scarlet wave mounted in the soft darkness where she now found herself, on the satin and the ruffles— with the hard-muscled body pressing against the trembling, yielding softness of her own as he found her.

Dorothy thought she heard a distant, strangling cry, and then her senses reeled into a deeper darkness. She was never able later to quite remember what actually happened that fateful night . . .

Nine

And if previously the lives and loves of the Hamilton Sisters, Siamese Twins, had captured the public interest and become the daily topic of newspaper headlines and private controversies, now the sudden and un-explained estrangement between Dorothy and Andre swept the city like a prairie fire. The headlines were huge. The comments of the columnists, frenetic.

One newspaper epitomized the situation briefly with the headlines: SIAMESE TWIN DESERTED, BY GROOM OF ONE NIGHT!

One famous wag sharpened his wit, on a paraphrase of the advertisement about permanent waves, to ask in a daily column: "Which Twin is the virgin?" And immediately drew upon himself a torrent of opprobrium. The Bijou, besides being a theatre, became also an armed camp, in which two factions, pro and con, glared at each other and engaged in arguments which sometimes led to blows. The uproar became national and then international, until the City Fathers began to wonder where all this was going to end!

Meanwhile, attendance at the Bijou became almost a mark of wealth and pull, for seats were at a premium. It was impossible to purchase a ticket—reservations had to be made for weeks in advance.

When the Hamilton Sisters went on the stage for their act, the other performers clustered in the wings watching them curiously, speculating on how Dorothy felt. They gazed at her with pity in their hearts and curiosity in their eyes, and each one of them would have given a great deal to find out just what actually happened to make Andre desert Dorothy the morning after their wedding night. Or was it the morning after?

But the Hamilton Sisters managed to mask their feelings; they didn't betray what had occurred either by word or expression. Dorothy tried to smile and sing and dance as if nothing had happened, but each lurid headline, each ribald comment in the various columns, was a fresh stab in her heart. She felt as life had lost all its savor—as if the very reason for her existence had dissolved into that darkness she had known her wedding night.

As for Vivian, there was a cold, purposeful hardness about her, which precluded questions or discussions. One or two had tried to question her, and they had withdrawn embarrassed and a little awed at the cold, ruthless look she gave them.

There had been a scene at their apartment, when the reporters and columnists and other representatives of the press had practically forced their way in, that Mabel would never forget. Vivian had almost gone berserk and thrown everything she could at them, screaming frenziedly for them to get out. That too had been recorded in headlines, but thereafter, they had been left alone.

Andre, featured with Renee in the second spot, continued with his act, following the Hamilton Sisters. He went blithely about it, as if Dorothy and Vivian didn't exist, secure in the knowledge that he had achieved his objective—from now on, he was a headliner—wherever he went, the women mobbed him.

✑

It was the last night of their engagement, and the restless audience that filled the Bijou shouted itself hoarse as the Hamilton Sisters finished their duet—"Love Thief."

Vivian felt spent and dull as if from a long expense of spirit. She dared not look at Dorothy, feeling the anguish in her sister's heart. She would not see Andre again. It was over. Incredibly, it was over! A dreadful nightmare which had left only the dregs of a profound hatred in Vivian's own heart.

Vivian could see Andre out of the corner of her eye, standing in the wings, blatantly male, waiting for them to leave the stage so he could enter triumphantly and begin his act. Something like a flame swept through her, blinding her as she bowed to the thunderous applause. Then with her arm around Dorothy's waist, they exited, and stood in the wings.

Andre was already on stage. They heard the first shot as he fired and shot the cigarette out of Renee's mouth, then the burst of sound from the audience.

"I . . . I want to watch him," Dorothy said wistfully. No anger, no pride, no resentment possessed her now, only the inexpressible anguish of a woman in love.

"It's . . . our last . . . night!" She turned to her sister Vivian, pleading with her eyes, in which the tears were beginning to gather.

It was the last thing Vivian wanted to do, to watch Andre strut and pose and display his wares. But Dorothy pulled her towards a spot where they could watch. They walked to where a tree of the garden setting stood in the middle of a narrow space. They tried one side, then the other, but each was too narrow for both of them to stand, so they stood slightly behind the tree, with the trunk between them, as they gazed out, their heads on either side of the tree-trunk.

They saw myriad faces in the audience, then Andre, bowing on the stage at the applause, placed the gun with which he had shot the cigarette out of Renee's mouth on a small roller table; without even looking, he sent the table rolling towards the wings with a push. The rolling table came to rest on Vivian's side of the tree. She looked down at the gun lying on the velvet case and her hand closed around the gun.

On the stage, Renee had wheeled another table, on which there are several rifles, over to Andre, who raises his hand for attention, then with a broad smile, he says: "Ladies and Gentlemen . . . I believe that what I am about to perform, on this stage tonight, is the only act of its kind in the world! I will use these rifles to play that organ. My first selection will be a Bach Fugue."

Renee, smiling, hands him the first rifle. Andre turns to the organ in the background, up stage, he aims and fires. The first chord of the Bach Fugue is heard clear and sonorous. Renee hands Andre one rifle after another and the music swells floating over the hushed audience.

In the wings, Dorothy, completely oblivious to everything but Andre, gazes at him with all the hurt, and love and anguish in her heart.

On the other side of the tree, Vivian calmly raises the gun, aims at Andre and fires. She sees Andre's eyes widen in pain and terror, as he stiffens at the impact of the bullet, as he takes a few steps hesitantly, his mouth half-open, then crumples down, falling with his head twisted towards the audience.

Renee stood for an instant rooted to the spot, staring in horror at the fallen form of Andre, then the audience rose in a pandemonium of shouts and screaming, drowning her own scream of horror and grief.

"Close the curtain! . . . Close the curtain!" Mackenzie was yelling. A dense crowd gathered on the stage in seconds, as performers, members of the audience, stage-hands . . . everybody who could push their way on to the stage, gathered around the inert form.

Finally, the police arrived and managed to achieve some semblance of order. They took Vivian and Dorothy into custody, and immediately had to take them to the County Hospital because of Dorothy's condition. She was in deep shock, murmuring over and over in a voice that was more of a wail than anything else, "Let me die! . . . Oh, God, let me die!"

Hinkley was almost out of his mind. Deep in his heart, he felt responsible. Everything he had hoped for had been granted him—with a vengeance! But he was not prepared to cope with this situation.

Bail was immediately forthcoming, but the judge was reluctant to grant it. However after a wrangle of lawyers and the court, it was finally fixed, and the girls were able to return to their apartment, condemned to live in an endless atmosphere of scandal and sensation, as the days dragged into weeks, and the trial progressed slowly.

It seemed to Vivian as if it would never end, as the long line of witnesses were called to the stand. They were questioned and cross-questioned until their very thoughts were probed mercilessly. Dorothy was sworn to tell the truth, the whole truth and nothing but the truth! But could she? Vivian wondered.

Lawyer Price did everything he could as he defended Vivian. At times he seemed inspired. But there was no question but that Vivian had fired the shot that killed Andre Pariseau.

At last, the trial draws towards the end. To Vivian sitting with Dorothy at the Defense's table, it all was like a ghastly nightmare from which one presently awakes. She heard the prosecutor making his final plea to Judge MacAdoo, for Price had waved a jury trial, content to abide by the verdict of the judge.

"Your Honor," the prosecutor was saying. "There probably has never been a more unusual case presented in any court; nor has any court heard so much testimony that is irrelevant and immaterial!

"In an attempt to arouse your sympathy, the defense has taken you backstage into the life of the Hamilton Sisters, deliberately ignoring the fact that we are here only because murder has been committed!" He turned and looked at Vivian, who returned his hot gaze, calmly.

"The state is not concerned with the involvement in the lives and loves of the defendant, her sister, and the murdered man. It is only concerned with one question: Did or did not Vivian Hamilton, with premeditation and in cold blood, shoot and kill Andre Pariseau? . . . The answer to that is—Yes! . . . By her own admission!" This time he gazed at the judge, as he drew himself up and concluded, "I, therefore ask you to pronounce the only verdict possible—guilty . . . guilty of murder in the first degree!"

The Prosecutor bowed to the judge and sat down, looking grimly at Attorney Price, who rose as Judge MacAdoo said, "Counsel for the defense may proceed."

In the hushed courtroom, every eye was centered on Attorney Price. What would he say? What could he say that had not been said already in the seemingly interminable battle between the State and the Defense? For the moment, both Dorothy and Vivian were forgotten. They remained as mere symbols of a tragedy which, in the last analysis, went beyond the fact that a life had been taken. And of all this Price was profoundly conscious.

He was aware, as he walked a few paces to stand in front of the presiding judge, that the usual, legalistic and formal defense would fall far short of his objective. But he was aware too, that the time was past to elicit sympathy or understanding. It wasn't only that Vivian Hamilton's life was at stake—careers would be made and unmade in that small, hushed anteroom. The trial had ceased to be a local matter. It had transcended national boundaries and become an international affair. It had been established that Vivian Hamilton had fired the fatal shot. What would the verdict be? What could it be!

This was the moment for which Price had been waiting, throughout the harrowing ordeal. He permitted himself a backward glance at Vivian, who, pale and silent, gazed unseeingly straight ahead. He smiled at her out of the well of pity within him, then he turned to the judge, and began to speak in a low, vibrant voice, instinct with feeling.

"Your Honor . . ." Price paused. "The state has built a case against Vivian Hamilton which is punishable by law, and applicable to all human beings. The Prosecution demands the extreme penalty." He looked squarely into Judge MacAdoo's eyes as he continued, "When it comes to punishment, the law demands equality—but the actual fact is, that the law has never considered the Hamilton Sisters as equals . . ." He turned and pointed dramatically at them, then turned his head to gaze at the judge.

"They have been denied marriage. Children. Love! All normal fulfillment has been denied to them irrevocably. Has the law ever protected them! No! But when it comes to punishment, to the destruction of their lives, the law demands the extreme penalty . . .

"Yes, Vivian Hamilton is guilty . . . guilty of loving her sister Dorothy better even than her own life: Should you find that the defendant is guilty as charged, under the statutes of this state, the death penalty would be mandatory. But if the law is to be satisfied, the state becomes the murderer of an innocent person—Dorothy Hamilton. If you find Vivian Hamilton guilty of manslaughter, then the penalty is life imprisonment . . . and even then the state cannot deprive her sister Dorothy of her rightful liberty. In fact, the law cannot take Vivian Hamilton into custody without defeating the very purpose for which it was created—justice! . . ."

In the silent courtroom, not a sound could be heard—not even the breathing of that mass of humanity who now hung on every word of the Defense. Judge MacAdoo was leaning forward as Price paused, and so was the frowning prosecutor.

"Your honor," Price continued. "Do you know what the Book of Knowledge calls the Hamilton Sisters? I ask you your honor, are they abnormalities, or are they human beings? Are they one and indivisible or are they two entirely separate entities? . . .

"I cannot conceive, in my mind, any other verdict than *not guilty*! The defense rests its case in the hands of the court." He bowed to the judge and walked slowly over to the defense table and sat down.

Judge MacAdoo's voice sounded hoarse and strange in the ensuing silence as he said, "The prosecution may proceed."

"The prosecution rests!" was the answer, as the prosecutor mopped his forehead.

With a sigh, Judge MacAdoo rose, gathering the folds of his robe around him. "Court will remain in session until a verdict has been reached," he said slowly, then retired to his chambers to deliberate. As soon as he had left, the audience seemed to come to life noisily, like a long-dormant organism. Speculation was rife, as cigarettes were lighted; groups walked into the hall, others peered curiously at the girls sitting by the defense table. Hinkley came over and patted Vivian's arm wordlessly. He looked haggard and wan and spent, folds of skin hung in crosses where before there had been pudgy flesh. Dorothy was weeping softly, insistently into a handkerchief.

The wait seemed interminable—another phase of the endless nightmare which seemed to go on inexorably like a Greek tragedy.

At last, the Judge emerged from his chambers, and the Bailiff chanted his slurred ritual announcing that the court was again in session. And once more the electric silence pervaded the court, until the judge said, "The defendant will rise!" And both Vivian and Dorothy obediently rose to hear their fate.

Judge MacAdoo's face was grave, he gazed at the girls, then at the packed courtroom. "After twenty years on the bench," he said with feeling, "I can find no precedent that will serve me as a guide in this case! The purposes of justice are to protect the innocent as well as to punish the guilty. Were I Solomon, I might be given the supreme wisdom to do justice! But as it is, I cannot pass sentence and deprive an innocent person of her liberty and her life! Therefore, a higher court than mine will have to impose the final judgment!" He ceased speaking for an instant, then gazing at the courtroom with an all-embracing glance, he added, "I must point out that the defense chose to place the entire responsibility of this case on my conscience. Had the defense chosen trial by jury, anyone of you could have been selected to share the burden . . . And, if you were the jury, I wonder, what would your verdict be?" He stopped speaking and rose.

The entire courtroom rose in a tremendous salvo of sound. They saw in those two slim figures, so cruelly burdened by Fate, symbols of all that humanity can and must endure. Saw the truth for an instant, which unveiled the empty dark heart of revenge.

In those two figures standing free, they saw the ultimate meaning of life, to which death must add the somber magnificence of the last adventure, and they cheered and cheered, despite the hanging gavels, and the shouting Bailiff—cheering beyond the trial and the verdict and the freedom of the girls, to something so deeply felt that it went beyond the power of words, and could only be translated into that ultimate meaning which is the secret dictum of the heart.

And as Vivian swayed lifeless almost from the long, relentless expense of spirit, it was Dorothy this time who enfolded her in her arms, as Hinkley bent his head, for he, too, was crying.

THE END

Wisconsin Studies in Autobiography

William L. Andrews
General Editor

Robert F. Sayre
The Examined Self: Benjamin Franklin, Henry Adams, Henry James

Daniel B. Shea
Spiritual Autobiography in Early America

Lois Mark Stalvey
The Education of a WASP

Margaret Sams
Forbidden Family: A Wartime Memoir of the Philippines, 1941–1945
Edited with an introduction by Lynn Z. Bloom

Charlotte Perkins Gilman
The Living of Charlotte Perkins Gilman: An Autobiography
Introduction by Ann J. Lane

Mark Twain
Mark Twain's Own Autobiography: The Chapters from the North American Review
Edited by Michael J. Kiskis

Journeys in New Worlds: Early American Women's Narratives
Edited by William L. Andrews, Sargent Bush, Jr., Annette Kolodny,
    Amy Schrager Lang, and Daniel B. Shea

American Autobiography: Retrospect and Prospect
Edited by Paul John Eakin

Caroline Seabury
The Diary of Caroline Seabury, 1854–1863
Edited with an introduction by Suzanne L. Bunkers

Cornelia Peake McDonald
A Woman's Civil War: A Diary with Reminiscences of the War, from March 1862
Edited with an introduction by Minrose C. Gwin

Marian Anderson
My Lord, What a Morning
Introduction by Nellie Y. McKay

American Women's Autobiography: Fea(s)ts of Memory
Edited with an introduction by Margo Culley

Frank Marshall Davis
Livin' the Blues: Memoirs of a Black Journalist and Poet
Edited with an introduction by John Edgar Tidwell

Joanne Jacobson
Authority and Alliance in the Letters of Henry Adams

Kamau Brathwaite
The Zea Mexican Diary: 7 September 1926–7 September 1986

Genaro M. Padilla
My History, Not Yours: The Formation of Mexican American Autobiography

Frances Smith Foster
Witnessing Slavery: The Development of Ante-bellum Slave Narratives

Native American Autobiography: An Anthology
Edited with an introduction by Arnold Krupat

American Lives: An Anthology of Autobiographical Writing
Edited with an introduction by Robert F. Sayre

Carol Holly
*Intensely Family: The Inheritance of Family Shame and the Autobiographies of
    Henry James*

People of the Book: Thirty Scholars Reflect on Their Jewish Identity
Edited by Jeffrey Rubin-Dorsky and Shelley Fisher Fishkin

G. Thomas Couser
Recovering Bodies: Illness, Disability, and Life Writing

John Downton Hazlett
My Generation: Collective Autobiography and Identity Politics

William Herrick
Jumping the Line: The Adventures and Misadventures of an American Radical

Women, Autobiography, Theory: A Reader
Edited by Sidonie Smith and Julia Watson

José Angel Gutiérrez
The Making of a Chicano Militant: Lessons from Cristal

Marie Hall Ets
Rosa: The Life of an Italian Immigrant

Carson McCullers
Illumination and Night Glare: The Unfinished Autobiography of Carson McCullers
Edited with an introduction by Carlos L. Dews

Yi-Fu Tuan
Who Am I?: An Autobiography of Emotion, Mind, and Spirit

Henry Bibb
The Life and Adventures of Henry Bibb: An American Slave
Introduction by Charles J. Heglar

Suzanne L. Bunkers
Diaries of Girls and Women: A Midwestern American Sampler

Jim Lane
The Autobiographical Documentary in America

Sandra Pouchet Paquet
Caribbean Autobiography: Cultural Identity and Self-Representation

Mark O'Brien, with Gillian Kendall
How I Became a Human Being: A Disabled Man's Quest for Independence

Elizabeth L. Banks
*Campaigns of Curiosity: Journalistic Adventures of an American Girl in
    Late Victorian London*
Introduction by Mary Suzanne Schriber and Abbey L. Zink

Miriam Fuchs
The Text Is Myself: Women's Life Writing and Catastrophe

Jean M. Humez
Harriet Tubman: The Life and the Life Stories

Voices Made Flesh: Performing Women's Autobiography
Edited by Lynn C. Miller, Jacqueline Taylor, and M. Heather Carver

Loreta Janeta Velazquez
The Woman in Battle: The Civil War Narrative of Loreta Janeta Velazquez,
      Cuban Woman and Confederate Soldier
Introduction by Jesse Alemán

Cathryn Halverson
Maverick Autobiographies: Women Writers and the American West, 1900–1936

Jeffrey Brace
The Blind African Slave: Or Memoirs of Boyrereau Brinch, Nicknamed Jeffrey Brace
as told to Benjamin F. Prentiss, Esq.
Edited with an introduction by Kari J. Winter

Colette Inez
The Secret of M. Dulong: A Memoir

Before They Could Vote: American Women's Autobiographical Writing, 1819–1919
Edited by Sidonie Smith and Julia Watson

Bertram J. Cohler
Writing Desire: Sixty Years of Gay Autobiography

Philip Holden
Autobiography and Decolonization: Modernity, Masculinity, and the Nation-State

Jing M. Wang
When "I" Was Born: Women's Autobiography in Modern China

Conjoined Twins in Black and White: The Lives of Millie-Christine McKoy and
      Daisy and Violet Hilton
Edited by Linda Frost